The Economics of Poverty

Kevin Furey

The Economics of Poverty

ISBN: 978-1-943536-57-3
Edition 1.0 (Fall 2019)

Chemeketa Press

Chemeketa Press is a nonprofit publishing endeavor at Chemeketa Community College. Working together with faculty, staff, and students, we develop and publish affordable and effective alternatives to commercial textbooks. To learn more, visit www.chemeketapress.org.

Publisher: David Hallett
Director: Steve Richardson
Managing Editor: Brian Mosher
Instructional Editor: Stephanie Lenox
Design Editor: Ronald Cox IV
Manuscript Support: Steve Richardson, Brian Mosher, Steve Slemenda
Interior Design: Mackenzie Allen, Ronald Cox IV, Casandra Johns,
    Jess Kolman, Steve Richardson, Brandi Harbison, Leo Martinez
Cover Design: Ronald Cox IV
Cover photo: "Young Suits" by Joris Louwes is in the public domain
(https://www.flickr.com/photos/jorislouwes/8169811354).

Printed in the United States of America.

Contents

"Politics isn't about left versus right;
it's about top versus bottom."
— Jim Hightower

❖ 1

Finding Solutions to Poverty

"I am, somehow, less interested in the weight and convolutions of Einstein's brain than in the near certainty that people of equal talent have lived and died in cotton fields and sweatshops."
— Stephen Jay Gould

The goal of this book is to use economic analysis to determine the causes and solutions to one of the United States' most vexing social problems — poverty.

From 1959 to 1973, the US saw a significant decline in poverty. As the nation became richer, everyone's income increased. Because the poverty line stays constant, only moving by the amount of inflation, more people went from having incomes below the poverty line to having incomes above the poverty line. Improvement in Social Security[1] during this time period also lowered poverty rates of the elderly. As figure 1 on the next page illustrates, poverty rates fell from 22.4 percent in 1959 to 11.1 percent in 1973.

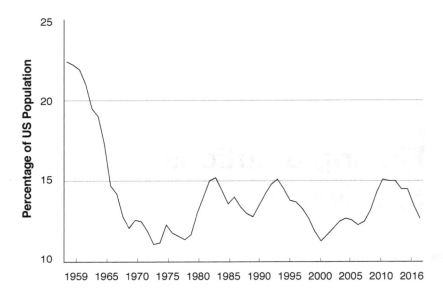

Figure 1. The official poverty rate, 1959 to 2016.

The growth rate of the economy has been slower since 1973 than it was from 1946 to 1973, but the economy *has* continued to grow. Correcting for inflation, per capita income has increased from $20,478 in 1973 to $34,489 in 2017. Abstracting from business cycle effects, we would expect the poverty rates to become lower over time. That clearly hasn't happened. In fact, the average poverty rate for the decade of the 1970s is lower than the average poverty rate for any decade since then.

The only way for per capita income to rise and for poverty rates to not fall is if the distribution of income became more unequal. In other words, while the average citizen became 68% wealthier between 1973 and 2017, those on the bottom of the income distribution did not. After correcting for inflation, the average income for those in the top twenty percent of the income distribution increased by $88,559. For those in the bottom twenty percent, the average income only increased by $702.[2] The growth in the US economy since 1973 somehow missed the poor.[3]

Using economic analysis, this book looks for solutions to this problem. Given the large number of social ills associated with poverty, we would expect a deep and robust literature on the subject. After all, economists are supposedly in the business of proposing solutions to social problems. However, economists have devoted surprisingly little effort to the study of poverty.[4] Furthermore, at least from the point of view of a social scientist attempting to determine the causes of and the solutions to poverty, the books that *have* been written are poorly organized. We would expect that a study of some economic problem would be structured as follows:

1. Define the problem.

2. Determine and show the relevant economic theory to address this problem.

3. Use that economic theory to explain the cause or causes of the problem.

4. Use that economic theory to devise solutions to the problem.

The problem of poverty is generally defined in terms of a lack of income. People are typically impoverished because they either don't have a job or they have one that pays a very low wage. Therefore, we would expect a book on poverty to have at or near the beginning a detailed section on the economic theory of labor markets. This section then provides an anchor for the rest of the book. However, economics books written on poverty are never organized in this way. Most don't talk about labor market theory at all, and none do so thoroughly.[5]

Two Theories of Labor Markets

To thus determine the causes and solutions to poverty, we start with a discussion of the economic theory of labor markets. This task is not as easy as might seem because there is no single theory of labor markets. Economists classify themselves into a broad range of perspectives — rational expectationists, neo-Keynesians, Marxists, post-Keynesians, quantity theorists, institutionalists, neo-Austrian, and so on. Some groups of economists have much in common with some groups while at the same time having little in common with others. To the introductory economics student, however, the precise theoretical differences that divide economists into certain groups are nearly meaningless. When it comes to labor markets, we can thus focus on the commonalities and divide economists into two basic groups, heterodox economists and orthodox economists.[6]

The theories of labor markets held by these two groups of economists are quite different, and most of this book will explore those differences in detail. As we will see, each sees very different causes and solutions to poverty.

Heterodox Theory

In the first half of this book, we will examine the heterodox theory of labor markets. In the heterodox theory, people are poor because they are un- or underemployed or because they work at jobs that pay low wages. As you'll see in coming chapters, macroeconomic forces determine the level of employment.

For heterodox economists, capitalist societies are excess capacity societies because they always possess idle capital equipment and unemployed and underemployed workers. These societies are never in equilibrium. They are always either expanding, which occurs most of the time, or they are contracting. During the expansions, firms meet the increased demand for their products by hiring unemployed laborers to work on previously idle or underused capital equipment. However, before full employment is reached, internal forces cause the expansion to collapse and a recession to begin. Because full employment is never or almost never reached, there are always or almost always more people looking for work than there are job openings. Those who end up unemployed for long time periods end up in poverty.

Others are in poverty because they work at jobs that pay low wages. In this model, microeconomic forces determine wages. Jobs are divided into a primary labor market, where firms pay high wages and high benefits, and a secondary labor market, where firms pay low wages and little or no benefits. Under certain conditions, following a high wage/high productivity strategy lowers a firm's cost of production and maximizes its profits. In other situations, following a low wage/low productivity strategy lowers the firm's cost of production. The low wages of the secondary market are the result of a low minimum wage and the fact that high levels of unemployment keep wages low. One of the reasons why poverty rates have not declined over the past forty years is that the relative size of the secondary market appears to be expanding.

Poverty in this model is the result of the natural operation of the social system. It is often referred to as a "blame the system" explanation of poverty. The solution is thus job creation through increased government spending, lower taxes, low interest rates, and direct public-sector hiring. In addition, there needs to be a significant increase to the minimum wage, support for those who are temporarily or permanently unable to participate in the labor market, increased funding for the enforcement of labor laws, and increased support of the formation of labor unions. The aim of these policies is that all workers have jobs, and the wages paid are high enough that all or nearly all households have an income above the poverty line.

Orthodox Theory

For orthodox economists, poverty is primarily a microeconomic problem. In the orthodox theory, labor markets are supply-and-demand markets that always clear in the long run so that for every job seeker, there is a job opening. While it takes time to match the unemployed with job openings, unemployed people find jobs quickly unless there are skill or geographic mismatches.[7] There is little, if any, long-term unemployment in this model, so if people are poor due to long-term unemployment, we have to ask why. Are they really trying to get jobs? Do they display such counterproductive or disruptive behaviors that they can't get or keep jobs? Are there other impediments to employment?

In this theory, workers are paid a wage that is equal to the value of what they add to output. If their wages are low, it's because they are not very productive or because what they produce has low value. If they are not very productive, this theory assumes that it is either due to a lack of skills or a lack of effort. People are thus poor because of their own short-comings. This is known as a "blame the victim" explanation of poverty.

There is a conservative and a liberal variant to this theory.

Conservative Orthodox Variant

In the conservative variant, people are poor because they are either natu-rally lazy or government programs give them an incentive to become lazy. In this view, people can always find a job if they actually try. In addition, if people aren't lazy, they will gain sufficient skills in school and else-where to get a well-paying job. Moreover, their pay will increase if they work hard and make themselves more productive. It is easy to see why government programs to aid the poor are so infuriating to conservative orthodox economists.

First, according to conservative orthodox economists, these pro-grams give people an incentive to be lazy. As a result, they don't develop their full potential. In the name of compassion, government programs attempt to help the poor, but they actually cripple the poor by robbing them of the incentives to develop the character necessary for success in life. The solution for conservative orthodox economists is to eliminate all or nearly all social safety net programs.[8] The poor either have to develop the grit and skills necessary to make a living, or they perish.

Second, social safety net programs cost money. The government must tax workers to pay for them. In this theory, workers are paid an income equal to the amount they produce. However, conservatives take this concept a step further. They imply that what people earn is purely of their own doing. A worker's income is not the result of technological advances made by prior generations but purely the result of what they accomplish by personal effort.

In this view, individuals owe society nothing, and for conservatives, mandatory government taxes are therefore a form of stealing.[9] This theft is even more galling when it is used to support people whom conservatives believe are lazy and could earn their own way if they tried. This sentiment is captured in this bumper sticker: "You have to keep working—millions of welfare recipients are depending on you." It is no wonder that discussions of welfare expenditures are a flash point for conservatives.

Conservative orthodox economists tend to have more in common with one another than those who are labeled as liberals. In general, conservative economists believe that markets work quickly and efficiently. They believe that when disruptions occur, market forces work rapidly to restore normalcy. As a result, they see little need for government intervention.

Liberal Orthodox Variant

Liberal orthodox economists believe that as a compassionate society, we need to support the less fortunate. The liberal variant assumes that the poor are, for the most part, as hard working as the rest of us but that due to unfortunate circumstances, they are caught in a position of earning low incomes. For some, the problems are temporary, such as a factory closing, a recession, or a divorce. For others, the problems are potentially permanent. They attended poor-quality schools, made bad decisions as teenagers, or face discrimination. Because such circumstances are too expensive to be resolved on an individual basis, we need government, representing the interests of society, to devise a series of programs addressing the different reasons why people are impoverished. These programs should be tailored to help individuals overcome the barriers that are holding them back.

Unlike conservative orthodox economists, liberals believe that there are times and places where markets fail or clear slowly and that society would be better off if the government were involved to improve outcomes. However, there is a large variation among liberals as to how many and how strong these market failures are. Their views on the areas and depth of government involvement also vary widely. In general, though, these economists all offer a mixture of programs from the following three categories:

1. Supporting individuals who are temporarily or permanently unable to participate in the labor market

2. Increasing the income of the working poor and near poor

3. Increasing the productivity of the poor

Some liberal economists also have programs from a fourth category:

4. Increasing employment

While conservative and liberal orthodox economists share the same basic economic theory, their different views on human nature and the speed with which markets clear produces different causes of and solutions to poverty. Because both of these positions are well known in the poverty literature, we will not only track the heterodox and orthodox theories, but within the orthodox theory, we will also track the conservative and liberal perspectives.

Measuring Poverty

The way that economists generally measure poverty is to designate a level of income as the poverty line. Those with incomes below the poverty line are counted as poor. That part is clear. What isn't as clear is how to set the poverty line.

There are many suggested methods for determining the poverty line, but they all fall within two theoretical approaches: an absolute poverty line and a relative poverty line. The absolute poverty definition focuses on the physical deprivation of poverty, and relative poverty focuses on the psychological deprivation. Shiller (2008) defines the absolute approach in this way:

> The absolute approach to defining poverty begins with the concept of minimum subsistence, that is, some bundle of goods and services that is regarded as essential to the physical well-being of a family unit. Those who do not possess the economic resources to obtain these goods and services are considered poor. (p. 36)

However, there is a certain degree of subjectivity in designing an absolute measure. What should this bundle of goods and services contain? Should the bundle change over time? While absolute measures capture one aspect of poverty, this approach ignores another aspect:

> The relative approach is simply more explicit about this subjectivity. In essence, it states that a person is poor when his or her income is significantly less than the average income of the population. For example, we might say that a person or family with less than one-half of the average income is poor . . . [or] anyone in the lowest fifth (or tenth, or third) of the distribution is regarded as poor. (Shiller 2008, p.38-9)

People who are in poverty suffer because they don't have the basic goods and services regarded as essential to the physical well-being of the family, but they also suffer psychologically because they have so much less than others. The relative approach tends to emphasize the psychological effects by drawing a poverty line relative to the average or median income of the nation.

In this book, we focus on absolute poverty. It is not that people's feelings are unimportant—they *are* important. However, given the way relative poverty is defined, it would be extremely difficulty to eliminate it. In fact, some measures of relative poverty claim that poverty could never be eliminated without having a perfectly equal distribution of income. There is, however, a more important reason for concentrating on absolute poverty.

Absolute poverty's focus on physical deprivation highlights the fact that in the short run, and potentially in the long run, an impoverished family's freedom[10] and ability to achieve their ultimate potential is severely limited. Poor people not only live less pleasant lives, but their lack of resources may prevent them from being able to accomplish life goals that might have been more feasible in a wealthier household. They may face a lifetime of unequal opportunities.

The Official Poverty Line

The official poverty line in the US was set in 1963, and the only change that has taken place over the years is to update it each year to reflect changes in prices—inflation. The original level was set at three times the US Agriculture Department's minimally adequate food budget, an absolute poverty measure. In 2016, the poverty line for a family of three was $19,105 a year.[11] Figure 2 shows the poverty line for various household sizes.

Anyone who has attempted to draw up a budget for a family of three with only $19,105 per year knows how constraining it would be to live on the poverty line. However, many poor people have incomes well below the poverty line. Every dollar reduced from their budget makes the fam-

Family Unit	Poverty Line
1 Person	$12,228
2 People	$15,569
3 People	$19,105
4 People	$24,563
5 People	$29,111
6 People	$32,928
7 People	$37,458
8 People	$41,781
9 or more	$49,721

Figure 2. The poverty line by household size.

ily's choices even harder. They often face tough choices such as whether to do without transportation or medical care. In 2016, over 40.5 million people lived in households with incomes below the official poverty line. That is 12.7% of the population or more than one in every eight people. This includes 18.0% or almost one in every five of children below the age of eighteen. This is a large portion of the population, and it is a particularly large portion of children. Furthermore, 2016 was not an unusually high year for poverty rates. In 2014, the overall poverty rate was 14.8%, and for children, it was 20.7%.

Not everyone who is in poverty is near the poverty line. Some have incomes that are far below that line. They are referred to as the "extreme poor" and are defined as having a household income that is below one half of the poverty line, or $9,553 for a family of three. In 2016, a little over 18.5 million people live in extreme poverty. That is almost half of all the poor.

Not everyone who has an income above the poverty line is far above that line. Many have incomes that are just above the poverty line. They are referred to as the "near poor." One measure of the near poor is those who have an income between the poverty line and 1.50 times the poverty line. For a family of three that would be between $19,105 and $28,658 per year. In 2016, more than twenty-seven million people were considered near poor by this definition. That is about 8.5% of the total population.

Alternative Measures of Poverty

It doesn't take long to see that the official definition of poverty comes with many potential difficulties:

- The original measure doesn't appear to be the result of a detailed analysis of what would constitute the "bundle of goods and services that is regarded as essential to the physical well-being of a family unit."

- The official measure was constructed fifty-six years ago. It is quite possible that this "bundle of goods and services" has changed in that time period.

- The official poverty line is the same for all parts of the country, but the cost of living differs considerably from one part to another. In 2008, for example, rent and utilities in New York City were two and a half times as high as those in Decatur County, Iowa.

- Payments from the government and gifts from family members are not included in the measure of income.

- Medical expenses differ considerably for those in different age groups.

We might think that a better measure would have been developed by now. Many have been suggested, in fact, but politics and ideology has gotten in the way. Conservatives, who believe that capitalism is the ideal economic system and prefer as little government interference and taxes as possible, tend to develop measures of poverty that minimize its existence. Meanwhile, liberals, who see much suffering and unfairness in our society, tend to develop measures that produce levels of poverty higher than the official measure.

Most alternative measures of poverty come to the conclusion that the actual poverty rate should be somewhat higher. The Census Bureau, which produces the official poverty count, has developed its own alternative measure, and it produces a poverty rate that is higher than the official. For 2016, their alternative rate was 14.0% while the official was 12.7%. However, even with the measures that produce lower poverty lines, the level of poverty in the US is still substantial.[12] For all its faults, the measure of poverty developed in 1963 lives on as the official poverty line. We will thus use the data from the official measure—not because it is the best but because the official data is what you see quoted elsewhere.

Understanding This Book

Conventional wisdom or common sense is often drawn from the writings of professional academics. These writings provided the rigorous academic rationale that forms more causal conventional wisdom. The current conventional wisdom about poverty is drawn from the orthodox economic theory. As we shall see in the pages that follow, both the economic rationale and the conventional wisdom that underlies most of today's discussions on poverty are wrong.

Positions from both the liberal and conservative viewpoints, reflected in the Democratic and Republican parties, are both anchored in the orthodox economic theory of labor markets. This theory is both unable to predict real world outcomes and is unable to explain how real-world labor markets operate. The errors of this model are not small, and it should never be used as a guide for making policies to eliminate poverty or as the basis for conventional wisdom. The heterodox model does a far better job.

Readers might question why we bother to show the orthodox model at all. Why not focus our attention solely on the heterodox model? There are a couple of reasons. First, the conservative and liberal viewpoints are what dominate public discourse on poverty. When "authorities" speak on the subject of poverty, students of economics should be able to recognize the perspective they are using and which parts of the orthodox model their statements rely on. A detailed description of both models is thus necessary for readers to be sufficiently well informed to evaluate and intelligently discuss the subject. Second, because this book concludes that the most accurate position is that held by the minority of economists, it is unfair to the reader to just assert that conclusion without proof.

When reading a textbook, sometimes the best and most efficient strategy is to skim over the material, looking for the key concepts. In those situations, the details are often unimportant as long as readers follow the general thread of the argument. Reading this book in that way is a colossal mistake. This book is all about the details, and readers need to understand all the details. If at any point readers find that they don't thoroughly understand the material, they need to slow down, go back, and reread.

This book has been written to be thoroughly enjoyed, like a good novel. Some points are to be pondered, others to be savored, and some to be examined from several angles. In a good novel, the action often slows for character development. While plunging ahead with the story might be more fun, to really understand the characters' actions later on in the novel, we need to know the backgrounds and motivations of the various characters.

In order to thoroughly enjoy, understand, and participate in a discussion about the causes and solutions to poverty, readers need to learn in detail how each of this book's models operates. Almost every point that is developed in the early chapters will be used later on. Reading with the goal of absorbing all the details in the beginning will make the later part of the book more interesting and easier to understand.

References

Danziger, Sheldon and Peter Gottschalk. 1995. *American Unequal.* Cambridge, MA: Harvard University Press.

Gould, Stephen Jay. 1992. *The Panda's Thumb: More Reflections in Natural History.* New York: W. W. Norton & Company, Inc.

Haveman, Robert and Melissa Mullikin. 1999. "Alternatives to the Official Poverty Measure: Perspectives and Assessment." University of Wisconsin. Working Paper.

Lang, Kevin. 2007. *Poverty and Discrimination.* Princeton, NJ: Princeton University Press

Lee, Frederic. 2009. *A History of Heterodox Economics: Challenging the Mainstream in the Twentieth Century.* New York: Routledge.

Mangum, Garth, Steven Mangum, and Andrew Sum. 2003. *The Persistence of Poverty in the United States.* Baltimore, MD: Johns Hopkins University Press.

Murray, Charles. 1984. *Losing Ground: American Social Policy, 1950–1980.* New York: Basic Books.

Phelps, Edmund. 1997. *Rewarding Work: How to Restore Participation and Self-Support to Free Enterprise.* Cambridge, MA: Harvard University Press.

Ravallion, Martin. 2016. *The Economics of Poverty: History, Measurement, and Policy.* New York: Oxford University Press.

Rycroft, Robert. 2013. *The Economics of Inequality, Poverty, and Discrimination in the 21st Century, Volume 1: Causes.* Santa Barbara, CA: Praeger.

Schiller, Bradley. 2008. *The Economics of Poverty and Discrimination,* 10th Edition. Upper Saddle River, NJ: Pearson Prentice Hall.

Wolff, Edward. 2009. *Poverty and Income Distribution,* 2nd Edition. Chichester, West Sussex, UK: Wiley Blackwell.

❖ 2

Economic Models

It may surprise students to learn that economists spend little time observing society. Instead, economists spend most of their time working in models. They create models as their own alternative universes, and then they work in these alternative universes as if they were reality. At first glance, it might seem irrational to base government policy decisions on the working of a model. Granted, this method does have its dangers, but it is the only practical way of determining the causes and solutions to most social problems.

The goal of this chapter to show why economic policy must be conceived within a model. We will also discuss how models are developed, the danger of using models that don't mimic the actions of the real world, and the need to test models to make sure that they predict accurately. Understanding these points is a necessary prerequisite for comprehending how social scientists actually work and for understanding the organization of this book.

Direct Observation and Models

To devise a solution to poverty, we need to know the cause or causes of poverty. A number of reasons have been suggested. However, determining the cause of poverty through direct observation of the poor is virtually impossible for the following reasons:

- There are, as of 2016, all most twenty-three million working-aged adults below the poverty line. Interviewing them all would be prohibitively costly and time-consuming.

- Interviewing the poor may not be a good way of determining why they are poor. In some cases, certain factors interact with one another, making it extremely difficult to determine which factor is the primary cause of poverty. For example, people who are unable to get steady employment due to a lack of jobs in one time period often develop anti-social behavior patterns and poor employment histories. This makes it difficult for them to get jobs later, even if jobs are more plentiful.

Simply stated, the world is too big and too complex to discover the causes and solutions to most social problems by direct observation. As a result, social scientists must use an indirect method for determining the causes of poverty. This is not only true for poverty but for most problems in the social and natural sciences. Using models is the tried and true method for handling these situations.

Economic Models

The indirect method of finding the causes and solutions to poverty or other social problem can be characterized by the following three-step process:

1. Build a simplified model that mimics the actions of the real world.

2. Determine what causes poverty to occur in the model.

3. Determine what policies will reduce or eliminate poverty in the model.

However, after reading this three-step approach, the dangers of using the indirect method should be clear to everyone. If the simplified model doesn't mimic the actions of the real world, the causes and solutions produced in the model will most likely be wrong. These models thus need to be tested to make sure that they react to changes in the same ways as the real world. When the indirect method is used, the quality of the explanations and the effectiveness of the solutions depends critically on the accuracy of the model.

The goal of model-building is to produce a model that is both simple and accurate. However, it is the second part of the goal — accuracy — that is the most important. If we can't find a simple model that mimics the actions of the real world, then a more complex model must be used.

Using data, a model is tested to determine whether its predictions match what actually happens. If it doesn't, then the model must either be altered so that it performs better, or it must be scrapped if no amount of altering can make the model predict well. The testing and alteration process repeats itself again and again until a usable model is developed.

Models and Reality

Economists spend much of their time thinking and playing within the alternative universes of their models. Then they leave and re-enter the real world to test their models, to make policy recommendations, to have dinner, and so on. They then return to their alternative universes to do more work, and so it goes, back and forth, over and over. The economists constantly move from models to reality and back to models.

One of the skills that we want to strengthen is our ability to think within a model. After learning how to think within one model, we'll learn how to think within a second model. And then we'll move back and forth between models. Finally, we'll move back and forth between reality and models. Clearly, we will be having a good time with all this moving around, but there is a pitfall that many economic writers fall into, and we should be aware of it.

Many economists fail to indicate to readers whether they are discussing a model or reality. The reader is often left thinking that X has been observed in reality, when in fact X is just a feature or prediction of the author's model. While we suspect that every economist has been guilty of this at one time or another in everyday conversation, it shouldn't happen in writing.

When authors discuss models as if they are the real world, it may be that they are unaware of the audience's misperceptions. However, the intention may also be more nefarious. The authors may be passing off their models as reality to avoid explaining unrealistic assumptions to the reader. Either way, being unclear as to whether they are writing about models or reality doesn't serve the reader, and it is especially harmful for introductory students. As we proceed through this book, we will regularly encounter phrases like "in the orthodox model" or "in the heterodox model." This may seem unnecessarily repetitive, but it is better said too often than not enough.

Hypotheses, Theories, and Models

Economists often use these three words interchangeably. While the dictionary definitions of these words are different, it isn't always clear in practice which word should be used and when.

A theory is "a coherent group of general propositions used as principles of explanation for a class of phenomena" (Random House Webster 2001). A hypothesis is essentially the same. The difference is that hypotheses are tentative explanations, while theories have undergone a certain amount of testing. How much testing of an explanation must occur before that explanation goes from being a hypothesis to a theory? There is no tried and true rule, so people tend to use the two interchangeably.

A model is "a simplified representation of a system or phenomenon, as in the sciences or economics, with any hypotheses required to describe the system or explain the phenomenon, often mathematically" (Random House Webster 2001). An economic model can either be presented verbally or mathematically. We can envision a model as being an outgrowth of a theory where the important variables and direction of causation are dictated by the theory. However, especially when what we call a model is presented verbally, it becomes difficult to definitively say this is the model and that is the theory because both are being presented verbally. At times, then, economists tend to speak interchangeably about hypotheses, theories, and models. It can be confusing for students, but however it is labeled, each is an attempt to explain how the world in which we live works. If we can get that explanation correct, then we can use that knowledge to help improve our world.

Developing Scientific Models

Setting aside for the moment that we might build a model with the objective of producing a particular result for ideological reasons, as we'll see later in this chapter, the goal of model building is to construct a model that is much simpler than the real world but operates exactly like it. For the sake of simplicity, we present the process of model building as if it occurs in distinct steps. This implies that the model builder does the first step, then moves to the second step, and so on.

In fact, nothing could be further from the truth. Model building is not cleanly structured. It is an iterative process in which the modelers bounce between these steps, adjusting here and there as they move closer and closer to the final version of the model.

Negligibility Assumption

The first step in constructing a model is to make what are referred to as negligibility or simplifying assumptions. Negligibility assumptions are supposed to simplify the model without compromising its effectiveness (Musgrave 1981). There are many factors that don't have an effect on the phenomena under study. For example, the eye color of wheat farmers probably has no effect on the amount of wheat produced. Therefore, if in reality the effect of factor F, the eye color of wheat farmers, is negligible, then modelers can assume that it doesn't exist when building their models.

The eye color example is trivial, but in other models, determining whether a factor's effect is negligible is not so obvious. For example, does trading on financial markets affect the demand for money? The NYSE has a clearinghouse attached to it. At the end of the day, the clearinghouse calculates how much money on net traders owe each other. The amount of money exchanged between stock traders at day's end is only a small fraction of the dollar value of stocks traded. Those who developed models attempting to explain changes in money demand originally assumed that stock market trading had a negligible effect on the demand for money.

Later, another channel was discovered by which stock trading affects the demand for money. Those who were asking their brokers to buy and sell stocks on the NYSE were, at least temporarily, shifting from holding stocks to holding money. As a result, the demand for money increased, and predictions of money demand improved when a variable for stock market trading was added to models of money demand (Furey 1993). In the ideal model, all the factors that have a negligible effect are assumed not to exist, and only those that matter are left.

Direction of Causality

After getting rid of all the factors that have little or no effect, modelers are left with the factors they believe have a significant effect on the phenomena under study. They must next hypothesize how these factors interact with each other. For example, during certain time periods, there has been a strong correlation between changes in the price level and changes in the amount of money in the economy. As one goes up, the other goes up, and vice versa.

However, do higher prices lead to an increase in the quantity of money in the economy? Does an increase in the quantity of money lead to an increase in prices? Or is there some third variable that causes both of them to move up and down simultaneously? These are the types of causal relations that modelers must initially specify.

Getting the order of causation correct is vital for finding the correct solution to problems. A good example comes from the world of healthcare. It's not uncommon for the elderly to suffer hip fractures from a fall. Because such injuries take a long time to heal, especially in the elderly, a fractured hip often sets off a downward spiral of health problems resulting in institutionalization or death. Efforts were therefore made to keep older individuals from falling with handrails and other safeguards. However, the effects of these measures were less successful than expected.

Finally, researchers started to suspect that the direction of causation was reversed, that for many of the elderly, loss in bone density and other factors actually resulted in hip breakage, which caused them to fall. Efforts to increase bone density—and not the installation of handrails—are thus a far more effective solution if causality primarily runs in this direction.

It's the same principle that guides economic theory. Getting the direction of causality correct is the key to developing an accurate model and effective solutions.

Domain Assumptions

No economic model can be used in all situations. For each model, there are circumstances where it will mispredict. This doesn't mean that all economic models are bad and need to be scrapped. It simply means that models can only be used effectively under certain conditions. Some models are flexible and can be used over a broad range of circumstances. Others can only be used in very specific situations.

Modelers must therefore specify under what conditions or in what domain each model can be used. The act of specifying the model's usability is what we call specifying the domain or conditional assumptions of the model. In order to illustrate the domain assumptions[13] of a model, we'll discuss two examples. One is pulled from economics, and the other is not.[14]

A Zombie Epidemic

Researchers in England attempted to model the effects of a zombie epidemic on the world population (Davies, Cheshire, Garratley, and Moore 2016a). They found that if such an epidemic occurs, the world's population will be virtually wiped out within one hundred days. Setting aside for the moment that there are no such things as zombies, how is it possible for that to happen? Judging from zombie movies, it appears that after a terrifying and harrowing adventure, the protagonist always manages to survive. How is it possible then for the total world population of humans to be eliminated in just over one hundred days?

The answer may lie in one domain assumption of the authors' model. They assume that there is no "possibility for the humans to kill the zombies." Would it make any difference if the domain assumption in their model had been that humans can kill zombies? As it turns out, the researchers produced a second study, "Another Zombie Epidemic" in which they changed several parts of their model, including allowing humans to kill zombies. The result is that while humans come close to extinction, they manage to survive (Davies, Cheshire, Garratley and Moore 2016b).

Our researchers thus have two models. If there is an actual zombie epidemic, which model should they choose? If the zombies have mutated into invincible super-zombies and the humans are unable to kill them, then the first model is best. The domain assumption in that model best fits the real-world situation, and we will mostly likely be roaming the streets looking for brains in one hundred days. Conversely, if the actual zombies are killable and each town has its own weapons caches and ruggedly handsome action heroes, then the second model is the best to use because its domain assumption best fits the real-world situation.

Model	Domain Assumptions
Perfect Competition	Many Small, Powerless Firms Homogeneous Products
Monopolistic Competition	Many Small Firms Heterogeneous Products
Oligopoly	A Few Large Firms Heterogeneous Products
Monopoly	Only One Firm in the Industry

Figure 1. Different models for different market structures.

A Decrease in Demand

How firms react when the demand for their product declines significantly, as often happens in a depression or recession, depends on the firm's relative power and the amount of competition it faces. To analyze real-world situations like this, economists have developed a series of models that have different domain assumptions about the size of the firm and whether its goods and services are homogenous, just like other firms' goods, or heterogeneous, not like other firms' goods. Traditionally, the discussion of these models falls under the topic of market structure. Introductory discussions usually focus on the four models in figure 1.

If we look historically at the question of what firms do in a depression or recession, we can once again see the importance of domain assumptions. With the onset of the Great Depression in 1929, economists of the day used the model of perfect competition. When perfectly competitive firms face a fall in demand, they lower their prices. Because each is small and powerless, each fears being stuck with unsold goods and cuts its price, hoping to get rid of its surplus goods. Because each firm has the same incentives, this leads to a price war, and prices fall. Based on this prediction and other parts of their model, the orthodox economists of the day predicted that depressions could not last for long. They could not have been more wrong about the Great Depression, which lasted for over ten years. Their models contained domain assumptions that didn't fit the actual conditions.

As the economist John Maynard Keynes pointed out at the time, most industries were dominated by a few large firms called oligopolies. When oligopolies face a decline in demand, their first reaction is to cut production, which increases unemployment, making the depression or recession worse. Keynes's model, which contains the domain assumption that firms are best described as oligopolies, does a far better job of explaining and predicting events during depressions or recessions than models that assume perfect competition.

The modelers' choices of domain assumptions take on a more important role than we might at first suspect. Once a model has been simplified through negligibility assumptions, the two major parts of model building are to determine the causal links and to make the domain assumptions. In many cases, the two are indistinguishable. Often, when modelers make a domain assumption, such as that wages are determined in a supply and demand labor market, they are determining the direction of causation for some, if not all, of the variables.

Testing Models

The key to the indirect method being able to successfully determine the causes and the solutions to social problems is that *the model must be able to mimic the actions of the real world.* Models that can't mimic the action of the real world will most likely suggest causes that are incorrect. The solutions suggested by these models may damage society. In order to tell whether a model is accurate, it needs to be tested.

Once an initial model has been constructed, there is a period of testing and alteration. This process continues until either the model is the most scientific model in this area of study, or it has been scrapped.

However, even if the scientific community agrees that the model is good, the testing never stops. This is because the world is continuously changing. At some point, the model may no longer predict accurately. If this happens, the model must once again go through a period of alteration and testing or be scrapped.

One of the keys to getting an accurate model is getting the assumptions correct. Getting the assumptions wrong can cause may types of problems.

Negligibility Errors

There are two types of errors that could occur if the model has an incorrect negligibility assumption.

One error is that a particular variable may be thought to be important but actually isn't. If, after testing a model in a number of different situations, this variable is shown to never have any effect, then it is dropped from the model. While it may seem to be an unproductive use of a modeler's time, the reassurance that this factor has no effect was probably worth the time and effort.

A second error is that the model's developer assumes that a factor has no effect when it actually does. Leaving this factor out means the model cannot explain or predict what is happening as well as it could if this variable is included. However, depending on the situation, discovering that there is a missing factor may be difficult. No model can explain the economic data perfectly. If a researcher has a model that seems to explain reality reasonably well, and if the missing factor is not changing dramatically, then the researcher may think all significant variables have been identified.

Stock market trading, for example, increased steadily for many years and at about the same rate as the growth in the overall economy. Not having this factor in a model of money demand made little difference because its effect was picked up by the much more important growth of the overall economy. However, when stock market trading exploded between 1983 and 1987, forecasts with the standard model consistently underestimated the demand for money. This was an indication that some factor was missing from the model. In such a scenario, it then becomes a question of finding the missing factor.

Domain Assumption Errors

The more problematic situation is when a domain assumption in the model is incorrect.

If a domain assumption is unrealistic, then the model's predictions will be inaccurate. This doesn't mean that the model's predictions are always wrong. However, when the false assumption plays a significant role in the analysis, the model will tend to mispredict. This is important to understand because models with unrealistic domain assumptions can predict accurately at times. However, they will not and cannot predict accurately all the time because these models can't mimic the actions of the real world. We can demonstrate this point with a simple example.

Let's assume that we built a model of a bicycle. Our model has one terrible domain assumption—it assumes there is no chain connecting the pedal sprocket to the rear wheel sprocket. We can do a couple of experiments with our model. First, let's take our model to the top of a hill and point it down and see what happens. The model coasts down the hill, picking up speed as it goes, and when it comes to the flat, it decelerates until it comes to a stop. Is this what a real bicycle would do? Yes. Did the faulty assumption come into play? No.

Our second experiment is on flat land. This time, we sit on the model and pedal rapidly. The model doesn't move. In fact, we and our model will probably fall over. Is this what a real bicycle would do? No. A real bicycle with a chain connecting the pedal sprocket to the rear wheel's sprocket would move forward. Did the faulty assumption come into play? Absolutely.[15]

While the actions of real scientific models are more complicated than this example, the basic principle is the same. If a model doesn't operate like the real world operates, then it cannot at all times predict accurately the actions of the real world. The more the analysis relies on the faulty domain assumption, the less likely the model is to predict accurately.

Testing for Errors

All models produce numerous predictions, so where should we start testing? The object of our testing is to discover whether the model can mimic the real world. If it can't, then it either needs to be altered or scrapped. We thus want to test the model at its weakest point. A good first step is to review the model's negligibility and domain assumptions, as well as the model's proposed directions of causality. If one of these seems unrealistic, then a good place to start testing is with the predictions that are highly dependent on the questionable assumption.

As we will see in coming chapters, the orthodox economic model is built on several unrealistic assumptions. Those assumptions are critical to the model's answers to the questions of whether labor markets tend to clear and what happens to wages during a recession. This is likely to be a weak point for that model, so it is an area that we should test. The heterodox model produces different answers to those same questions, so that gives us another reason for testing those questions. Because the predictions of the two models are so different, this is a good place to test which model does a better job of mimicking the real world.

There is an additional reason to test whether labor markets clear. The heterodox model predicts that labor markets rarely clear. The orthodox model predicts that labor markets always clear in the long run.[16] For each perspective, this feature is critically important to the operation of their overall model and for determining the causes and solutions to poverty. Knowing which model best mimics the real world on that question will be vitally important for devising solutions to poverty.

Building Models for Ideological Reasons

The scientific process can be corrupted. Economists are people just like everyone else, and they may succumb to incentives and pressures from both inside and outside the profession. The problem stems from the fact that the policies resulting from any economic analysis can have major effects on the distribution of income — that is, on who gets how much money. Those with much to gain or lose, and who have the financial and institutional means to affect the direction of research, have a strong incentive to influence economists to develop models that produce policies that they favor. These individuals are likely uninterested in furthering science or in improving society. They spend their financial resources as an investment, hoping to reap large returns.

Let's assume, for example, that a factory owner's factories produce a toxic sludge as a byproduct of their production process. They could ship the sludge off to a Class 1 dumpsite to be treated, but it is much cheaper to pour the sludge into the river. To avoid being forced by some law to ship the sludge off to a Class 1 dumpsite, the factory owner can try lobbying Congress. The owner can also donate to economic think tanks who have models arguing that government efforts to clean up pollution are bad for the economy and society. In this example, the factory owner does not care if the think tank's models are accurate — only how the models can be used to further a specific agenda. The oil and gas industry does this in the global warming debate.

The chances are small that a model developed for ideological purposes accurately mimics the actions of the real world. One reason is that non-scientific models are not subject to the full interactive process of testing and adjustment. When these models don't predict well, they can only be altered to the extent that the alterations improve predictions without changing the results. After all, the model is created to produce the desired results and nothing else. Therefore, when necessary alterations cause the results of the model to change, the creators of these models must then ignore the evidence that their models can't mimic the actions of the real world and proceed as if nothing has happened.

The orthodox theory of labor markets has a number of domain assumptions that most find highly unrealistic. As we will see, the orthodox model badly mispredicts basic labor market outcomes and is unable to explain basic features of real labor market. These problems have been known for many years. Outside of some minor adjustments, orthodox economists have basically ignored the problems with their model. In both micro- and macroeconomics, their model of labor markets has been used again and again to defend the interests of the business community and the well-to-do. As we will see, the orthodox model of labor markets also produces results favorable to the well-to-do when analyzing poverty.

We wouldn't expect the creators of these models to state publicly that they built them purely to produce a particular set of ideologically driven results.[17] However, we begin to suspect a model was developed purely to defend the interests of the powerful group when the following is true:

- The model is built with a series of unrealistic assumptions.

- These assumptions are critical to producing the primary results and predictions of the model.

- The predictions of the model are routinely wrong.

- The users and creators of these models ignore these wrong predictions.

- The model is incapable of explaining how the real world works.

- The model is used primarily to protect and promote the interests of a powerful group in society.

This problem isn't just true for the orthodox theory of labor markets. We will see the same pattern with the orthodox theory of money creation. In that theory, there are two assumptions that are clearly false. These assumptions are critical to producing the basic results and predictions of the model. Like the orthodox labor market model, this model is unable to explain how the real banking system works, its predictions are routinely wrong, and the model is used by itself and with other models to defend the interests of the rich.

Many of the models used by orthodox economists are constructed using highly unrealistic assumptions, and these models have come under criticism for that reason. However, a defense of this practice was put forward by the famous conservative economist Milton Friedman in *Essays in Positive Economics* (1953). His position is that a hypothesis can only be judged worthy or unworthy based on the accuracy of its predictions, not by the realism of its assumptions.[18] Many have questioned Friedman's argument, but within the economics profession, his position that models should be judged by how well they can predict has become the gold standard for determining whether a model is worthy or unworthy.[19]

However, Friedman's position is not held by the wider scientific community. For the scientific community, explanation and not prediction is the primary goal of science.[20] For them, the ability of the model to explain the real world is more important than its ability to predict. Later, we will see how well our two models can predict economic outcomes and how well they can explain what happens in real-world labor markets.

References

Clark, John Bates. 1899 (1956). *The Distribution of Wealth: A Theory of Wages, Interest and Profits*. New York: Kelley & Millman, Inc.

Davies, C.T., K.J. Cheshire, R Garratley, and J. Moore. 2016a. "A Zombie Epidemic." *Journal Physics Special Topics: An undergraduate physics journal*. November 22: A2_5.

Davies, C.T., K.J. Cheshire, R Garratley, and J. Moore. 2016b. "Another Zombie Epidemic." *Journal Physics Special Topics: An undergraduate physics journal*. November 22: A2_6.

Friedman, Milton. 1953. "The Methodology of Positive Economics." *Essays in Positive Economics*. Chicago: University of Chicago Press, 3-43.

Furey, Kevin. 1993. "The Effect of Trading in Financial Markets on Money Demand." *Eastern Economic Journal* 19, Winter: 83–90.

Haack, S. 2003. *Defending Science—Within Reason*. Amherst, MA: Prometheus Books.

Henry, John F. 1983–84. "On Equilibrium." *Journal of Post Keynesian Economics*. 6, Winter: 214–29.

Hesse, Mary. 1967. "Laws and Theories." *The Encyclopedia of Philosophy, Vol 4*, edited by Paul Edwards. New York: Macmillan and the Free Press, 404-10.

Musgrave, Alan. 1981. "'Unreal Assumptions' in Economic Theory: The F-Twist Untwisted." *Kyklos* 34: 377–87.

Random House Webster. 2001. *Random House Webster's Unabridged Dictionary*. 2nd ed. New York: Random House.

Webb, James. 1987. "Is Friedman's Methodological Instrumentalism a Special Case of Dewey's Instrumental Philosophy? A Comment on Wible." *Journal of Economic Issues* 21: 393–429.

❖ 3

The Simple Keynesian Model

According to heterodox theory, the natural workings of a capitalist economy always produce individuals and families with income below the poverty line. In other words, "the system is to blame." In this theory, expansions normally end before full employment is reached. As a result, there are almost always more people looking for work than there are job openings. Some people go through long periods of unemployment or underemployment and have incomes below the poverty line. Others fall below the poverty line because they work at low-wage jobs.

To understand the causes and solutions to poverty in the heterodox model, we thus need to know what determines the level of employment and unemployment and what determines wages. The major questions are why the economic system doesn't produce full employment and why some jobs pay very low wages. We'll start with the question of employment in this and the next chapter. After that, we will look at wages.

Employment in a Heterodox Model

In a heterodox model, employment is determined by macroeconomic forces. If the economy is at full employment, then aggregate supply determines the level of employment and output. When the economy is at less than full employment, aggregate demand determines the level of employment and output. According to the heterodox model of business cycles, the economy rarely achieves full employment. Therefore, during most if not all time periods, employment is determined by the level of aggregate demand. The best vehicle for studying changes in aggregate demand and employment is the simple Keynesian model.

The model is named for the father of macroeconomics, John Maynard Keynes. While Keynes never put forward this model, it is a simplified version of what appears in his classic work, *The General Theory of Interest, Employment and Money* (1936), which was published during the Great Depression. The model conveys many of Keynes's ideas in an easily digestible form.

If we survey the different macroeconomic theories, we find that the aggregate supply side differs dramatically from one theory to another. This difference is particularly large between orthodox and heterodox models. On the other hand, with the exception of how different models handle financial markets and the role of the Federal Reserve,[21] which we will take up in Chapter 11, the aggregate demand sides are fairly similar.

The simple Keynesian model focuses on aggregate demand, though without the effects of financial markets. It is reasonable, then, to say that all macroeconomic models contain a simple Keynesian model within them. As we study the simple Keynesian model in a chapter on heterodox theory, we could just as well be studying the same topic in an orthodox textbook. Before starting our discussion, however, there are a couple of terms that need to be clarified.

Measuring Growth

People often ask how the economy is doing. Answering that question requires investigating a number of dimensions. One part of the answer revolves around measuring whether the economy is growing or shrinking and how fast it's growing or shrinking.

In order to answer that part of the question, we need a measure of the nation's output. We could add up the number of goods and services produced. However, if the nation produced one million more cars this year but produced two million less peanuts, would we say that the economy was shrinking? Probably not. One car takes far more effort and resources to produce than one peanut. One car is also more valued by the person who receives it than one peanut. Those who developed a measure of US output therefore looked for something that reflected the value of the goods and services produced. Gross Domestic Product (GDP) is what they used to measure output.

GDP is the dollar value of all final goods and services produced within the US borders over some time period, which is generally a year. The word "final" in this definition means that we only count a sale when it goes to the person who ultimately uses the good. This is so we don't double- or triple-count items. For example, the farmer sells wheat to the miller who then makes flour from the wheat. The miller sells the flour to the baker who makes bread from the flour, and then the baker sells the bread to a shopper. If we count all of these transactions, we count the wheat three times, and we count the flour twice. We don't want that to happen, so we only count the transaction of the baker selling the bread to the shopper.

There is another problem with the definition of GDP that surfaces when we compare different years. GDP can increase for two reasons. One reason is that the nation is producing more goods and services. The other reason is inflation, which means that the price of goods and services increases. If we divide GDP by a measure of inflation, we can remove inflation from our measure, leaving only the change in output, which is what we want. GDP is divided by something we call the GDP deflator, which removes inflation, to get to the real gross domestic product (RGDP). In the US, we use the RGDP to measure changes in the level of goods and services produced. However, RGDP measures more than just output.

The Relationship of Output to Income

It seems as if the output of the nation and the income of its citizens should be different concepts with different numerical values. However, they are actually different sides of the same coin, and they have the same numerical value. Part of the reason they seem so different is that we live in a monetary economy. If we lived in a barter society, the connection between the two would be clear.

Let's say, for example, that we have a number of people with connections to Papa Bee Soup Company and its famous minestrone soup. Some people are suppliers, some are workers, and some are managers. There is also Papa Bee, the owner. On Monday, under the guidance of the managers and with a constant supply of vegetables, hot Italian sausage, pasta, and Italian herb and spices, the workers start producing cans of minestrone soup. When the product is finished, it's put into boxes, placed onto pallets, and stacked in the warehouse. At the end of work on Friday, it's time to be paid.

In a barter society, these people aren't paid with money, but with products. Based on the contracts that they have signed, each supplier, worker, and manager receives a certain number of cans of soup. If there are cans left over after everyone with a contract has been paid, then Papa Bee receives those cans. When they all leave with their weekly income and Papa Bee leaves with his leftover cans, the warehouse is empty, just as it was on Monday morning.

As you can see, what these people produce each week is thus both the output of the factory and the income of the group. The same is true for us in a monetary society. Income and output are the same. These terms are often used interchangeably by macroeconomists. In textbooks, economists often use the capital letter Y to designate both income and output, and its numerical value is that of the RGDP.

Introduction to the Model

Now that we have those terms in mind, it's time to turn our attention to the simple Keynesian model. This model can be summarized by the following equation:

$$AD = C + I + G + NX \text{ (3.1)}$$

The equation highlights the four basic actors who demand goods and services in macroeconomics. Demand in this model is not what people wish to have but what people actually purchase. In a simple Keynesian model, we assume that firms hold inventories and always have the ability to expand production. If a person wishes to purchase a good, there is always a good available to sell them. Therefore, aggregate demand (AD) is the actual purchasing of US made goods and services by one of our four actors—households, businesses, government, and foreigners.

Household purchases of goods and services are known as consumption (C). Business purchases of plant and equipment are referred to as investment (I).[22] Government purchases of goods and services are known as government spending (G).[23] When people in other countries purchase US-made goods and services, those purchases are referred to as exports. When US citizens purchase foreign-made goods and services, those purchases are referred to as imports. Exports minus imports is known as net exports (NX), the fourth and last component of aggregate demand. Net exports can be a negative number if we import more than we export.

We can think of aggregate demand as a stack of four blocks that build a tower. The higher the tower is, the more goods and services need to be produced, so the more people firms need to hire. Figure 1 illustrates that stack of blocks. While this metaphor is useful, there is an inaccuracy hidden within it that we will look at when we examine the multiplier.

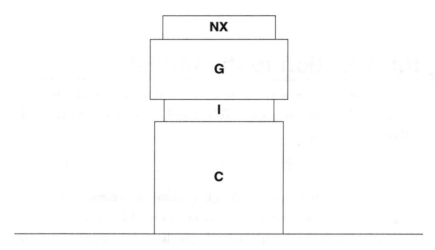

Figure 1. The tower of aggregate demand.

When envisioning an economic model, there is a tendency to think of something that has both a supply and demand side. But the simple Keynesian model appears to have only the aggregate demand side. That is not actually true. What this model assumes is that there are unemployed individuals and that there is unemployed capital equipment. As the demand for products increases, firms increase their output by hiring unemployed laborers and putting them to work with the previously unused capital equipment. Therefore, the aggregate supply, the amount of goods and services that firms produce, is determined by aggregate demand. While aggregate supply exists in this model, there is no independent action that arises from aggregate supply. Aggregate supply adjusts passively to the level of aggregate demand.

In a simple Keynesian model, then, we can say that demand determines supply. We therefore only need to focus our attention on what is happening to aggregate demand. If the economy were to continuously expand, then at some point, society would either run out of unemployed individuals or unused capital equipment. However, the simple Keynesian model implicitly assumes that this never happens.

Given that an increase in aggregate demand results in an increase in employment and a decline in unemployment, it is natural to ask what causes the four components of aggregate demand to rise and fall. Can we use government policy to increase aggregate demand? Let's start with consumption, the largest component of aggregate demand.

Consumption

The major factors that affect household purchases of goods and services are disposable income, expected income, wealth, and availability of credit.

Disposable Income

Disposable income is by far the most important factor in determining how many goods and services households will purchase. Disposable income is calculated using this formula:

$$DI = Y - TA \quad (3.2)$$

In other words, disposable income (DI) is income (Y) minus taxes (TA). If everything else is constant, higher income leads to greater disposable income and greater consumption. If everything else is constant, higher taxes lead to lower disposable income and lower consumption.

It is important to understand that in macroeconomics, households can only do two things, spend and save. Any disposable income that is not spent on goods and services is saved. It doesn't matter whether the funds are put into a savings account, used to buy stocks and bonds, or used to buy oil futures—it is all saving in macroeconomics. It doesn't matter how risky the asset is. With any increase in disposable income, the household spends a portion and saves the rest. While spending and saving varies dramatically from household to household, these proportions for the economy as a whole are fairly constant in the short run and normally change slowly over time.

In developing his theory, Keynes gave specific names to these interlinked proportions of spending and saving. The marginal propensity to consume (MPC) is the proportion of additional disposable income spent on goods and services. The marginal propensity to save (MPS) is the portion of new income not spent on goods and services:

$$1 = MPC + MPS \ (3.3)$$
$$MPS = 1 - MPC \ (3.4)$$

Thus:

$$\Delta Y = MPC \times \Delta Y + MPS \times \Delta Y \ (3.5)$$

How much does consumption increase when the disposable income of the nation increases by—this is macroeconomics, so let's use a big number—$100 billion? If MPC = 0.95 and MPS = 0.05 and national income increases by $100 billion, then spending increases by $95 billion. Savings increase by $5 billion.

Not everyone in society has the same MPC. This is not surprising because a larger proportion of the income going to the poor and middle class is spent on necessities. They have far less income left over to save.

The fact that the MPC is higher for the poor and middle class has an interesting implication for public policy. Often during recessions, the government has attempted to increase consumption spending by lowering taxes. To get the largest increase in consumption, whose taxes should the government cut? The government should cut taxes for the poor and middle class. However, that is not what happened in 2001 and in 2008, where the lion's share of the tax cuts went to the rich.

Expected Income

People often look ahead. If in the near future they foresee their fortunes changing dramatically, they change their consumption patterns in the present. Assume, for example, that you are a low income student—not that your grades are bad but that you don't have much income. It's the spring of your senior year, and you'll be graduating soon. You get a call from the First Bank of Godzilla, a multinational financial corporation, which says that upon graduation they wish to hire you. They offer you a good salary and full benefits. What is likely to happen to your current spending patterns?

When asked this sort of question, most reply that they will spend more now. If a large portion of the population believes that the economy will do well in the future and that they will personally prosper, then consumption increases. If people believe that a recession will occur soon and that they will personally suffer, then consumption falls as people save more in preparation for bad times. Because government economists worry about spooking the public and causing a fall in consumption, their public announcements tend to be optimistic.

Wealth

Household spending is not only affected by income and expected income but also by household wealth. Wealth is generally defined as objects that can be sold for money. Stocks, bonds, bank accounts, and real estate are the primary assets that constitute wealth. As the dollar value of wealth increases, people feel richer and spend a higher proportion of their income.

The increase in spending caused by an increase in wealth is not large. For every $100 increase in wealth, it's estimated that yearly spending increases by $2 to $3 dollars. During many time periods, the year-to-year fluctuations in wealth are not large enough to make much of a difference in consumption. However, over the past twenty-five years, there have been several periods in which the dollar value of wealth changed rapidly due to rapid increases or decreases in the price of stocks or housing.

Availability of Credit

As the availability of credit increases, there is a strong tendency for households to increase their purchases of goods and services. This availability comes largely from two sources.

The first source is an increase in the willingness of banks and credit card companies to lend to households. This can happen because times are good, and as a result more people qualify for credit. This can also happen because banks and credit card companies lower their standards of creditworthiness, extending credit to those who in the past would have been considered uncreditworthy. The expansion of credit due to falling credit standards can lead to an increase in defaults during a recession. An excellent example of this is the expansion of the sub-prime mortgages and the implosion of financial markets from 2007-09 .

The second source is an increase in home equity loans. This is primarily a function of rapidly rising house prices. An increase in these types of loans can occur without a drop in credit standards. This can also be thought of as an increase in consumption resulting from an increase in wealth. There are really two steps to this increase in consumption. First, wealth needs to increase in the form of higher home prices. Second, banks need to be willing to grant loans based on that increase in wealth. In this day and age, banks seem very willing to do that.

While consumption is the largest component of aggregate demand, investment is normally considered the most important in both heterodox and orthodox models—but for different reasons in each model.

Investment

In macroeconomics, the purchasing of plant and equipment by firms is known as investment. The purchasing of stocks, bonds, and other financial instruments is *not*. While businesses buy many goods and services, most go into the products that the firms sell to consumers and thus are not counted as investment. The only final goods that businesses buy, often referred to as plant and equipment, are the buildings to house the firm's activities and the machines and tools used to produce the firm's goods and services. Economists also refer to plant and equipment as "capital" or "physical capital."

The factors that affect investment are interest rates, the rate technological progress, capacity utilization, the availability of credit, business taxes, and what Keynes calls the "animal spirits" of business people. We'll start with that last factor.

Animal Spirits

The reason businesses buy plant and equipment is that they expect to make a profit from using the capital to make goods and services. But because capital lasts a long time it is impossible to calculate profits from buying the new plant and equipment. The most important factor for determining investment is thus what Keynes referred to as the spontaneous optimism of businesspeople—or the animal spirits.[24] To understand this factor, it is worth quoting Keynes at length:

> Even apart from the instability due to speculation, there is the instability due to the characteristic of human nature that a large proportion of our positive activities depend on spontaneous optimism rather than on a mathematical expectation, whether moral or hedonistic or economic. Most, probably, of our decisions to do something positive, the full consequences of which will be drawn out over many days to come, can only be taken as a result of animal spirits—of a spontaneous urge to action rather than inaction, and not as the outcome of a weighted average of quantitative benefits multiplied by quantitative probabilities. Enterprise only pretends to itself to be mainly actuated by the statements in its own prospectus, however candid and sincere. Only a little more than an expedition to the South Pole,

is it based on an exact calculation of benefits to come. Thus, if the animal spirits are dimmed and the spontaneous optimism falters, leaving us to depend on nothing but a mathematical expectation, enterprise will fade and die;—though fears of loss may have a basis no more reasonable than hopes of profit had before. . . .

We should not conclude from this that everything depends on waves of irrational psychology. On the contrary, the state of long-term expectation is often steady, and, even when it is not, other factors exert their compensating effects. We are merely reminding ourselves that human decisions affecting the future, whether personal or political or economic, cannot depend on strict mathematical expectation, since the basis for making such calculations does not exist; and that it is our innate urge to activity which makes the wheels go around, our rational selves choosing between the alternatives as best we are able, calculating where we can, but often falling back for our motive on whim or sentiment or chance. (Keynes 1936 p. 161–63)

Keynes is simply pointing out that firms only invest if they believe the investment will be profitable. However, most of the information necessary to make the calculation of profits is unavailable. They don't know, for example, what the price of copper will be ten years from now or what inventions will affect demand for their product over the next twenty years. However, even if business people can't make these calculations, they still have to make a decision. They can't wait for the information to come in. They have to ask themselves, even after all the research has been done, "Do I feel lucky?"

College students are in exactly the same situation when deciding whether to invest in a college education or when choosing a major. While the costs of going to college may be known with some degree of certainty, the benefits for each individual are largely unknown. In the end, the decision to invest in new plants and equipment, like the decision to invest in a college education, rests on optimism. Research shows that what tends to make business people optimistic about the future is how well their firm is doing now (Fazzari 1993). A strong economy tends to promote investment, and a weak economy doesn't.

Interest Rates

Another important factor is the interest rate on business loans. The higher interest rates are, the more expensive it is to borrow money to purchase new plant and equipment.[25] This plays a smaller role in heterodox theory than it does in orthodox theory. The reason that interest rates play a relatively small role in heterodox economics is that studies have shown that the purchasing of plant and equipment is relatively unresponsive to changes in interest rates.[26] In orthodox theory, it is the movement of the interest rate—and as a result, the level of investment—that brings the loanable funds market into equilibrium. Interest rates thus play a more important role in that theory.

Higher interest rates also have a secondary effect on investment. Many firms have loans outstanding for either previous investment or for working capital.[27] Most bank loans to businesses are variable-rate loans whose rates change whenever there is a change in the prime rate.[28] If the prime rate goes up, then the cost of those previous loans goes up, reducing profits and depressing the animal spirits. For the most part, short-term interest rates in the US are set by the Federal Reserve. Long-term rates are strongly influenced by the short-term rates set by the Federal Reserve.

Technological Progress

In a world where there is no technological progress and all firms produce the same quantity of output year after year, the total demand for investment each year would be equal to the amount of capital equipment that wears out. However, technological progress is the hallmark of a capitalist society. As time goes by, the productivity of capital equipment improves.

Output produced with older capital thus costs more than output produced with newer capital. A firm may be forced to replace older capital that has not worn out simply because the cost of producing with the older capital makes their product uncompetitive. This capital is termed obsolete.

The total demand for investment can thus be captured with this formula:

Total Demand for Investment = Worn Out Capital + Obsolete Capital + New Capital (3.6)

If the pace of technological progress increases, capital equipment becomes obsolete at a faster pace, and firms are forced to purchase more capital. In the 1990s, rapid developments in the computer industry kept capital investment strong during the period that otherwise would have witnessed slow investment growth.

Capacity Utilization

Firms never wish to miss a sale due to a lack of product. Firms prevent this from happening by carrying inventories and having excess capacity. They meet short-term increases in consumer demand out of inventories. They meet long-term increases by increasing production. This means hiring new workers, purchasing more raw materials, and using more capital equipment.

Capital generally takes time to order, make, and install. Sometimes the process takes years. In order to meet potential increased demand, most firms have excess capacity—capital equipment that they are not using or are underutilizing. Since 1967, the Federal Reserve has collected data on capacity utilization. As figure 2 shows, the average level of excess capacity has been 19.6 because the average level of capacity utilization was 80.4%. At no time has it been less than 11.5%.[29] If the firm's excess capacity becomes low, it has a strong incentive to buy more capital equip-

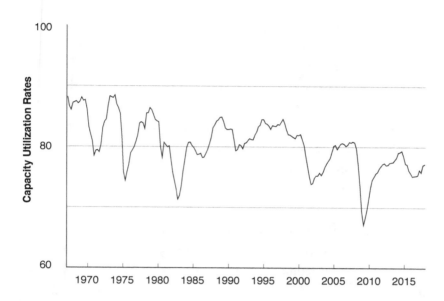

Figure 2. Quarterly capacity utilization rates, 1967 to 2018.

ment. As the aggregate rate of capacity utilization increases, more and more firms find themselves in this position.

Availability of Credit

In the modern period, the cost of capital is large even for small businesses. The vision of the experienced workers saving up their money and then launching themselves into business is largely a thing of the past. For those wishing to go into business or attempting to expand their business, it is necessary to find financing — somebody willing to loan them money. Some can ask friends and family. Most must go to a bank.

However, banks aren't willing to hand out money to just anyone. They only loan it to those they believe have a high chance of paying them back. For small and medium firms, and those with short or non-existent credit histories, the availability of credit from banks is crucial to their investment plans.

Just as in the case of consumption, there are two basic reasons for an expansion in credit. The first reason is that during expansions, banks become more optimistic and firms become more profitable. More firms are thus judged to be creditworthy. The reverse happens during recessions. The second reason is that banks may reduce their standards of creditworthiness in order to attract new customers, purposely taking on risky loans. As a number of banks found out in the 2007–09 recession, this strategy can have dire consequences.

Business Taxes and Subsidies

Firms purchase a piece of capital equipment if the expected net profits are positive. A reduction in business taxes or an increase in subsidies could switch the net expected profits from negative to positive, thereby increasing the purchases of capital.

However, we should expect this effect to be fairly small, and studies have shown it to be small to nonexistent (Fazarri 1993). We should expect the smallest effect from a reduction in general business taxes, which are simply a tax on profits. The largest effect will come from tax reductions or subsidies that are given to firms when they purchase new capital equipment.

Government Spending

Government spending in the simple Keynesian model is spending by government agencies at all levels—city, county, state, and federal. Governments provide many services such as schools, roads, police, recycling, parks, employment services, health care, mental health support, national defense, and the justice system, just to mention a few. There is a tendency in macroeconomics, however, to focus on the federal government because state and local governments are required by law to balance their budgets.

On the state and local level, any increase in spending must be matched by an equal increase in taxes, and vice versa. An increase in government spending increases aggregate demand, and an increase in taxes decreases it. The effect of these two is not equal. An increase in government spending and taxes by the same amount leads to an increase in aggregate demand and employment.[30] However, that increase is small.

The federal government, on the other hand, can have a larger effect because it is not required to balance its budget and can run a sizable budget deficit or surplus. An increase in government spending without an increase in taxes has the exact same effect on aggregate demand and unemployment as an increase in consumption or investment.

Consequently, when the economy falls into recession, the president and executive branch often increase government spending or cut taxes in order to inject aggregate demand into the system. This slows the decline in the economy. Hopefully, this injection of aggregate demand also slows down the decline in consumption and investment by slowing down the decline in household and business optimism. During the 2007–09 recession, the Bush and Obama administrations both attempted to stimulate the economy in this way. While their efforts no doubt helped, these injections of aggregate demand were too small to prevent the economy from falling into the worst recession in the post-WWII period.

While we won't go into detail, we should briefly discuss two related concepts that are often in the news. The size of each has, at times, been a political football. The first is the federal budget deficit, which is government spending minus taxes:

Budget Deficit = G – TA (3.7)

The budget deficit is normally reported for the federal government's fiscal year, which runs from October 1 to September 30. If taxes are greater than government spending, the budget deficit is negative and is referred to as a budget surplus. The last time the US government ran a surplus was at the end of the Clinton Administration and the first year of the Bush Administration, from 1998 to 2001.

The other concept is the national debt. It's a terrible name. Most people believe that the national debt is the amount the US owes the rest of the world, but it's not. It's the amount that the federal government owes others. Most of those others are US individuals, companies, and institutions. In fact, the largest individual holder of US debt is the US Social Security Administration. The formula for calculating the national debt is the sum of all budget deficits minus the sum of all budget surpluses, from 1790 to the present:

$$\text{National Debt} = \textstyle\sum \text{Budget Deficits} - \textstyle\sum \text{Budget Surplus} \quad (3.8)$$

The size of the national debt changes every day, so it is reported at a specific point in time. On May 30, 2018, for example, the national debt was $21.11 trillion.

Political ads have illustrated the national debt with a small child chained to a giant ball of debt, implying that our grandchildren will be stuck paying off our national debt. Others have calculated the national debt owed by each man, woman, and child. The implication is that a day of reckoning is coming soon. However, neither of these images is even vaguely correct.

In 1790, George Washington and his administration ran a budget deficit and had to borrow money. As a result, the US government had a national debt in 1791. The US has never paid that debt off. While the federal government paid back the original lenders, it has never paid off the national debt as a whole because it paid back the original lenders by borrowing more money.

This is known as rolling over the debt, and as a nation, we have been doing it for over two hundred years. George Washington's grandchildren didn't have to pay off national debt, and neither will ours. Those running those ads know full well that the dynamics of the federal government budget and its national debt are not the same as a household's budget and debt. All industrialized countries have sizable national debts, with some being larger than ours and some being smaller.

Net Exports

The next factor in the simple Keynesian model is net exports (NX), which is explained by this equation:

NX = Exports − Imports (3.9)

There are a number of factors that affect net exports. These factors can be broken up into two groups, long-term effects and short-term effects.

Long-Term Effects

Long-term factors tend to shift slowly over time, but they often have profound effects. The general trend of these long-term effects has been to increase imports into the US.

An example of a long-term factor would be reduced shipping costs. When shipping costs are high, the production facilities need to be close to the markets they serve. Over time, technological advancements have steadily reduced shipping costs. Two hundred years ago, the markets served were only citywide. As shipping costs fell, they became regional, national, and eventually international. This has allowed large corporations to set up routine production facilities where wages are low and then import these items back into the home country. The result is a large increase in imports. Other long-term effects include the following:

- Increase in urbanization and industrialization of developing countries: In order to locate routine production facilities in low-wage, third-world countries, those facilities require a sufficient number of urbanized semi-skilled workers.

- Improvement of the quality of manufacturing in other industrialized countries: Japan went from a producer of cheap plastic toys to becoming a producer of high quality goods. Eventually, China is likely to do the same.

- The negotiation of regional trade agreements has opened up countries that were either closed or less open before.

Short-Term Effects

Short-term effects tend to attract more attention because movements in these factors will affect aggregate demand in the near future. We will look at four of these effects — strength of the US economy, strength of foreign economies, exchange rates, and tariffs.

First, the strength of the US economy affects the level of US imports. As the US economy becomes stronger, the income of US households increases. As incomes go up, US citizens buy more goods and services. Some are domestically produced and some are produced aboard, so as the US economy gets stronger, imports increase and, as a result, net exports decrease.

Second, the strength of the economies of our best trading partners affects US exports. The rationale is just the same as above, but it applies to foreign citizens buying US exports. As a result, if the economics of our best trading partners become stronger, US exports rise, as do net exports.

The third factor is exchange rates. A change in the value of the US dollar affects both US exports and imports. For example, assume that the exchange rate between the US dollar and the Japanese yen is that one US dollar buys 100 Japanese yen ($1 = 100¥).[31] For the sake of this example, assume that shipping costs are zero. A US car with a price tag of $20,000 in the US sells for 2,000,000¥ in Japan, and a Japanese car with a price tag of 2,000,000¥ in Japan sells for $20,000 in the US.

The value of the US dollar is said to have "appreciated," "gotten stronger," or "increased" if one US dollar buys more yen. We'll assume then that the value of the US dollar increases to $1 = 110¥. The US car with a price tag of $20,000 now sells for 2,200,000¥ in Japan. Because the car is now more expensive, sales in Japan fall, as do US exports. The Japanese car with the 2,000,000¥ price tag now sells for $18,182 in the US, so the sales of Japanese cars and imports to the US rise. Therefore, if the value of the dollar increases, net exports fall because exports fall and imports rise.

It should be clear from this example that a stronger US dollar is not good for everyone, even though that is how it is often portrayed in the news. If the dollar becomes stronger, the price of imports goes down. People buying imports are better off, but the owners, managers and workers in export goods industries are worse off. Without going into detail about how exchange rates are determined, which is code for "trust me on this one," if the Federal Reserve increases interest rates, then with all other things being equal, the value of the dollar also increases.

The fourth factor is tariffs. This factor is not as straightforward as it might seem. A tariff is like a tax on imports. If the tariff increases, then the foreign producers must either increase the price of their product or take lower profit margins. If they increase the price, sales and hence imports fall and net exports rise.

However, increasing tariffs in order to increase the nation's aggregate demand and employment doesn't work this easily. If the US increases its tariffs on Chinese goods, then China is likely to increase its tariffs on US goods. This cancels out the effect of increasing US tariffs. This is exactly what happened in country after country during the Great Depression. The result was a significant decline in international trade. This section was originally written before President Trump started his trade war with China. Unlike many before us, we may get a chance to observe the effects of an actual trade war, which is something that is usually just talked about in theory.

Trade Imbalances

A natural question is whether net exports tend to be positive or negative. Positive numbers mean that exports are greater than imports, creating a trade surplus, and negative numbers mean imports are greater than exports, creating a trade deficit. As you can see from figure 3, the US has run a trade deficit every year since 1975.

Over the last twenty years, the size of trade deficits appears to have gotten quite large. In fact, they have, although it may be a little difficult to tell given that the *y*-axis is defined as the size of the trade deficit divided by GDP rather than the dollar value of the trade deficit. The reason economists use the size of the trade deficit divided by GDP is to make it easier to compare different time periods.

Because of inflation and the growth of the US economy, the dollar value of trade deficits or surpluses are larger today than in the past. Using the dollar value makes it appear that in recent times trade imbalances have been much larger than they were in the past, but in fact, that may not be true. To get rid of the bias caused by inflation and economic growth, we compare the size of the deficit or surplus to the overall size of the economy by dividing the deficit or surplus by the GDP.

Looking at figure 3, of course, it's clear that US trade imbalances have gotten considerably worse recently. If you're curious about the actual

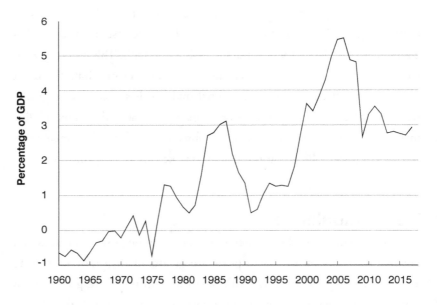

Figure 3. Trade deficits as a percentage of GDP, 1960 to 2016. (US Commerce Department)

dollar amounts, the US imported $762 billion more goods and services than it exported in 2006. In 2017, this number was $568 billion. These are truly massive numbers, and it is interesting that this subject, unlike the budget deficit, has received little attention in the press.

The Multiplier

At the beginning of the chapter, we characterized aggregate demand as a stack of four blocks—consumption (C), investment (I), government spending (G), and net exports (NX). The higher the stack, the more output and employment. However, this vision of four blocks is flawed. If the animal spirits become more optimistic and investment increases by $100 billion, for example, we might expect that the investment block and the stacks as a whole to increase by $100 billion. However, while the investment block *does* grow by $100 billion, the consumption block also grows. To understand why this happens, we need to consider the concept of the multiplier in the simple Keynesian model.

If firms purchase an additional $100 billion of plant and equipment, the owners, managers, and workers in the capital goods producing industries receive an additional $100 billion in income. They take that additional income home and spend some (MPC) and save some (MPS). If the MPC is 0.8, then consumption increases by $80 billion, but the additional increase in aggregate demand and consumption doesn't stop there. The additional $80 billion of consumption spending becomes an additional $80 billion of income to the owners, managers, and workers in the sector that produces consumption goods.

These owners, managers, and workers from the consumption good sector then take that income home and spend the MPC of it. In this case, consumption spending increases again by .80 times $80 billion, or $64 billion. This additional round of consumption spending becomes additional income to yet another group of individuals. In theory, we have an infinite number of rounds of additional consumption. Each round adds to aggregate demand. Each round also adds to the size of the consumption block. This process is known as the multiplier because it multiplies any change in spending into a much larger change in aggregate demand and output (RGDP).

Calculating the Simple Multiplier

At first glance, calculating the simple multiplier seems extremely difficult because it entails adding up an infinite number of rounds of increased spending. That could take a long time. Fortunately, mathematicians have developed a simple formula that approximates this calculation. If one has an infinite series of the form

$$= 1 + X + X^2 + X^3 + \ldots + X^\infty \ (3.10)$$

where X is $0 < X < 1$, then the series converges to

$$= 1/ (1 - X) \ (3.11)$$

Because the MPC is a fraction between zero and one, for every additional investment dollar spent, our series (equation 3.12) has the exact same form as equation 3.10:

$$= 1 + MPC + MPC^2 + MPC^3 + \ldots + MPC^\infty \ (3.12)$$

The formula for the simple multiplier, which is denoted by the Greek letter α, is thus

$$\alpha = 1/(1 - MPC) \ (3.13)$$

In our $100 billion example, the MPC is 0.8, and as a result the multiplier is 5:

$$\alpha = 1/(1 - MPC) = 1/(1 - 0.8) = 1/0.2 = 5 \ (3.14)$$

How much would a $100 billion increase in investment spending cause aggregate demand and output to increase? We now have a formula that allows us to calculate that value. That formula is the multiplier times the change in investment:

$$\Delta AD = \Delta RGDP = \alpha\, \Delta I \text{ (3.15)}$$

Substituting in the values for the simple multiplier and for the change in investment, we get

$$\Delta AD = \Delta RGDP = 5 \times \$100 \text{ billion} = \$500 \text{ billion (3.16)}$$

In addition, a change in spending for any of our other three actors can be substituted for the change in investment:

$$\Delta AD = \Delta RGDP = \alpha \times \Delta C \text{ (3.17)}$$
$$\Delta AD = \Delta RGDP = \alpha \times \Delta G \text{ (3.18)}$$
$$\Delta AD = \Delta RGDP = \alpha \times \Delta NX \text{ (3.19)}$$

The multiplier also works in both the upward and downward direction. How much will aggregate demand and output decline if the federal government reduces government spending by $50 billion without changing taxes? Assume that the MPC is 6/7. The formula is now

$$\Delta AD = \Delta RGDP = \alpha \times \Delta G \text{ (3.20)}$$

Plugging in the value for the MPC, we can calculate the simple multiplier:

$$\alpha = 1/(1 - MPC) = 1/(1 - 6/7) = 1/(1/7) = 7 \text{ (3.21)}$$

Plugging in the values for the simple multiplier and the ΔG into equation 3.20 we get

$$\Delta AD = \Delta RGDP = \alpha \times \Delta G = 7 \times (-\$50 \text{ billion}) = (-\$350 \text{ billion})$$
$$\text{(3.22)}$$

The result of the government's $50 billion reduction in spending is a $350 billion decline in aggregate demand and output.

The Actual Multiplier and Taxes

We refer to α as the simple multiplier because it leaves out a couple of important pieces of reality, each of which make the actual multiplier smaller. One of these you probably spotted as we developed the concept of the multiplier:

> If firms purchase an additional $100 billion of plant and equipment, the owners, managers, and workers in the capital goods producing industries receive an additional $100 billion in income. They take that additional income home and spend some (MPC) and save some (MPS).

This description assumes no taxes. In a world with taxes, however, these owners, managers, and workers have taxes subtracted from their paychecks before they leave the plant for home. If the tax rate is 25%, households in the example received not an extra $100 billion in disposable income but an extra $75 billion, and they spent 80% of that or $60 billion.

The resulting $60 billion in increased consumption is less than the extra $80 billion in the original example. A smaller level of consumption occurs with every round of the multiplier because with every round, taxes are subtracted from the increase in income. If we include taxes in our calculation of the multiplier, the size of the multiplier is smaller. The larger the tax rate, the smaller the multiplier.

The Actual Multiplier and Imports

The other piece left out of the simple multiplier is imports. Unlike purchasing a domestically produced good, when people purchase imports, a portion of the additional income flows abroad. The merchants that sell the imports keep some of the sale price to pay their salespeople and other expenses and for their own profits, but a large chuck of the money is sent aboard, reducing the next round of spending in the US. The existence of imports thus causes the multiplier to be smaller. The more goods we import, the smaller the US multiplier.

Estimating the actual size of the US multiplier is thus difficult. Multiple rounds of spending take time. How many months or years of data should be included in an estimate? The estimate is also dependent on the state of the economy. If we are at full employment, for example, the size of the multiplier is zero because an expansion in output is impossible without additional laborers. If the economy has large amounts of unemployment, then the multiplier is relatively large. In addition, we always assume all else is constant, but the real world is never so accommodating. Other things are changing all the time, and separating the effects of various forces is imprecise.

Ideological factors seem to play a role in these estimates, too. Conservatives think government should be small, and they also like to think that the government is ineffective. If the multiplier is small, then increases in government spending will be relatively ineffective at stimulating the economy. When conservative economists make estimates of the size of the multiplier, they thus tend to be small.

Liberals, on the other hand, favor large government, and they like to think that government can play a significant role in stimulating the economy. If the multiplier is large, then increases in government spending will be relatively effective at stimulating the economy. When liberal economists make estimates of the size of the multiplier, they not surprisingly tend to be large.

Using the Simple Keynesian Model

Using the simple Keynesian model is fairly easy because it unfolds in the exact same manner every time. We can think of it as having three steps.

Step one: An event occurs, such as a significant increase in stock prices. We then determine, within the simple Keynesian model, which of the four components of aggregate demand is affected by this event. A change in stock prices affects wealth, so it affects consumption. In this example, consumption increases.

Step two: We then determine how this affects aggregate demand. This step is actually redundant because we assume, at least initially, that the other three components have not changed. If the component increases, then aggregate demand increases. If the component decreases, then aggregate demand decreases. In our example, consumption increases, so aggregate demand increases.

Step three: We then determine the effect of the change in aggregate demand on real GDP and unemployment. The simple Keynesian model assumes that if aggregate demand increases, the first effect is a decline in inventories. As inventories fall below the level firms wish to hold, firms increase production rates, thereby increasing real GDP. This increase in production is also accomplished by hiring unemployed workers and putting them to work on previously idle or underutilized capital equipment, thus reducing unemployment.

Therefore, in our example, stock price increases can be outlined as the following process:

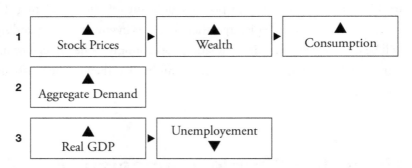

If we have a situation where the effected component causes aggregate demand to fall, then the line of causation reverses.

Examples

Let's look at a few more examples of the simple Keynesian model at work.

A Recession for Our Trading Partners

Let's say that the economies of our best trading partners go into recession. Here is how we apply the model:

1. This causes the purchasing of all goods and services in those countries to fall. Some of those goods are goods produced in the US, so US exports fall and net exports will go down as a result.

2. If net exports fall, then aggregate demand falls.

3. If aggregate demand falls, then real GDP falls, causing unemployment to increase.

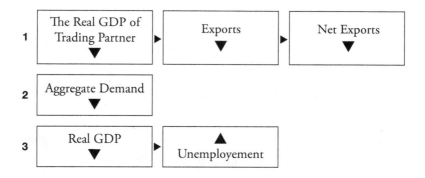

Lower Interest Rates

Assume that the Federal Reserve lowers interest rates. Here is how we apply the model to this situation:

1. In the simple Keynesian model, if interest rates fall, then it becomes cheaper for firms to borrow money to purchase new plant and equipment, so investment increases.

2. If investment increases, then aggregate demand increases.

3. If aggregate demand increases, then real GDP and employment increases. As a result, unemployment decreases.

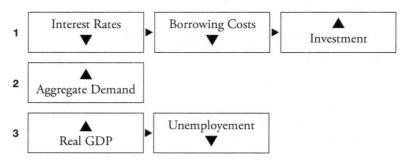

Increased Government Spending

We'll assume that the Federal government increases its spending. Here we go:

1. Because the federal government can run an unbalanced budget, an increase in government spending can occur without an increase in taxes. That is exactly what we assume here.

2. If government spending goes up, then aggregate demand goes up.

3. If aggregate demand increases, then real GDP and employment increase. As a result, unemployment decreases.

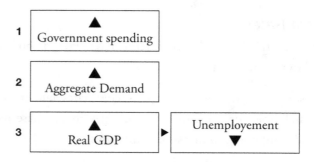

The Indirect Effect on Investment

In the simple Keynesian model, the most important determinate of investment is the animal spirits or spontaneous optimism of business people. The biggest factor affecting their optimism is how profitable their businesses are. In the short run, then, the major factor affecting businesses profits is the sale of a firm's goods and services. The stronger sales are, the higher are profits, the more optimistic business owners tend to be, and the higher investment will be.

As a result, if a change in aggregate demand is large enough to affect the animal spirits of businesspeople, then there is a secondary effect on aggregate demand that runs through investment. This change in investment will be in the same direction as the original change in aggregate demand. For an example, let's go back to the increase in stock prices that lead to an increase in consumption and aggregate demand. If that increase is large enough to increase the optimism of business people, then there is also a secondary increase in investment:

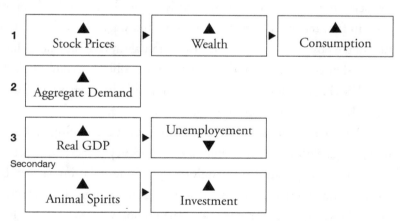

Similarly, if aggregate demand falls, this may cause business optimism to fall, which then causes investment to fall.

This secondary effect doesn't always happen. If changes in aggregate demand are small, they do not affect overall business optimism. There may also be some other reason why a change in aggregate demand doesn't affect the animal spirits. However, any change in aggregate demand *can* trigger a secondary effect on investment, and this secondary effect always reinforces the initial effect, making it larger than expected.

Domain Assumptions

As long as unemployment is high, the simple Keynesian model is an excellent guide to how certain events affect the economy and what policies the government should pursue. The famous liberal orthodox economist Paul Krugman was convinced during the 2007–09 recession, and for many years thereafter, that unemployment was high and needed addressing in both the US and Europe. In his *New York Times* columns from 2008 to at least 2013, readers could understand most of the economic analysis by understanding the simple Keynesian model.

We must then wonder about the drawbacks to the simple Keynesian model. One is that it doesn't explain how the banking system and financial markets affect investment. Second, there is nothing in the model about inflation. In fact, the model assumes that prices and wages don't change. Given that in the post-WWII period we have almost always had inflation, this is a serious shortcoming. Third, the model is not flexible. It doesn't work if we don't have high levels of unemployment and aggregate demand increases. It can only analyze a situation with high unemployment.

The simple Keynesian model also assumes that the economy is stationary, that aggregate demand and output have no tendency to increase or decrease. In this model, aggregate demand only changes if one of the four factors above changes, and those factors are just as likely to go down as up. Capitalist economies, however, are never stationary. The economy is always either in the process of growing or shrinking. The model is thus incapable of explaining one of the unique features of a capitalist economy, the business cycle.

As the name indicates, this is a simple model. It is often studied to develop understanding of aggregate demand as a precursor to introducing more complicated models.

References

Federal Reserve. 2005. *The Federal Reserve System: Purposes and Functions*. Washington, DC: Board of Governors of the Federal Reserve System.

Federal Reserve. "Industrial Production and Capacity Utilization—G.17." *Statistical Releases and Historical Data*. Washington, DC: Board of Governors of the Federal Reserve System.

Keynes, John Maynard. 1936. *The General Theory of Employment, Interest and Money*. New York: Harcourt, Brace and Co.

❖ 4

Business Cycles

One of the unique features of capitalism is the business cycle. The business cycle is a recurring pattern of sustained growth, measured by rising RGDP and falling unemployment, that is followed by a period of contraction, measured by falling RGDP and rising unemployment. The periods of growth, which are known as expansions, normally last much longer than the periods of decline, which are known as recessions.[32]

Business cycles are far from uniform, not like the cycles on an oscilloscope. They differ dramatically from one another, and as a result, they are difficult to predict. Not counting the current expansion that started in June of 2009, there have been ten expansions in the US since 1946, each lasting an average of sixty months. As figure 1 on the next page shows, there is significant variation in length, and the most recent ones have been longer.

The length of the recessions has been more uniform, averaging 11.4 months, with a range of six to eighteen months. However, the impression that recessions are more uniform is largely a result of the official measure-

Length of Expansion before Recession	Length of Recession	Peak Unemployment (Increase during Recession)
37 Months (1945-48)	11 Months (1948–49)	6.9% (3.4%)
45 Months (1949-53)	10 Months (1953–54)	5.9% (3.4%)
39 Months (1954-57)	8 Months (1957–58)	7.4% (3.5%)
24 Months (1958-60)	10 Months (1960–61)	6.9% (1.7%)
106 Months (1961-69)	11 Months (1969–70)	5.9% (2.5%)
36 Months (1970-73)	16 Months (1973–75)	8.6% (4.0%)
58 Months (1975-79)	6 Months (1980)	7.8% (2.1%)
12 Months (1980-81)	18 Months (1981–82)	10.8% (3.6%)
90 Months (1983-91)	9 Months (1990–91)	7.8% (2.6%)
121 Months (1991-2001)	8 Months (2001)	6.4% (2.5%)
72 Months (2001-07)	18 Months (2007–9)	10.0% (5.4%)

Figure 1. US business cycles since 1945.

ment of recessions. It is not a reflection of how they are perceived by the average person. A recession is officially over when RGDP increases, and not when the economy returns to a state of good health. If we look at peak unemployment rates and the increase in unemployment, we notice a considerable variation in the depth of recessions.

In some business cycles, the unemployment rate only increased to around 6%. In those cases, it did not take long before the general consensus was that the economy is doing well. But in times when the recession was deep, the economy had to grow for years before the average person believed that the recession was over. The recession of 2007–09, for example, ended in June 2009. Four years later, many considered the economy to still be in recession. With jobs hard to find and an unemployment rate of around 7.5%, that was a reasonable position.

The question for economists is why does an economy that is growing suddenly start to shrink. This might be just a curiosity question if not for the damage caused by recessions — increases in unemployment, business failures, foreclosures, and poverty. That leads to increases in robberies, heart attacks, strokes, murders, child abuse, and spousal abuse. Furthermore, business cycles inject a degree of uncertainty into many long-term decisions. For society, it would be beneficial if we can limit the number and depth of recessions.

The pain of recessions is not shared equally. There are those who suffer little during recessions, while others are greatly impacted. The wealthy are hurt by recessions because profits decline in the short run and because recessions cause a temporary decline in the paper value of their assets, including stocks and real estate. In the long run, however, recessions benefit this group because they re-establish conditions for higher profits in the future. This happens through the increase in both unemployment and inventories of raw materials.

Many members of the poor and middle class are injured by recession when they become unemployed or their income falls due to a fall in economic activity. Others members of the poor and middle class are injured because they are unable to push up their wages because of the poor economic conditions and their lack of bargaining power. Many feel lucky just to have a job. Actions to prevent recessions or limit their depth are often muted and far less aggressive then is needed because they threaten the long-term financial interests of the wealthy.

In this chapter, we will develop a framework for understanding business cycles and for explaining why capitalist economies rarely reach full employment. With our business cycle model, the focus shifts away from such things as providing the poor with more incentives to take a job or providing better opportunities through job training to strategies for creating more jobs.

The starting point for our model of business cycles is a statement by the famous British economist Nicholas Kaldor (1938), who wrote that an expansion was like "a peculiar steeplechase, where the horse is bound to fall at one of four obstacles." While Kaldor's statement can be viewed as just a metaphor — there are more than four ways for an economy to stumble and fall—his statement points out one of the difficulties of studying business cycles. What causes an expansion to end is not always the same. Therefore, composite data on business cycles, while useful for some purposes, is not necessarily a good guide for determining the shape or cause of business cycles.

The Basic Mechanism

In creating our model of business cycles the first step is to develop the "basic mechanism" for the end of the expansion. This might be thought of as Kaldor's last hurdle, the barrier that always trips the economy if some other force hasn't done so already. We then add to our model those forces that tend to amplify the basic mechanism, the Federal Reserve increasing of interest rates and banks increasing their standards of creditworthiness. After that, we discuss other mechanisms that can bring expansions to an end. In Kaldor's metaphor, these are the first three hurdles — although there are more than three other mechanisms.

For an economy to go from an expansion to a recession, aggregate demand must go from increasing to decreasing. Of the four components of aggregate demand, our basic mechanism focuses on investment, as do most theories of business cycles. Investment increases when firms expect new investment to be profitable.

Unfortunately, as Keynes (1936) points out, calculating whether a piece of investment will be profitable or not is undoable. A piece of capital lasts well into the future, so determining whether it will be profitable depends on knowing all the factors that affect profits now and in the future. It is impossible to know the future values of almost any of the factors that are necessary to make this calculation. Firm managers are thus left to make decisions with incomplete information.

As a result, Keynes believed that investment decisions are based to a large degree on the spontaneous optimism or animal spirits of business managers.

Businesspeople tend to be optimistic about the future when the business is currently doing well. We should expect investment to rise when current profits rise, and fall when current profits fall.[33] Because profits are total revenue minus total cost, our model focuses on the movement of revenues and costs over the business cycle. The basic mechanism is a profit squeeze model that is illustrated by a box flow diagram with two arms. One arm represents revenues, and the other arm represents costs.

The squeeze of profits can come from either a decline in revenues or an increase in costs. Underconsumptionist models focus on a decline in revenues that come from a decline in consumption. In an underconsumptionist model, as the economy expands, household incomes rise, and the marginal and average propensity to consume falls (Knoop 2010).[34] As a result, total consumption lags behind the total production of consumption goods, so the revenue going to consumption goods producers falls.

However, data in the post-WWII era doesn't support the idea of underconsumptionism. This is either because it doesn't occur at all or because its effect is being swamped by other factors influencing consumption. If the latter is true, then this underconsumptionist tendency may show itself in the future. The basic mechanism is built to handle underconsumptionism, but the model presented here revolves around rising costs as the main cause of falling profits.

Upper Arm

During an expansion, the economy is by definition growing, and RGDP is rising. As RGDP increases, household income increases and consumption increases. Revenue going to businesses thus increases. If everything else is constant, current profits rise, which causes expected profits to increase and animal spirits to rise. That causes investment and aggregate demand to go up, which causes RGDP to rise. Because RGDP is rising, the process repeats itself, causing the economy to grow larger and larger. The above steps in logic are represented in the upper arm of the basic mechanism diagram, as shown in figure 2 on page 74.

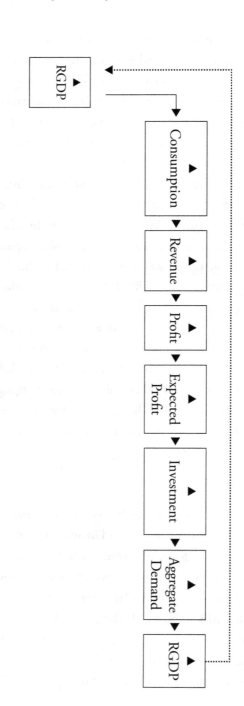

Figure 2. The upper arm of the basic mechanism.

Lower Arm

When RGDP increases, more goods and services are produced. This requires firms to hire more workers and purchase more raw materials. As the expansion progresses, this causes both raw material prices and wages to increase faster than the price of the firm's product, thereby reducing profits. According to Sherman (1991), this normally occurs first with raw material prices. At the beginning of the expansion or end of the recession, there is a surplus of raw materials, so their prices are low.

However, raw material producers typically can't expand production as fast as final goods and service producers. Once the inventories of raw materials are gone, raw materials become increasingly scarce. This forces final goods and service producers to bid against one another, sending the price of raw materials upward.

Wages also rise at some point, but this usually occurs later in the expansion. As the economy expands and RGDP rises, firms normally need to increase the size of their workforce to meet the increased demand for their goods and services. As a result, unemployment tends to decrease.[35] As unemployment goes down, the number of potential employees an employer has to choose from goes down, and the number of jobs offers a worker receives over a given period goes up. As the unemployment rate goes down, then, the employers' power over employees diminishes. As the employers' power diminishes, workers are better able to bargain for higher wages. As wages rise, with all other things held constant, current profits go down.

There is the possibility of a third cost that is not pictured in the diagram. The reason for its omission is that depending on the firm, this increase in costs may or may not occur. As we discussed earlier, most firms have capital equipment that is either underutilized or sitting idle. Quite naturally, excess capacity is largest during a recession and tends to decline during an expansion. It only makes sense for a firm to use its newest and most productive capital as much as possible and its older and less productive capital as little as possible. Having already employed its newest and most productive capital, a firm tends to use its least productive capital more intensely as the expansion continues. Because that capital is less productive, the cost of producing goods and services rises.

However, this idea that a firm progressively uses more of its less productive capital as the economy expands is not always true if the firm has multiple plants of various ages. Let's assume, for example, that we are in the depth of the recession and that Mountain Man Tim, the maker of quality mountain bikes, is only using 70% of his capital stock. Tim has two new plants and one old one. To keep from losing his productive veteran employees, Tim must run his plants at least at 60% of capacity. Tim thus runs the two new plants at 75% of capacity and the old one at 60%. As the economy expands, Tim increases the use of his new plants, thereby lowering his overall costs of production. It is only late into the expansion that Tim is forced to expand the use of his older, less productive plant. In a situation of multiple plants, therefore, it is not always true that as production expands, firms are forced to use older, less productive capital.

However, there will be some firms whose costs of production rise as the expansion continues due to having to use older, less productive capital. For those firms, there is a third avenue by which rising costs squeeze profits.

We thus have two and possibly three costs that, at some point during the expansion, start to rise. And as the expansion continues, this tendency for costs to increase intensifies. At some point during the expansion, the increase in these costs causes total costs to rise faster than total revenue. This causes profits and expected profits—and thus the animal spirits—to fall, which causes investment to fall. As this manifests itself, some companies either cancel orders for machines or do not order machines in the first place.

As a result, machine makers lay off workers, and these workers reduce their purchase of consumption goods. Consumption goods producers then lay off consumption goods workers. A downward spiral in aggregate demand and RGDP follows, and the economy plunges into recession. The above logic is represented by the lower arm of the basic mechanism, as we see in figure 3.

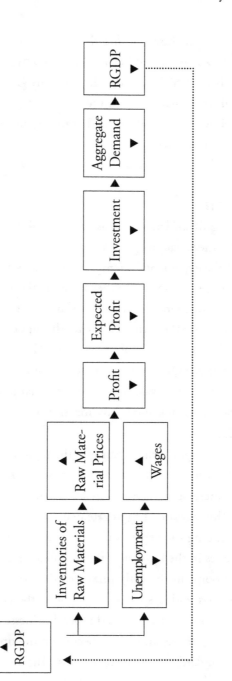

Figure 3. The lower arm of the basic mechanism.

The upper arm shows profits rising as the economy expands. The lower arm shows profits falling as the economy expands. The overall effect depends on which arm dominates. This gradually changes as we move through the expansion. For most of the expansion, the upper arm dominates. However, towards the end, if the expansion lasts long enough, the lower arm dominates.

Expansion

The beginning of an expansion is the end of a recession. We expect the unemployment rate to peak at or near that moment.[36] During the early part of the expansion, unemployment rates are high and workers' bargaining power is weak. Furthermore, at the end of the recession, inventories of raw materials are at or near their peak. In the beginning stages of the expansion, the values in the upper arm increase while those in the lower arm do not. This is because even if unemployment declines, it is still high, and workers see no increase in their bargaining power. The same can be said about raw material prices. A small decline in inventories does not allow raw material producers to increase raw material prices.

In the early stages of the expansion, then, profits and expected profits increase and so does investment. This increases aggregate demand directly through the increase in investment and indirectly through the multiplier effect. The increase in aggregate demand causes RGDP to increase, thereby continuing the expansion. Values in the upper arm continue to rise while values in the lower arm remain unchanged.

At some point in the early phases of the expansion, optimism that the recession has ended spreads throughout the economy. Consumers become more optimistic and spend more, businesses become more optimistic and invest more, and banks become more optimistic and start to lower their standards of creditworthiness. The result is an even larger increase in aggregate demand and RGDP.

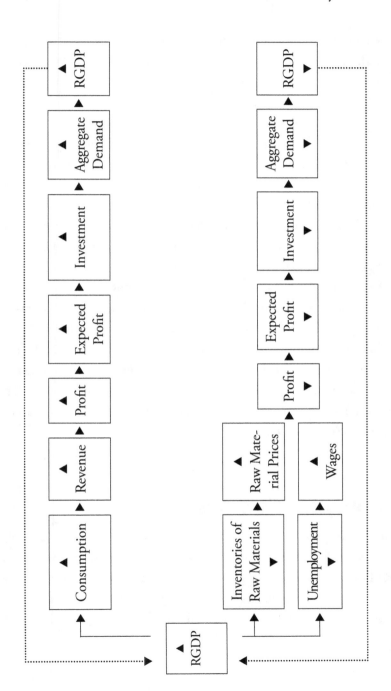

Figure 4. The basic mechanism.

We can think of the two arms as neon signs. Whichever one glows the brightest is the one that dominates. In the early part of the expansion, the upper arm is the only arm that glows, and this state may continue for some time. In time, however, the inventories of raw materials decline, and raw materials become scarcer, so raw material producers can charge higher prices. In addition, unemployment rates decrease over time to the point where the bargaining power that employers have over employees begins to diminish. Workers can then push up real wages, making wages increase faster than prices.

At that moment, the lower arm starts to glow a little. The upper arm still glows brighter. Profits continue to increase, as do expected profits and investment. If all other things are held equal, however, then as raw materials become scarcer and the unemployment rate continues to decline, the lower arm glows brighter and brighter until the increases in costs are greater than the increases in revenue. When this occurs, profits start to fall.

Once it becomes clear that profits are not only falling but will continue to fall, then expected profits and the animal spirits of businesspeople declines, as does investment and aggregate demand.[37] When aggregate demand goes from increasing to decreasing, the expansion comes to an end, and the recession begins.

Amplifying Factors

In our model, rising raw material costs or rising labor costs eventually become sufficiently large to cause profits, expected profits, and investment to decline. Two other factors—increasing interest rates and increasing standards of creditworthiness—often happen at about the same time. These factors amplify the effects of rising costs.

Interest Rates

The Federal Reserve, often referred to as "the Fed," sets short-term interest rates by targeting the federal funds rate. By moving short-term interest rates, the Fed hopes to influence the economy's rate of growth. If the Fed wishes to slow down the economy because inflation is high, it raises interest rates. This makes borrowing money more expensive, thereby reducing the demand for goods that people typically borrow money to purchase — houses, cars, and business fixed investment. If the Fed wishes to speed up economic growth, it lowers rates.

The Fed has two main economic goals. First, it wants to keep inflation rates low and stable. Second, if inflation is under control, it wants to minimize unemployment. Besides keeping inflation low, the Fed also wishes to keep public expectations about future inflation low. It is the Fed's belief that if it lets inflationary expectation rise, it will have to inflict more pain on society through higher interest rates to lower inflation. As a result, the Fed is hypervigilant for any signs of a *permanent* increase in inflation. Increases in the price of oil or food are often temporary, so the Fed will often not respond to these.

Since the recession of 1981–82, the Fed has kept a close eye on wage increases, especially real-wage increases. If the expansion is sufficiently long that real wages start to increase, the Fed fears increases in inflation and inflationary expectations, and it increases short-term interest rates. This decreases investment both directly and indirectly. Higher interest rates directly decrease investments because it costs more to borrow money for those investments. Higher interest rates indirectly affect investment because most businesses owe money on investments they made in the past or for working capital loans. The vast majority of these loans are variable rate loans, meaning that as the Fed increases interest rates, the cost of those old loans goes up, and the firm's profit goes down. This further depresses investment.

This indirect effect may be larger than we might first expect. According to Minsky (1986), when the economy is coming out of a recession, firms are conservative about how they finance new investment and working capital expenditures. However, it is more profitable to finance expansion through debt than it is from cash flow. As an expansion continues, firms become more optimistic and turn more to the use of debt — in some cases, large amounts of debt.

While more profitable, this strategy is also riskier. The viability of the strategy often depends on a certain expected cash flow. If that doesn't materialize, then the firm's optimism vanishes and their expansion reverses into a contraction for survival purposes. This may be catalyzed by some unexpected rise in costs, a fall in demand, or an increase in interest rates by the Fed.[38] Therefore, as real wages increase, the Fed tends to increase interest rates, and this increase in interest rates may have a bigger effect on investment than expected because of the indirect effect. Figure 5 shows both the direct and indirect effects of an increase in interest rates on investment.

Orthodox economists—primarily conservative orthodox economists—see the Federal Reserve's actions as far more important than just an amplifying effect. In fact, they see the Fed as the primary cause of recessions. Their stance appears to be largely ideological. In their desire to defend capitalism against its critics, they imply that the only reasons for recessions are outside forces that throw the economy out of its natural full employment equilibrium, and the primary culprit is the incompetent Federal Reserve. In discussing the possibility that 2007–09 recession was the result of the inherent instability of financial markets, Frank Shostak of the Ludwig Von Mises Institute offered this typical orthodox response:

> The heart of Minsky's framework is that capitalism is inherently unstable and has self-destructive tendencies. An important mechanism for this destructive tendency is the accumulation of debt. Contrary to Minsky, our analysis shows that it is the existence of the central bank that makes modern capitalism unstable. It is this factor alone that is responsible for the current financial instability. (qtd. in Davies 2010)

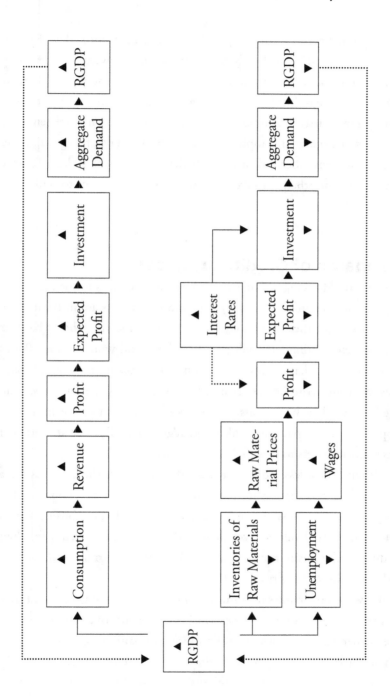

Figure 5. The basic mechanism with increasing interest rates

What makes this argument possible is the fact that the Federal Reserve has raised interest rates shortly before the economy went into recession on numerous occasions. However, the position that the Federal Reserve is the root cause of instability in US capitalism relies on two improbable assumptions. First, it assumes that the economy has a natural tendency towards some stable full employment equilibrium, a fact this group never attempts to prove. Second, it assumes that members of Federal Reserve never learn from their mistakes, an idea that runs counter to both logic and data.[39]

Standards of Creditworthiness

There is an old saying in banking: "What really counts is not the return *on* your money but the return *of* your money." Banks are in business to make profits for their stockholders. The most important choice bankers make is determining who will pay them back and who will not. Banks need to choose a large number of winners to make up for a single loser. They typically write off less than 1% of their loans (Ritter, Silber and Udell 2009). If a bank consistently takes losses by loaning money to people who don't pay the bank back, regulators will close it, and that causes stockholders to lose their investment.

When a business requests a loan, the bank asks the business for a great deal of information to determine if the firm is creditworthy. The firm's creditworthiness depends on the quality of their business plan and whether the bank believes there will be sufficient demand for their product. If the business owner meets the bank's minimum standard for creditworthiness, the firm gets the loan.

However, the bank's minimum standard does not stay constant over the business cycle. During the expansion, standards of creditworthiness creep downward as business profitability and bank optimism improve. When banks foresee a recession, they tighten credit standards rapidly. As the potential profitability of businesses declines, banks' financial

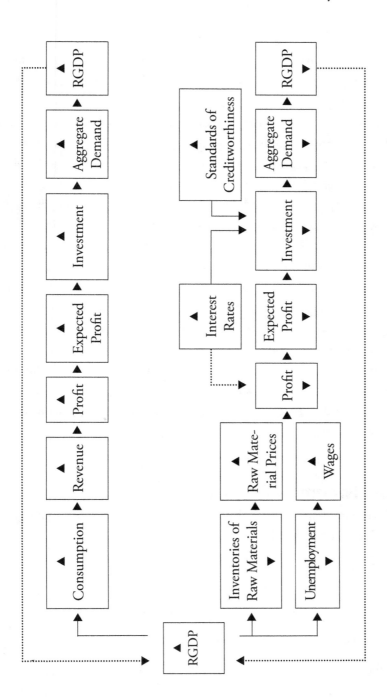

Figure 6. The basic mechanism with both amplifying effects.

conditions decline, and their own tolerance for risk declines (Federal Reserve 2011). As a result, some firms face reduced credit limits and more stringent loan conditions while others lose access to bank credit altogether.[40]

This is particularly true for small businesses because they have a higher probability of going under during a recession. The more severe the recession, the greater is the markdown of firms' projected profitability and the greater is the aversion to risk by banks. As a result, the restriction of credit will be more severe.[41] Therefore, when rising raw material prices, wages, and interest rates threaten to bring an end to the expansion, banks tighten their credit standards, further reducing investment and amplifying the effects of the basic mechanism, as shown in figure 6.

A number of authors have attempted to blame the end of the expansion on a single cause, but this is rarely the case. Normally, at least a couple of factors are at work. In particular, banks are always monitoring the pulse of the economy because their survival depends on making a high percentage of performing loans, which are loans in which the borrower is paying the bank back. If there are any signs of an oncoming recession, banks tighten credit, becoming at least a second factor in the ending of an expansion.

Fluid Nature of Amplifiers

The basic mechanism and the amplifying factors, which we consider to be Kaldor's last hurdle, have three parts:

- Rising business costs, primarily from increasing raw material prices and increasing wages.

- Increased interest rates from the Federal Reserve.

- Tightened standards of creditworthiness by banks.

Each part causes investment to fall, but there is nothing static about the relative strengths of these three forces in any given business cycle. As we compare different time periods or different business cycles in the same time period, the relative contributions of these three parts may change.

In the 1950s and 1960s, for example, labor unions and labor in general were more able to push up wages. Since then, labor has become continuously weaker. We should expect this trend to continue, as business interests increasingly dominate US politics regardless of which party is in office.

As for the Federal Reserve, exactly how much of an increase in inflation or real wages it takes to trigger the Fed's increase in interest rates and how rapidly the Fed will increase those interest rates depends, in part, on the chairperson of Federal Reserve and the other members of the Fed's decision-making body, the Federal Open Market Committee.[42] As the strength of labor changes and the personalities at the Federal Reserve change, the relative strengths of our three forces associated with the basic mechanism change over time.

Other Causes of Recession

An expansion comes to an end and a recession begins when aggregate demand goes from expanding to contracting. There are many events outside of the basic mechanism that can conceivably cause one or more of the four elements of aggregate demand to contract.

This section focuses on six causes that are either most often mentioned in the economic literature or that have been strongly suspected of causing economic downturns over the past fifty years:

- A collapse of financial markets.
- A severe cut in government spending or increase in taxes.
- A rapid rise in oil prices.
- A rapid increase in interest rates.
- An increase in the size of the capital stock.
- The anarchy of production.

Collapse of Financial Markets

In a modern capitalist society, most businesses are dependent on borrowing money. Firms can borrow money by getting a loan from a bank, issuing bonds, or issuing commercial paper. Households can also borrow money to purchase cars, houses, and other durable goods. If financial markets stop functioning properly—through the bankruptcy of several financial firms or the freezing of key financial markets—then investment and consumption declines significantly as the ability of firms and households to borrow and spend decreases.

What may be equally as important as the decline in availability of credit is that this causes business and consumer optimism to plunge. If the event is large or widespread enough, the result is a recession. The 2007–09 recession is an excellent example of a recession that was primarily caused by a collapse of financial markets, which was largely the result excessive risk-taking by financial firms (Stiglitz 2010, Financial Crisis Inquiry Commission 2011).

According to theories advanced by Hyman Minsky (1986), modern capitalist societies are driven to periodic financial market collapses unless government constrains the actions of the financial markets. While much of Minsky's work is rather complicated, one part of his theory can be expressed in the simple metaphor of teenagers skating on a partially frozen lake. In order to impress the others, a teenager skates out onto the unproven ice. In financial markets, assets and strategies with higher returns have greater risk. Once one teenager has successfully skated out on the unproven ice, others follow, so to continue to impress people, the first teenager must skate out even further. Likewise, after one financial firm uses a risky, high-return strategy without disaster, other firms follow in order to keep their customers and attract new ones. To out-do their competitors, financial firms have a tendency to engage in even riskier strategies. Without a barrier, skaters tend to go too far, and after the most daring skater falls through the ice, cracks in the ice spread toward shore, imperiling all the skaters. Without regulation and its active enforcement, financial firms may take on too much risk, and when one firm collapses, it often imperils the whole system.

In the 1990s and 2000s, financial firms engaged in increasingly risky strategies involving various aspects of the housing market in an attempt generate higher returns. Those in charge of regulating financial markets did little to prevent this growth in risk. These risky strategies were based on the idea that housing prices will always increase. In hindsight, this seems a foolish notion. Because of the recession of 2001, the Fed was keeping interest rates low to spur economic growth, but they would have to raise them at some point to be in position to fight the next recession.

From 2004–06, the Fed increased its interest rate target from 1% to 5.5%. Many people with sub-standard credit were allowed and often encouraged to purchase houses using adjustable rate mortgages, which were often pegged to the one-year T-bill rate.[43] When the Federal Reserve raised its rate, the one-year T-bill rate increased by almost as much. Unable to pay their rapidly rising mortgage payments, many holders of these adjustable rate mortgages were forced to sell their homes. As a result, house prices started to fall in 2007, and the financial house of cards collapsed soon after.

Cuts in Government Spending

Typically, we don't anticipate national governments to slash spending in amounts sufficient to drive their economies into recession. That's normally a sure recipe for electoral defeat. However, if forced by other events, it's entirely possible that this can happen. It occurred in many European countries in the early 2010s. In one country after another, and especially in Greece, national governments either chose or were forced to institute austerity programs that cut government spending and increased taxes. Contrary to what proponents predicted, these austerity programs drove their economies into recession.[44]

Rapid Rise in Oil Prices or Interest Rates

Before the basic mechanism kicks in, an expansion can be halted by a sizeable rise in the price of oil or any significant group of commodities or by a sizable increase in interest rates.

The 1973–75 recession has been largely attributed to rising oil prices. Between July 1973 and January 1974, oil prices increased 163%, going from $19.18 a barrel in 2015 dollars ($3.56 in actual prices) to $50.48 ($10.11). This rapid rise in prices drove up the cost of production and reduced profits. In the early 1970s, many production processes were based on the expectation that energy costs would always be low, so facilities weren't built to conserve fuel. As a result, production costs increased significantly. Because the price increases had been engineered by the oil cartel OPEC, many predicted this increase in oil prices would be permanent. This decreased animal spirits and caused investment spending to fall.

The recessions of 1980 and 1981–82 are generally attributed to sky-rocketing interest rates. In 1979, world oil prices spiked again, increasing by 124% from $51.89 ($14.85) per barrel in January 1979 to $116.37 ($39.50) in April 1980. As a result, inflation in the US increased to 13.2% in 1980. The Federal Reserve, under Paul Volker, reacted with massive increases in interest rates. In April 1979, the Federal Funds rate was 10.5%, and by April 1980, it was 17.61%. It fell to 9.03% in July 1980, only to increase to 19.08% in January 1981.[45] Mortgage rates also went skyward, going from 10.5% in April 1979 to a high of 18.45% in October 1981. The results for the housing industry were disastrous, and the US economy plunged into a deep, double-dip recession.[46]

The Rising Size of the Capital Stock

John Harvey (2014) has produced a model of business cycles based on the work of Paul Davidson (1978, 2011). Our presentation of this model is much simpler than what is presented by Harvey. The Harvey/Davidson model shares with the Basic Mechanism the ideas that business cycles are driven by changes in investment, that changes in investment are driven by changes in the animal spirits of business people, and that booms are bigger and recessions are deeper because of fluctuations in the optimism of banks. The critical features of the Harvey/Davidson model are:

- Firms purchase additional units of capital if the amount they are willing to pay for an additional unit of capital is greater than the price of an additional unit of capital. The amount a firm is willing to pay is based on their expected profit from an additional unit of capital.[47] Expected profits are based on the optimism of businesspeople.

- If actual profits turn out to be greater than expected profits, then the animal spirits rise, and the demand for new capital increases. If actual profits turn out to be the same as expected profits, then the animal spirits remain the same, as does the demand for new capital. If actual profits turn out to be less than expected profits, then the animal spirits become depressed and the demand for new capital falls.

- As a firm's capital stock gets larger, its expectations for profits from an additional unit of capital goes down, and so does the firm's the demand for new capital.

The model thus has two forces that shift the demand for new capital.[48] We might suspect that when expected profits are different from actual profits, this will have a far greater effect on the demand for capital than the gradual change in the size of the firm's capital stock. Hopefully, when you contemplate the second effect, you can already see how the expansion sows the seeds of its own destruction.

In this model, the business cycle unfolds in the following way. During the early stages of an expansion, firms are tentative, and their expectations are low. Actual profits tend to be greater than expected profits, and as a result, animal spirits increase. Even though the size of the capital stock is increasing, the effect an increase in the animal spirits greatly outstrips the effect of a larger capital stock and the demand for capital goes up. The increasing demand for capital may go on for some time, but at some point, actual profits will equal expected profits, and the animal spirits and the demand for capital from this effect stays constant.

However, because the size of capital is rising, this causes the overall demand for capital to fall. Therefore, investment starts to decline, and with it, aggregate demand falls. As aggregate demand falls, the sale of goods and services falls, and so do actual profits. As actual profits fall below expected profits, the animal spirits decline, and the demand for capital now falls for two reasons. This causes investment to seriously decline, and the economy plunges into recession. It is the decline in expected profits caused by the increasing size of the capital stock that eventually causes the economy to stumble and fall into recession. If this occurs before the Basic Mechanism takes hold, then we have yet another reason why expansion will come to an end before full employment is reached.

The Anarchy of Production

In recent history, there hasn't been a recession that economists primarily blame on the anarchy of production. However, because it is a basic feature of a capitalist economy, and because it can either lead to the end of an expansion or a deeper recession, the anarchy of production is worth considering.

For those who praise capitalism, a frequently cited feature is that businesses have the freedom to use their ingenuity without any directive from the government—as long as their actions are legal. This includes decisions about the level of output and investment. For those who decry capitalism, a frequently cited feature is that businesses have the freedom to use their ingenuity without any directive from the government. It is a double-edged sword. The freedom of individual decision-making means that some of the most important decisions for industries and the nation are made on an unplanned and uncoordinated basis (Dobb 1958).

The problem lies in the fact that it takes time to plan, order, make, and install new plants and equipment. A firm that undertakes new investment because current profits are high may find out that all its rivals have also undertaken the same new investments, so the productive capacity in the industry now outstrips demand. Under those conditions, firms must either reduce their prices or produce less. Either way, the anticipated level of profits cannot be realized.

As a result of investment decisions not being coordinated — that is, the anarchy of production — we may have situations of investment booms followed by investment busts. Well-known industry-wide examples of this are the designer jean craze of the 1970s and the office building boom and bust of the 1980s and 1990s. If widespread enough, the anarchy of production can lead to the end of the expansion.

Predicting the Length of Expansions

We can use our basic mechanism model to make some elementary predictions about factors that affect the length of expansions. While these predictions will not be precise enough to make money in financial markets, they can point to reasons why recent expansions have tended to be longer and whether this is good or bad for the nation. The factors we will look at are the pace of economic growth and weaker labor unions.

Pace of Economic Growth

If we assume that the basic mechanism breaks the expansion and if the economy grows at a slower pace, this leads to longer expansions. According to the basic mechanism, the expansion ends when the costs of primarily raw material and wages rise to the point where they cause current profits and the animal spirits to fall, as we see in figure 7 on page 94.

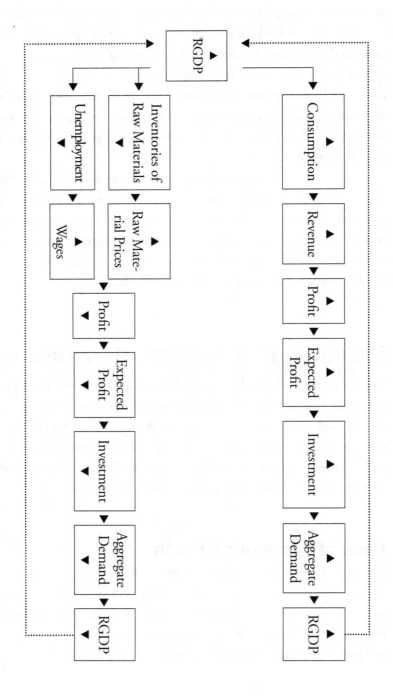

Figure 7. The basic mechanism.

Decade	Average Annual Real GDP Growth
1950s	4.3%
1960s	4.5%
1970s	3.3%
1980s	3.1%
1990s	3.2%
2000s	1.8%
2010–2018	2.3%

Figure 8. Average annual of real GDP growth per decade since the 1950s.

When the economy grows slowly, it takes longer for raw material inventories to fall to the point where raw material prices rise. Additionally, it takes longer for the unemployment rate to decline to the point where workers can force up wages. Thus, the expansion lasts longer when the economy grows slowly. Expansions before 1982 were generally shorter than expansions that have occurred since. The rate of economic growth, shown in figure 8, was much faster in the first twenty years than it has been in the last forty-plus years.[49]

If everything else is constant, longer expansions and shorter recessions are good for society. However, longer expansions that are the result of a slow-growing economy are, for the most part, a negative. With a slow-growing economy, we have fewer disruptions to the economy due to recessions, but the standard of living of the average citizen also grows more slowly. Furthermore, periods of high unemployment, which occur at the end of a recession and the beginning of the expansion, last longer with a slow-growing economy. High unemployment has many negative effects for both individuals and their communities. Those negative effects are compounded when people are unemployed for long periods of time.

Weaker Labor Unions

Weaker labor unions also cause expansions to be longer. Over time, the strength of the linkages between the boxes in the basic mechanism change as the economy evolves. For example, the effect of an oil price increase on the cost of production is now half of what it was in the 1970s. After being harmed by oil price spikes in the 1970s, businesses found ways to economize on their fuel consumption.

Year	Union Membership
1956	25.2%
1960	23.6%
1970	22.6%
1980	20.9%
1990	16.1%
2000	13.5%
2010	11.9%

Figure 9. The percentage of workers who are union members.

Over the last sixty years, labor unions have become progressively weaker. Figure 9 shows what has happened to union membership in the US over that period.[50] As a result, workers are less able to push up wages as unemployment falls. It takes a lower unemployment rate before laborers are sufficiently powerful to increase wages to the point where profits and expected profits fall. Expansions will thus be longer.

There is a trade-off. On one hand, weaker unions lead to longer expansions, resulting in fewer disruptions from recessions. On the other hand, if wages grow slowly, then profits grow more rapidly, and the wealthy get more while the rest of society gets less. As Stiglitz (2013) points out, as the distribution of income becomes increasingly unequal, it leads to a less stable,[51] more fractured, and more unpleasant nation.[52]

Could the Economy Reach a Stable Point of Low Unemployment?

As of this writing, the current expansion is in its tenth year, with unemployment rates a little below 4%. There are some who are acting like this could go on forever. It's worth asking whether an economy could walk a knife-edge for an extended period of time where unemployment is low but the Basic Mechanism and its amplifying effects are not triggered. While this would be unusual, I believe that at least in theory, the answer is yes.

Under what conditions could this happen, and could this occur during the current expansion? To answer those questions, we need to look at each of the variables that tend to squeeze profits in the Basic Mechanism and at the amplifying effects. Then we must ask if there is a situation in which all of them would not act to bring an expansion to an end when unemployment is low.

If the economy grows slow enough, it is possible that raw material producers can keep up with the demand for raw materials without reducing their inventories of raw materials. If this happens, then raw material prices will not increase. While there are those who say that our current economy is the greatest ever, the reality is that economic growth during this expansion has been anemic. There have been no recessions during the 2010s, but economic growth during this decade is only averaging 2.3% per year.

The decades of the 1950s and 60s saw two recessions each, but the average growth rate during those two decades, including the recession years, was almost double the current rate of growth. There has been no expansion in the post-World War II periods where the economy has grown so slowly. If the economy continues its slow rate of growth, then raw material prices may not rise. While it is not a perfect measure of raw material prices, the Producer Price Index (PPI) would show if raw material prices were surging, and that doesn't appear to be the case. Recently the PPI has been growing at the relatively tame pace of approximately 2% per year.

If labor is extremely weak, then unemployment can get quite low without wages rising fast enough to squeeze profits. While wages are now rising faster than prices, it's not by much. It's not clear how much tighter can labor markets get before shortages drive wages up at a faster pace. However, if the economy grows slow enough, then unemployment will not decline and labor markets will not tighten anymore.

If the expansion is slow enough, then firms can meet the increased demand for goods and services through increases in productivity and without using less efficient idle capital equipment. We are in the tenth year of the expansion, and the current capacity utilization rate is still below 80%. No expansion since data was first collected has the capacity utilization rate been so low.

Instead of preparing for the next recession, it appears that the Federal Reserve is trying to keep federal government borrowing costs down by keeping interest rates low. While the Fed has increased rates lately, they haven't increased them by much, and they have been increasing them at a slow rate. The key here is inflation. If it starts to rise, then the Fed will need to increase interest rates more quickly. However, if the economy continues to grow slowly, then inflation is less likely to rise.

If banks don't believe a recession is coming soon, they are likely to keep their standards of creditworthiness low. The Federal Reserve's January and April 2019 Senior Loan Officer Opinion Survey shows that after easing credit standards for years banks have recently left them unchanged, and while banks say they are likely to tighten credit over the next 12 months, this tightening is expected to be modest.

The reoccurring theme has been a slow growing economy. So, could our economy walk the knife edge and continue to expand for a long time? According to our model, if the economy grows slow enough that is at least theoretically possible.

Business Cycles and Poverty

When it comes to poverty, one major result of the heterodox models is that there are always or almost always more people looking for work than there is work available.

We would expect that as the unemployment rate falls, so would the poverty rate, and vice versa. Figure 10 shows that there is indeed a strong correlation between increases and decreases in unemployment and increases and decreases in poverty.

As long as the economy expands faster than the rate of productivity growth and labor force growth, unemployment falls and poverty decreases. However, as the economy approaches full employment, the power of workers to push up their wages increases. At the same time or perhaps earlier, raw material prices start to increase. For some firms, costs from using less efficient capital also increases.

Businesses do their best to pass these rising costs on to their customers. To the extent that they are unable to do so, their profits fall.

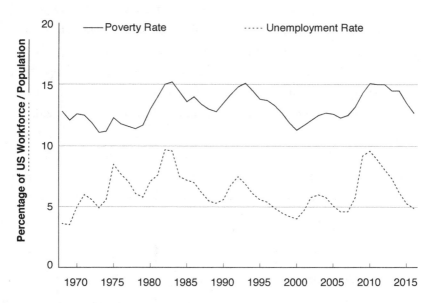

Figure 10. Poverty and unemployment rates, 1969 to 2016.

To the extent that they are able to do so, inflation rates rise. Therefore, at the same time that businesses are being squeezed by their own rising costs, the Federal Reserve starts increasing interest rates to fight inflation, further squeezing profits and increasing the cost of borrowing. In addition, banks see this scenario of rising business costs, increasing inflation, and increasing interest rates. They start to worry that the expansion is coming to an end and increase their standards of creditworthiness.

When business costs increase faster than revenues, then profits, expected profits, and investment fall. When interest rates go up, investment falls. When banks cut the availability of credit to small and new businesses, investment falls. As this fall in investment becomes widespread, the economy stops growing and falls into recession. According to heterodox economists, unless there is a strong countervailing push on aggregate demand from the government, as occurred during World War II and the Vietnam War, this plunge into recession occurs before full employment is reached.

The business cycle model thus shows us that there are always or almost always be more people looking for work than there is work available.[53] Moreover, if the economy trips and falls into recession before making it to the basic mechanism hurdle, then the economy will obviously not make it to full employment. According to heterodox economists, then, there will always or almost always be people who are unemployed and underemployed due to the natural operation of the capitalist system.

With this in mind, government policy should attempt to mitigate the negative effects of unemployment and the increased poverty that comes with it. Because business cycles are a natural feature of a capitalist system, it would be best for society if we can achieve the following:

- Reduce the number of recessions.
- Reduce the depth of recessions.
- Reduce the length of recessions.
- Cushion those most affected by the effects of recessions.

It may not be possible to achieve all these goals simultaneously, or it may not be possible to achieve these goals and still have a strong and healthy economy. As we have seen, a slow-growing economy reduces the number of recessions, but that is not necessarily good for the overall health of the nation. On the other hand, the following government policies can help achieve many of these goals:

- Implement spending programs to increase aggregate demand during recessions.

- Have the Federal Reserve lower interest rates to increase aggregate demand during recessions, as they already do.

- Increase unemployment benefits.[54]

- Hire the unemployed.

Societies of Excess Capacity

Orthodox economists characterize economics as the study of how society makes decisions under conditions of scarcity. However, according to heterodox theory, the basic feature of a real capitalist economy is excess capacity. The Federal Reserve has kept data on capacity utilization rates of capital since 1967. At no time has the level of excess capacity been less than 10%.

In finance, orthodox economists occasionally contemplate whether the financial world and Wall Street are optimally using the nation's scarce level of loanable funds (Stiglitz 2010). However, every bank can create money out of thin air for any customer they deem creditworthy with almost no restrictions (Moore 1988, Wray 1990). We discuss this in far more detail later in the book. Therefore, outside of the extremely rare time periods when financial markets freeze, there is a nearly unlimited supply of loanable funds for creditworthy businesses.

In this chapter, we have developed a model that concludes that we are at less than full employment in all but the rarest of situations. If the heterodox model is correct, we also have excess capacity in labor markets.

The fact that capitalism is an excess capacity society is as one would expect. Capitalism operates for the benefit of the owners of capital. When opportunities to increase profits through an increase in production occur, as is often the case during an expansion, there must be excess capacity in capital, finance, and labor for firms to be able to expand. If there isn't, the owners of capital make changes to ensure that there is excess capacity next time.

The downside of economies of excess capacity, much like the downside of Aztec society, is the necessity for human sacrifices. Societies of excess capacity require that a segment of the population be marginalized in order to make others prosperous. To function, societies of excess capacity must always have a portion of the population that is poor or nearly poor who can be called upon to fill productive rolls when necessary. I don't mean to imply that there is some conspiracy by businesspeople to keep a section of the population poor. The excess capacity in labor in our society comes from the natural operation of the social system and our business cycle model shows why this is true.

One of the keys to eliminating poverty within a capitalist society, without relying on massive welfare expenditures, is to devise a system that allows everyone to have a job but still allows the economy to maintain the feature of excess capacity.

References

Boddy, Radford and James Crotty. 1975. "Class Conflict and Macro-Policy." *Review of Radical Political Economics* 7, Spring: 1–17.

Brown, Christopher. 2008. *Inequality, Consumer Credit, and the Saving Puzzle*. Northampton, MA: Edward Elgar.

Davidson, Paul. 1978. *Money and the Real World*. London: Palgrave Macmillan.

Davidson, Paul. 2011. *Post Keynesian Macroeconomic Theory*. Cheltenham: Edward Elgar Publishing.

Davies, Howard. 2010. *The Financial Crisis: Who is to Blame?* Malden, MA: Polity Press.

Dobb, Maurice. 1958. *Capitalism Yesterday & Today*. London: Lawrence & Wishart Ltd.

Fazzari, Steven. 1993. "Investment and US Fiscal Policy in the 1990s." Washington DC: Economic Policy Institute Briefing Paper.

Federal Reserve. 2011. *"Senior Loan Officer Opinion Survey on Bank Lending Practices."* (available at federalreserve.gov/ boarddocs/snloansurvey/, Accessed 3 January 2011).

Federal Reserve. 2005. *The Federal Reserve System: Purposes and Functions*. Washington, DC: Board of Governors of the Federal Reserve System.

Financial Crisis Inquiry Commission. 2011. *The Financial Crisis Inquiry Report: on the Causes of the Financial and Economic Crisis in the United States*. New York: Public Affairs.

Harvey, John. 2014. "Teaching Keynes's business cycle: an extension of Paul Davidson's capital market model." *Journal of Post Keynesian Economics* 36, Summer: 589-606

Kaldor, Nicholas. 1938. "Stability and Full Employment." *The Economic Journal* 48, December: 642–57.

Keynes, John Maynard. 1936. *The General Theory of Employment, Interest, and Money*. New York: Harcourt, Brace and Co.

Klein, Naomi. 2007. *The Shock Doctrine: The Rise of Disaster Capitalism*. New York: Picador.

Knoop, Todd. 2010. *Recessions and Depressions*. Santa Barbara, CA: Praeger.

Minsky, Hyman. 1986. *Stabilizing an Unstable Economy*. New Haven, CT: Yale University Press.

Montague, Peter. 1998. "Major Causes of Ill Health." *Rachel's Environment & Health Weekly* 584.

Moore, Basil. 1988. *Horizontalists and Verticalists: The Macroeconomics of Credit Money*. Cambridge: Cambridge University Press.

Ritter, Lawrence, William Silber, and Gregory Udell. 2009. *Principles of Money, Banking and Financial Markets*. Boston: Addison-Wesley.

Sherman, Howard. 1991. *The Business Cycle: Growth and Crisis Under Capitalism*. Princeton, NJ: Princeton University Press.

Sherman, Howard, E. K. Hunt, Reynold Nesiba, Phillip O'Hara, and Barbara Wiens-Tuers. 2008. *Economics: An Introduction to Traditional and Progressive Views*. Armonk, NY: M.E. Sharpe.

Stiglitz, Joseph. 2010. *Freefall: America, Free Markets, and the Sinking of the World Economy*. New York: W.W. Norton & Co.

Stiglitz, Joseph. 2013. *The Price of Inequality: How Today's Divided Society Endangers Our Future*. New York: W.W. Norton & Co.

Tapia Granados, Jose. 2012. "Statistical Evidence of Falling Profits as Cause of Recession: A Short Note." *Review of Radical Political Economics* 44, (4): 484–93.

Wachtel, Howard. 1988. *Labor and the Economy*. Second Ed. New York: Harcourt Brace Jovanovich, Publishers.

Wilber, Charles and Kenneth Jameson. 1983. *An Inquiry into the Poverty of Economics*. South Bend, IN: University of Notre Dame Press.

Wolfson, Martin. 1986. Financial Crises: Understanding the Postwar US Experience. Armonk, NY: M.E. Sharpe Inc.

Wolfson, Martin. 2003. "Credit Rationing." *The Elgar Companion to Post Keynesian Economics*. Edited by John E. King. Northampton MA: Edward Elgar Publishing, 77-81.

Wray, L. Randle. 1990. *Money and Credit in Capitalist Economies: The Endogenous Money Approach*. Northampton, MA: Edward Elgar.

❖ 5

Wage Determination

Broadly speaking, wages are determined by a combination of institutional structure, negotiations, and minimum wage laws. Over the past forty years, and for most of US history, the output per worker has steadily increased. However, as we've seen, the poverty rate is now higher than it was in the 1970s. We would have expected poverty rates to have declined considerably, as they did from 1959 to the 1973. The question is, why haven't they?

To answer that question, we need develop a comprehensive theory of wages with a focus on low-wage work. To do so, we will focus on what has happened over the past forty years and discuss the following three elements:

1. The structure of employment and how it has shifted towards low-wage jobs.
2. The real minimum wage and its decline.
3. The market power of firms over workers and how it has increased.

Labor Markets

Segmented labor market theory is the basic heterodox microeconomic theory of labor markets. Simply stated, jobs can be segmented into various large groups. The jobs within each group are not identical, but they have enough in common that researchers can make some powerful general statements about these jobs, and researchers can contrast them with jobs in other segments.

The easiest of the segmented labor market theories to understand is the dual labor market theory. In this theory, there are two segments, the primary labor market and secondary labor market. In the primary labor market, the jobs have good wages, good benefits, and management by rules. In the secondary labor market, the jobs have low wages, few or no benefits, and idiosyncratic management. A slightly more compli-cated segmented labor market theory breaks the primary sector into three parts—blue-collar production workers, pink-collar office workers, and white-collar professional and managerial workers. We will revisit this towards the end of this section.

We start our investigation by examining the primary labor market.

Primary Labor Market

In a book on economics of poverty, it might seem odd to study the primary labor market because that segment contains jobs that pay good wages and have good benefits. These are not the jobs of the poor. However, through studying the primary labor market, we learn about the overall structure of jobs in the US and why the percentage of low-wage jobs appears to have increased over the past forty years.

When we look at the primary sector, a common feature among most of these jobs is that they are organized into internal labor markets (ILMs). Wolf (2009) characterizes internal labor markets in this way:

There are a well-defined and limited number of positions into which workers from the external labor market are hired.... [I]nternal labor markets typically have well-defined promotional ladders. A promotional ladder indicates the normal progression of jobs through which advancement takes place. These ladders usually consist of related jobs requiring similar but increasingly more advanced skills. Promotion may depend on ability, but more often on seniority.... Furthermore, there is a relatively rigid wage structure, which does not respond or change much in relation to changes in outside conditions such as unemployment and shifting wage rates. Internal consistency in the wage structure is therefore considered more important than external consistency. (p. 319–20)

Promotions in an ILM are generally a competition between current employees. Outsiders are excluded. Why would a firm voluntarily limit the number of competitors for a job? At first, the answer may seem counterintuitive, but by internalizing their labor markets, firms lower their costs of production by increasing worker productivity.

There are two theories as to why firms have structured employment into ILMs. These two theories are not mutually exclusive. Some firms may have formed ILMs for the first reason, and other firms may have done so for the second. In addition, firms that formed ILMs for the first reason may have later realized the benefits from the second reason, and vice versa. We assume that the reasons given in both theories play a role in the decision by firms to form ILMs and that they also play a role in firms continuing or not continuing to use ILMs for part or all of their employees.

Crisis in Control

The first theory is articulated by Richard Edwards (1979) in his book, *Contested Terrain: The Transformation of the Workplace in the Twentieth Century*. His basic premise is that one hundred fifty to two hundred years ago, firms were small and the owners oversaw every part of the production process:

> Alone or perhaps in concert with a few managers, [the entrepreneur] watched over the entire operation of the firm. He supervised the work activities directly; he maintained a close watch on his foremen; and he interceded immediately with full power to solve any problems, overriding established procedures, firing recalcitrant workers, recruiting new ones, rearranging work schedules, reducing pay, handing out bonuses and so forth.
>
> The entire firm was, in a way, the capitalist's own workshop. His knowledge of and involvement with his employees was great. . . . His success depended on his ability to get work out of his workers, whether by harsh discipline or by inspiration; undoubtedly, most attempted to use both. . . . Workers undoubtedly were oppressed and exploited by such employers, but they also became enmeshed in a whole network of personal relations. They had someone with whom to identify. (p. 26)

However, with the natural evolution of capitalism, firms grew in size, and in some cases, they became extremely large. Owners and upper level managers no longer oversaw the entire operation. In many cases, the owners were absentee stockholders. The question then became how the owners and upper-level managers could ensure that their employees were working hard every day, and that the job was being done correctly when they were not directly supervising their workers.

There emerged a "crisis in control," and the years between 1890 and 1940 became a period of experimentation with different mechanisms of control. According to Edwards, none of the experiments were a complete success, and none were a total failure. Each provided information and experience. The post-1945 period saw the full-fledged development of what Edwards calls "bureaucratic control" but what others refer to as internal labor markets. Edwards uses the example of Polaroid to illustrate some of the features of bureaucratic control:

> The nonsalaried employees are first divided into "job families"—eighteen groups of jobs such as "general clerical," "metal trades," or "chemical mixing and processing" that are "similar in nature and involve similar skills." Within every job family, the proliferation of job titles permits a far more fertile basis for distinguishing each worker from his or her coworkers. . . . Overall, the company has about three hundred job titles for its hourly staff alone. . . .
>
> Then there is the pay scheme. Each individual job is assigned a "Polaroid Classification Value" (PCV). . . . In Polaroid's theory, as many as twenty or twenty-five PCV levels are possible, although only fourteen were actually in use in 1975. . ., each job is now further positioned along the pay scale so that for any given job (or PCV value), seven distinct pay steps are possible, from entry-level through 5% increments to top pay for the job. (p. 134)

Whether employees are new hires or have been transferred or promoted, each is given a detailed job description upon taking a new job. It explains exactly what they are supposed to do and the expectations for how to do it. This description not only ensures that the job is performed correctly, but it also provides the employers' expectations as to what constitutes a good day's work.

At least once a year, employees are evaluated based on how well they performed their jobs as outlined in the job descriptions. Satisfactory job evaluations normally result in a step raise. A series of good evaluations puts an employee in position for a promotion within the job family. As a result, the company almost always has a carrot dangling in front of their employees' noses. A poor evaluation or a series of poor evaluations can result in loss of employment, and because these are jobs with good wages and benefits, each employee thus faces a stick to go with that carrot.

The system is not just for employees but for managers, too. Everyone faces yearly evaluations based on how well they perform their jobs. Even though the owners and upper-level managers are not directly observing the employees' daily work, the system ensures that the jobs are done properly and that the company receives a good day's work every day. In the end, a system of bureaucratic control results in greater productivity.

There are other productivity-increasing benefits of ILM for the employer, too, as noted in the next theory.

Firm-Specific Skills and On-The-Job Training

The second theory was produced by Peter Doeringer and Michael Piore (1971) in their book, *Internal Labor Markets and Manpower Analysis*. It appears that Doeringer and Piore wanted to walk a line between orthodox and heterodox economics. However, their work received little acceptance from orthodox economists. Doeringer and Piore contend that

> internal labor markets are a logical development in a competitive market in which three factors (usually neglected in conventional economics theory) may be present: (1) enterprise-specific skills (2) on-the-job training, and (3) custom. Enterprise-specific skills are those which can only be utilized in a single enterprise in contrast to general skills which can be transferred among many enterprises. The effect of skill specificity is twofold: it encourages employers, rather than workers, to invest in training; once the investment has occurred, it leads employers to stabilize employment and reduce turnover so that they can capture the benefits of the training.
>
> On-the-job training is characterized by its informality. In many ways, it appears to occur almost automatically by "osmosis" as the worker observes others or repeatedly performs his job. . . . Moreover, because skill specificity is often the result of elements of work which are difficult to codify in a formal training curric-

ulum, on-the-job training may be the only way to transmit skills from one worker to another. (p. 39)

Employers will want to reduce turnover for any job that has significant levels of firm-specific skills and/or a significant amount of skills that need to be absorbed through informal on-the-job training. The greater the level of firm-specific skills and/or the greater the amount of on-the-job training required for the job, the more the firm will want to reduce turnover. This is particularly true if the firm has "job families" with relatively long promotion ladders that require firm-specific skills and/or on-the-job training at each rung.

The reason for reducing turnover is twofold. First, it reduces the cost of recruiting, screening, and training new employees. Second, it promotes continuous skill learning and keeps productive employees with a large amount of firm-specific skills. The result of reducing turnover rates is a fall in unit labor costs (ULC), even in the presence of higher wages and benefits. ULC is the wages and benefits paid to laborers divided by output. This is often summarized as ULC= W/Q (wages/output). The function of internalizing the labor market is to reduce ULC by giving skilled, productive employees a strong incentive to stay with the firm.

Doeringer and Piore also point out an important firm-specific skill that normally goes unrecognized in the economic literature:

> Moreover, performance in some production and most managerial jobs involves a team element, and a critical skill is the ability to operate effectively with the given members of the team. This ability is dependent upon the interaction of the personalities of the members, and the individual's work "skills" are specific in the sense that skills necessary to work on one are never quite the same as those required on another. (p. 15-16)

Therefore, in a workplace where output is partially dependent on a team effort, not only will new employees be less productive, they will also slow down everyone who is dependent on them.

The third element that the authors mention is "custom." Their discussion of this element is multifaceted and of only limited application for us. However, it is worth noting that workplace interactions are an intricate web of human relationships. Within that web, what was once a new way of doing things is now habit and becomes part of the customary way. An outgrowth of custom is a collective sense of what is right and fair. Management may find that it is not worth making incremental changes to the workplace because the cost of disrupting custom may be greater than the benefit. However, custom will not stand in the way of firms making major cost saving changes.

In summary, firms that have a high degree of firm-specific skills—especially where a large portion of those skills must be absorbed through on-the-job training—will be prone to form internal labor markets in order to minimize turnover and maximize skill learning. The structure of internal labor markets tends to reduce turnover and promote skill learning:

- In general, jobs in internal labor markets pay good wages and good benefits, where good work is normally rewarded with a step increase per year.

- Promotions are a competition among other employees within the firm, so the chance that a good employee receives multiple promotions over a working lifetime is high.

- Because many of the skills are firm-specific, after an employee has been with the company for several years, the employee is more valuable and receives higher pay from their current employer than they would from another firm.

- Management is based on a set of personnel rules, so it is more predictable and less autocratic. While it may not be perfect, the workplace environment is tolerable in most cases. In order to reduce turnover, the firm has an economic incentive to discipline autocratic, out-of-control managers, and internal labor markets provide a mechanism to accomplish that goal.

- While this varies from firm to firm, promotions are often based to some degree on seniority. This may be explicit for firms with union contracts, or it may just be part of unwritten custom. When senior workers have a good chance of getting promotions over junior employees, they are more willing to share their knowledge.

The degree to which firms internalize their labor markets, how rigidly the ILMs are structured, and how well job descriptions are developed varies from firm to firm. Firms may also internalize or strongly internalize one part of their labor force and then weakly internalize or not internalize another part of their labor force. Because of the focus on job security by unions, it is not surprising that firms with unions tend to have more strongly internalized markets than firms without unions. Long ago — but not so long ago that old people can't remember — a person could go to work for one of the large US corporations, and if they worked hard, they could and often would spend the rest of their working lives at that firm.

Combining the two theories, we should expect to observe ILMs in firms that have a large amount of firm-specific skills, especially those who have skills that are absorbed through on-the-job training. We should also observe ILMs in firms that are too large for owners and top-level managers to effectively oversee the operation of the firm, which includes most government work.

Size of Internal Labor Markets

Estimating the amount of employment that is organized into internal labor markets is difficult. There are no national surveys or agreed-upon definitions as to what is or is not an ILM. Based on data from the late 1960s, Doeringer and Piore estimated that a little over 80% of employment was structured into in internal labor markets. However, the world is not static. The hallmark of capitalism is innovation and change. It was innovation and change that led to the formation of ILMs. The same forces could — and we believe have — led to a reduction in the need for ILMs.

Before the invention of the personal computer and office software, for example, billing and other forms of paperwork had to be done at some central office where actual pieces of paper could be transferred from place to place. In addition, firms tended to use systems specific to their own business. With the development of software like Word and Excel, firms converted to using these programs. Potential employees could receive training for this software at most colleges. Firm-specific knowledge was thus converted into general knowledge, and these pink-collar jobs no longer needed to be internalized.

With the rise of the Internet, much of the routine paperwork that used to be done in a central US location can now be subcontracted to the lowest bidder anywhere in the English-speaking world. Therefore, a number of pink-collar jobs have vanished from the primary sector. We see the same type of process in the subcontracting out of routine manufacturing work to oversees employers.

Even though there may be a decreasing percentage of jobs currently in ILMs, however, we should still expect that the vast majority of jobs are organized into ILMs. One indicator of this is the provision of health care benefits and pension plans by employers, a hallmark of the ILM. According to the 2018 Statistical Abstract of the United States, 67% of private sector workers had access to employer-provided health insurance in 2016, and 66% had access to employer-provided pensions.

Secondary Labor Market

Jobs in the secondary labor market can best be characterized by contrasting them with primary-sector jobs. First, these jobs require fewer skills. In particular, they have limited firm-specific skills. Employers in the secondary labor market thus have little reason to invest in their employees. Providing workers with incentives to stay with the firm is not a priority. As a result, these jobs have a high degree of turnover. Second, many of these jobs are in small firms or franchises where the owner has direct oversight of the operation.

These tend to be low-wage jobs with low or no benefits, high turn-over, little chance of advancement, and idiosyncratic, sometimes capricious management. Many of those jobs are part time and are not seen as the foundation of a career unless a worker is able to move into management. Wages are often at or not far above the minimum wage.

The workers in the secondary labor market can be divided into two groups—those who are said to be voluntarily in the secondary labor market and those who aren't. The term "voluntary" is not meant to imply that this group likes being paid low wages, or that they might not be members of the poor or near poor. The distinction between voluntary and involuntary is purely for explaining why a worker is in the secondary labor market.

People who are voluntarily in the secondary labor market are those who at this time can't accept employment in the primary sector because they are unavailable for full-time work or because they require flexible schedules. These are generally high school students, college students, and stay-at-home parents. According to 2018 Statistical Abstraction of the United States, this group made up approximately 13% of the labor force.

People who are involuntarily in the secondary labor market are those who can't secure jobs in the primary labor markets. The limited number of good jobs is ultimately determined by primary-sector employers because they do the hiring. When firms have more applicants than jobs, they rank potential employees from highest to lowest. Given how many openings need to be filled, employers start at the top when offering jobs, and they continue down the list until all openings are filled. Those who are consistently rated low by primary employers either end up with no job or with a poor job in the secondary labor market.

What are the characteristics of those who end up at the back of the line? What businesses want from their employees differs from firm to firm. The ideal employee for a firm that sells drugs to doctors is not the same as for a firm that needs an assembly line worker. However, those who are placed at the bottom of the list tend to have little education, a poor-quality education, little work experience, no connections, an anti-social attitude, an unstable work history, and inflexible schedules. For an employer who is prejudiced or who believes their current workforce is prejudiced, minorities or women may also be placed at the bottom. In addition, those who don't have access to transportation to primary sector employers are simply not in the hiring pool at all.

Labor Market Structure

Firms are in business to maximize profits, and profit equals total revenue minus total cost ($\pi = TR - TC$). Employees affect both sides of the profit equation. They produce goods and services that the firm sells, which is revenue. The employer must also pay the employees for their time and effort, which is a cost. While paying laborers low wages and no benefits would minimize costs, it may also result in reduced or low-quality output. Instead of minimizing the compensation paid to workers, the firm wants to minimize its unit labor costs.

For some firms, minimizing their ULC requires a high-wage/high-productivity strategy. These are the firms in the primary labor market, and their need to use that strategy revolves around firm-specific skills, on-the-job training, and control issues. If those conditions change for all or some segment of their workers, then the firm stops using the high-wage/high-productivity strategy. In the secondary labor market, higher wages don't result in a great enough increase in output to lower their ULC. Firms in this sector thus follow a low-wage/low-productivity strategy.

In the heterodox theory, there are only so many primary sector jobs. Those who can't obtain a job in the primary sector must look for work in the secondary sector. Those who can't get work in the secondary sector end up unemployed.

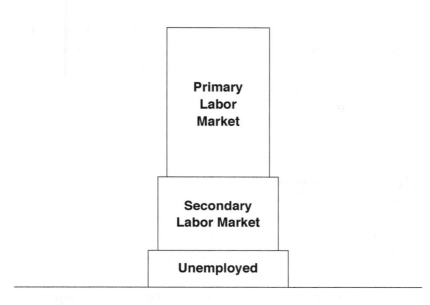

Figure 1. The labor force, broken down by the type of jobs that workers have or don't have.

Determining Pay in Segmented Labor Market Theory

While it should be clear from the above discussion, we want to emphasize that in the heterodox model *what determines a worker's pay is the job that they hold.* It is not determined by the individual's productivity, as is true in the orthodox model that we will see later on. It is true that those who are better educated, more skilled, more experienced, harder working, and as a result more productive, have a higher chance of landing a primary sector job and thus receiving higher pay. However, their pay is still determined by the job they have and not by their productivity.

For example, let's say that primary-sector Firm A has an entry level job opening that requires a college education. Two recent college graduates, Workers X and Y, apply for the job. Each has exactly the same education and background. The firm has only one job opening, though, and they chose Worker X. Worker Y, who has the exact same education, takes a job stocking the clothing racks at Walmart. Even though they both have a good education and are equally productive, one has a well-paying job, and the other has a poor-paying job. In the heterodox model, it is the job that the worker holds that determines worker's pay, not their productivity.[55]

Size of Labor Markets

While there is no direct measure, we can infer from several different pieces of information that the relative size of the primary labor market has been shrinking while the secondary labor market has been growing. A number of indirect statistics point to this conclusion. In addition, over the past twenty or more years, economists have been discussing how large corporations have restructured their operations so that the people who used to work for them directly are now working for them indirectly. These indirect workers are employed by firms who operate in more competitive environments where the pressures to lower all costs, including wages, are more intense.

Statistical Evidence

One indicator that the primary sector has been shrinking is the fact that the percentage of private sector employees who have access to employer-provided health insurance has declined from 77.3% in 1991 to 70.2% in 2012 and to 67% in 2016 (Dwork-Fisher, Gittleman and Moehrle 2014; 2018 Statistical Abstract of the United States).

Data on industrial and occupational composition of employment suggests that there has been a decline in blue- and pink-collar jobs in the primary sector. In manufacturing, employment peaked at 20.3 million workers in 1980 and fell to 12.3 million by 2016 (2018 The Statistical Abstract of the United States). Because of recent changes to the definition of certain occupations, it is difficult to compare the current number of clerical workers to the past. However, Wolf (2009) reports that the number of clerical workers increased as a percentage of total workers from 12.3% in 1950 to 17.4% in 1970 but then declined to 15.6% in 1993 and to 13.9% in 2005.

A recent study by Katz and Krueger (2016) gives the impression of a large recent shift towards secondary market work. They found that the percentage of workers in "alternative work arrangements," which they defined as "temporary help agency workers, on-call workers, contract workers, and independent contractor or freelancers" has been growing rapidly. Few of these workers are part of an internal labor market. According to Katz and Krueger, the percentage of workers whose *main* job is categorized as an alternative work arrangement increased from 10.1% of the labor force in 2005 to 15.8% in 2015—this is after the percentage remained relatively constant between 1995 and 2005. This is a massive increase in a short time span. According to the Bureau of Labor Statistics, there were approximately 142 million workers in 2015, the last year of Katz and Krueger's study. A 5.7% increase in the number of workers in "alternative work arrangements" is thus an increase of approximately 8.1 million workers in just ten years.

Corporate Restructuring

In the 1980s and early 1990s, business gurus said that large corporations had ossified, that they were dinosaurs, too internally bound to be able to keep up with fast, nimble small companies. Small firms were the engines of growth, they said, and these flexible and nimble firms would soon compete the large corporations out of existence.

Those futurists could not have been more wrong. The information that was, in part, driving their predictions was that employment growth was happening at small companies, and that employment at large corporations was declining. However, as Bennett Harrison (1994) points out, rather than being ossified, slow, or out-competed, large corporations were the ones calling the shots.

Technological developments, along with a kickstart from the leveraged buyout movement, propelled corporations into restructuring themselves into a core-periphery structure. Like a planet with moons, the large corporation resides at the center, and a large number of small firms, which compete against one another to provide services, orbit around the corporation. This is what Harrison refers to as a "lean and mean" structure. Part of process of becoming lean and mean is to transfer many of functions and jobs that used to be a part of the corporation to the small orbiting moons. Technological changes are what allow this. They reduce the firm-specific skills, on-the-job training, and control issues to the point where these jobs and functions can be profitably externalized.

While Harrison chronicles the beginnings of this movement, David Weil (2014) describes this process in a more advanced stage. He shows how more jobs and functions have been moved to the periphery, and he discusses the different ways or models for moving jobs to the periphery. Three forms of employment-shifting are subcontracting, hiring independent contractors instead of employees, and franchising. We will consider each in a moment.

This division is a little different from what Weil presents, but it better fits our proposes. Besides understanding how this restructuring of jobs has occurred, there are two other lessons to take from Weil's work. First, in the absence of significant law changes, this process will most likely continue. There are substantial benefits for large corporations to move employment to the periphery. If further technological developments allow it or if other industries realize how they can utilize existing models, the movement of jobs to the periphery will continue.

The second lesson is that efforts to reduce poverty must make efforts to improve conditions in the periphery. A successful anti-poverty program should include subtle and maybe not-so-subtle legal changes that reduce the benefits of shifting employment to the periphery. In addition, it should increase funding for the enforcement of labor laws to reduce wage theft, forced unpaid work, and health and safety violations.

Subcontractors

The traditional reason for a firm to hire a subcontractor is that the firm has a task that they do only periodically and that requires specialized equipment or workers with specialized skills. It doesn't make financial sense for the firm to purchase the equipment and hire the labor necessary to do this task if the firm is only going to use them every once and awhile. The firm instead subcontracts with specialists to do the work, and those specialists have similar contracts with other firms in the industry.

That's not what is happening today. Large corporations are now taking jobs that they do all the time, jobs that used to be done by their own employees, and hiring subcontractors to do them. The model used by many corporations is to hire a large subcontractor, who then hires many small subcontractors to do the actual work. In some cases, there may be three or more layers of subcontractors.

You may think that having multiple layers of subcontractors is more expensive. After all, each layer of subcontractor is expecting to make a profit. The more layers of subcontractors there are, the more the large corporation has to pay to get the work done. However, it turns out that this structure reduces both the costs and the liabilities facing the corporation.

One of the keys to this is there must be a large number of small contractors who are willing to bid for the work. Because it is the small contractor who hires the worker, the corporation not only transfers the cost of wages to the subcontractor but also contributions to Social Security, Medicare, unemployment insurance, worker compensation payments, and liability for safety violations and on-job accidents. The use of subcontractors allows firms in the coal industry to transfer pension payments and the obligations for lifetime health care to the subcontractors.

In a contract between firms of equal strength, we wouldn't expect any savings from shifting these costs to subcontractors. The subcontractors understand that they have to pay these costs and build them into the cost of the contracts. The price that the corporation has to pay subcontractors then reflects these costs. However, this isn't a contract between equals. The subcontractors are bidding against similar contractors for work. The corporation can thus get a price that is below the level that reflects all these costs. According to Weil, the reason for this is "perhaps because of the contractor's potential ability to fly under the radar, its inexperience in business, or simply the higher likelihood of insolvency" (p. 103).[56] Because the profit margins on these contracts are so thin, there is a strong incentive for subcontractors to violate basic labor law and safety regulations with wage theft, forced unpaid work, failure to provide a safe work environment and so on. One of the advantages of multilayer contractors is that it puts distance between these types of violations and the corporation. In October 2011, the California Labor Department inspected two small subcontractors, Premier Warehousing Ventures and Impact Logistics Inc. Their "murky and opaque payroll records" and inability to "produce records verifying hours for workers" led to citations for labor law violations (Weil 2014, p. 166).[57] The large subcontractor, Schneider, who hired both of these small subcontractors, eventually bore some responsibility for the situation, but Walmart didn't.

Weil uses a series of examples to show the different ways that large corporation have used subcontracting to move employment from the core to the periphery—the building and maintaining of cell towers, production of Hershey's Chocolate, cable TV installation, and even though he uses it as an example of franchising, janitorial services. One of his examples deserves special attention because of its sheer size—supply chains.

Supply chains are either the movement of manufactured goods from the manufacturer to the retail store or the movement of intermediate goods from the intermediate good producers to the factory floor in a timely fashion. With the increase in overseas production, these supply chains have become longer and more complicated. A container ship pulls into harbor from China, for example, and a truck driver picks up a container at the dock. The driver then drives the container to a warehouse, where its contents are unpacked and then repacked into other trucks that are bound for retail stores, factory floors, or warehouses where this process is repeated. Much of this work uses low-skilled labor that is subcontracted out instead of being done as it once was by employees of the corporation. This is a large shift from the primary labor market to the secondary labor market.

Independent Contractors

FedEx has long treated those who deliver their packages as independent contractors who are paid by the delivery. These drivers must purchase a truck specified by FedEx with its logo on it. The independent contractor is responsible for the gas, insurance, and maintenance. In addition, Weil reports that

> drivers are not covered by overtime or other labor standards or protections against discrimination, health and safety laws, or provisions that would allow them to take leave or care for a sick child or family member. Contributions for Social Security and Medicare taxes fall entirely on the driver, and because drivers are in business for themselves, they are not eligible for unemployment insurance or worker's compensation. (p. 161)

It is not hard to see how hiring drivers as independent contractors reduces FedEx's costs.

In recent years, the use of this model has exploded. According Arun Sundararajan (2016), Professor of Business at New York University, the "gig economy" is the result of technological change. Most of these "new on-demand services rely on a population equipped with computers or GPS-enabled smartphones." Uber, Lyft, Elance, Airbnb, Etsy, GrubHub, Dynamex, and TaskRabbit all rely on people who work for them being independent contractors.

However, the gig economy recently ran into a bump in the road. On April 30, 2018, the California Supreme Court ruled that "employers must treat workers who do work related to a company's 'usual course of business' as full-fledged employees" (qtd. in Finley 2018). Andrei Hagiu estimates that "converting contractors to employees can increase an employer's costs by about twenty-five to forty percent per worker" (qtd. in Finley 2018).

The ruling only affects California. However, the gig economy depends heavily on the use of independent contractors. Whether these firms will be able to continue to treat employees as independent contractor depends on how the laws defining what is an employee are interpreted by the courts. Part of the heterodox solution is to rewrite these laws to afford workers, especially low-wage workers, better protections.

Franchises

Franchising has long been associated with the fast-food industry. Building stores in every neighborhood in America would take a massive capital investment. However, once a company has built a brand that everyone recognizes, it can receive returns without sinking money into building new stores. If the company can find a person or group who wants to go into business, has access to enough funds to build a store, and is willing to follow strict instructions about every aspect of the products' delivery, then the two can enter into a franchisor/franchisee relationship.

In such agreements, the protection of brand is imperative. The key is to be able to write and monitor the agreement so that the franchisee provides the service just as franchisor would. The idea of having franchisees is not new, but it is spreading to other industries.

Weil highlights the hotel/motel industry, which employed 1.86 million workers in 2011. Fifty-five percent of those workers were "low-wage workers making $11.61 or less" (p. 154). Weil writes:

> Because of the significant capital investment in the industry, investors, brands and managers all have a stake in management

of hotel properties. This has given rise to a complicated mix of organizations with hands-on roles in day-to-day hotel operations. A given property may have four or more businesses with some impact on how work is organized, managed, supervised and compensated. This complexity leads to downward pressure on wages and benefits.... For the workforce, this can mean at best confusion over who is minding the store and at worst significant violations of workplace labor standards. (p. 157)

As a result, compliance with labor laws is low in the hotel/motel industry. Looking at major chains from 2002 to 2008, Weil reports that "only 31% of all investigated properties were in compliance with [Fair Labor Standards Act] provisions" (p. 155).

With franchising, employment is essentially moved from the large parent company to the small franchisee. In the case of the hotel/motel industry, employment at those franchisees is often subcontracted out to staffing companies. This trend is not good for the low-wage worker. Weil reports that a study of the fast-food industry showed that noncompliance with labor laws was 24% higher "among franchisee-owned outlets than among otherwise similar company-owned outlets" (p. 131).

In studying US poverty, one of the big questions is why poverty rates didn't fall after the 1970s. Many believe that an important part of that answer is that technological changes have reduced firm-specific skills, the need for on-the-job training, and control issues to the point that corporate American can now restructure itself into a core/periphery model. This restructuring has led to the movement of employment from primary to secondary markets. And as a result, the number and percentage of low-wage jobs has increased.

Given the advantages for large corporations, we should expect this trend to continue in the absence of legislative changes that would make it more difficult.

Minimum Wage

Another important part of the answer to why poverty rates have not fallen over the past forty years is that over this period, the real value of the minimum wage has gone down.

For those at the bottom of the secondary market, minimum wage laws are the most important determinate of wages. The federal government sets a minimum wage that covers the entire US. However, there are two caveats. First, approximately 20% of all low-wage jobs are not covered by the federal minimum wage law, so these employees can be paid a wage below the minimum wage. Second, states, counties, and cities may pass laws that require a higher minimum wage than the federal government, and they may also pass laws that cover more jobs.

Figure 2 shows the federal minimum wage for the years 1955 to 2015. The first column is the actual federal minimum wage that was paid in that year. The second column takes the actual minimum wages and corrects it for inflation so we know what that minimum wage was worth in 2014 dollars. The wages in the second column are sometimes referred to as the real minimum wage. The real minimum wages peaked in 1968, when it was worth $9.54 per hour in 2014 dollars. After correcting for inflation, the federal minimum wage has been generally lower from 1983 to the present than it was between 1963 and 1982. This fact is surprising because the productivity of the labor force has been continuously increasing. Had the minimum wage kept up with both inflation and increases in net total output per hour, which is a proxy for the increase in productivity, it would have been $18.33 per hour in 2014.[58]

Minimum Wage and Poverty

According to heterodox economists, the reason that fully employed people find themselves in poverty is that the wages at the bottom end are so low that they are unable to make an income sufficient to escape

Year	Current Dollars	2014 Dollars	Year	Current Dollars	2014 Dollars
1955	$0.75	$5.79	1986	$3.35	$6.90
1956	$1.00	$7.60	1987	$3.35	$6.68
1957	$1.00	$7.36	1988	$3.35	$6.44
1958	$1.00	$7.16	1989	$3.35	$6.18
1959	$1.00	$7.11	1990	$3.80	$6.67
1960	$1.00	$6.99	1991	$4.25	$7.20
1961	$1.15	$7.96	1992	$4.25	$7.03
1962	$1.15	$7.88	1993	$4.25	$6.86
1963	$1.25	$8.45	1994	$4.25	$6.71
1964	$1.25	$8.34	1995	$4.25	$6.56
1965	$1.25	$8.21	1996	$4.75	$7.14
1966	$1.25	$7.98	1997	$5.15	$7.57
1967	$1.40	$8.67	1998	$5.15	$7.47
1968	$1.60	$9.54	1999	$5.15	$7.32
1969	$1.60	$9.13	2000	$5.15	$7.08
1970	$1.60	$8.71	2001	$5.15	$6.89
1971	$1.60	$8.35	2002	$5.15	$6.78
1972	$1.60	$8.10	2003	$5.15	$6.63
1973	$1.60	$7.62	2004	$5.15	$6.46
1974	$2.00	$8.66	2005	$5.15	$6.25
1975	$2.10	$8.40	2006	$5.15	$6.05
1976	$2.30	$8.70	2007	$5.85	$6.68
1977	$2.30	$8.18	2008	$6.55	$7.20
1978	$2.65	$8.83	2009	$7.25	$8.00
1979	$2.90	$8.81	2010	$7.25	$7.84
1980	$3.10	$8.48	2011	$7.25	$7.63
1981	$3.35	$8.37	2012	$7.25	$7.48
1982	$3.35	$7.89	2013	$7.25	$7.37
1983	$3.35	$7.57	2014	$7.25	$7.25
1984	$3.35	$7.27	2015	$7.25	$7.17
1985	$3.35	$7.03			

Figure 2. The value of the minimum wage.

poverty. Therefore, an important question is how the minimum wage relates to the poverty line.

In 2016, the poverty line for a family of three was $19,105 per year. The federal minimum wage was $7.25 per hour. Someone working forty hours per week for fifty weeks at the federal minimum wage made $14,500 per year or 76% of the poverty line for a family of three.

If the minimum wage is $9.54, which was its real value in 1968, then this individual's yearly income is $19,080, or a little under 100% of the poverty line. If it is $18.33 per hour, which is what the minimum wage would be if adjusted for both inflation and productivity, then the yearly income is $36,660 or 192% of the poverty line for a family of three.

Obviously, increasing the minimum wage can reduce the level of poverty if there were a large number of people working at the minimum wage. So how many people are working at or near minimum wage?

In response to the proposed Raise the Wage Act, David Cooper (2015) of the Economic Policy Institute produced a paper analyzing the effect of the legislation. The Raise the Wage Act would have raised the federal minimum wage to $12.00 hour by increasing the minimum wage by one dollar each year between 2016 and 2020. Figure 3 shows the number of workers who would have been directly affected by these increases.

Increasing the minimum wage would also affect other low-wage jobs that pay above the minimum wage. This is known as the spillover effect. If the minimum wage is $7.00 per hour, for example, and if there are firms paying their employees $8.00 per hour, what happens to these higher wages if the minimum wage increases to $7.50 per hour? According to studies done by Card and Kruger (1995), firms don't all react the same. Some don't change their wage, while others do, presumably to allow these firms to attract the best low-wage workers.

The key point is that an increase in the minimum wage affects more than just minimum wage jobs. However, according to Card and Kruger, the spillover effect doesn't appear to extend much beyond one dollar

Year	Minimum Wage	Directly Affected
2016	$8.00	2.5 Million
2017	$9.00	8.1 Million
2018	$10.00	13.5 Million
2019	$11.00	24.6 Million
2020	$12.00	28.4 Million

Figure 3. Number of workers directly affected by minimum wage increases. 28.4 million workers is a little over 20% of the work force.

above the minimum wage. Given the time period of their analysis, that was approximately 125% of the minimum wage or closer to $2.00 per hour now.

In his paper, Cooper assumes that all workers who have wages between $12.00 and $13.00 dollars per hour see some amount of increase in their pay as a result of the minimum wage increasing to $12.00 per hour. On one hand, this is a conservative estimate because it only reaches one dollar above the minimum wage. On the other hand, it's a liberal estimate because it assumes all firms will adjust their wages. The size of his spillover effect is an additional 6.7 million workers. An increase in the minimum wage to $12.00 per hour would thus affect a total of 35.1 million workers or more than 25% of the workforce.

It is often implied that there is no real urgency to increase the minimum wage because it has little effect on the level of poverty. Those making these statements assume that most of those earning the minimum wage are middle-class teenagers who are working a few hours after school. As it turns out, this characterization of minimum wage workers as young, well-off, and working relatively few hours is largely false. According to Cooper, those who would be affected by increasing the minimum wage to $12.00 per hour have the following characteristics:

- 89.3% are twenty years old and older, 66.6% are twenty-five years old and older, and 36.7% are forty years old and older.

- 50% have a family income of less than $40,000 per year, and 21.5% have family incomes of less than $20,000.

- 57.4% work thirty-five or more hours per week, and 87.4% work twenty or more hours per week.

While this data doesn't allow us to know precisely who would be helped or to what degree, it certainly indicates that a substantial increase in the minimum wage would most likely result in a significant increase in the family incomes of a large segment of the poor and near-poor.

Employment Effects

As we will see in the next chapter, whether increasing the minimum wage causes employment to rise or fall doesn't have any effect on the heterodox solutions to poverty. However, students often ask about the employment effects of an increase in the minimum wage. Because recent legislative proposals asking for large increases in the minimum wage have not contained the rest of the heterodox package for eliminating poverty, it is worth addressing that question.

According to some orthodox economists, an increase in the minimum wage will decrease employment. The full details of why employment falls in the orthodox model when the minimum wage increases will have to wait until Chapter 8. In brief, though, this theory proposes that an increase in the minimum wage causes the firm to pay a wage that is greater than the dollar value of what the employee produces. As a result, when the minimum wage increases, the firm either lays off workers or cuts their hours. To the extent that this happens, unemployment and underemployment increases.

However, this theory overlooks an effect that works in the opposite direction. An increase in the minimum wage shifts income from the rich to the poor and middle class. Because the poor and middle class spend a higher proportion of their income, this redistribution of income causes aggregate demand to increase, thus increasing employment. Empirical estimates of the employment effects of the minimum wage are mixed.

The difference seems to fall largely along methodological lines. Those who use an estimating technique called "fixed effect" find that increases in the minimum wage cause employment levels to fall. The most well-known researchers from this camp are Neumark and Wascher.[59] Those who use an estimating technique called "matching" find that in most cases, an increase in the minimum wage has no effect on the level of employment (Kuehn 2014).[60] This group is best represented by Card and Kruger in the 1990s and over the past ten to fifteen years by Arindrajit Dube.

Which technique is the most accurate? The gold standard for scientific research, like research in medicine, is to randomly choose a large number of test subjects and divide them into two groups. One group receives the treatment, and the other group, called the control group, does not. It is rare in economic research to have a situation where there is a control group. Therefore, economists normally must use other, inferior testing methods.

However, the matching technique comes very close to testing with a control group. Because states and cities can enact minimum wage laws that are higher than the federal minimum wage, there can be situations where cities or counties in one state have an increase in their minimum wage, but adjacent cities and counties in another state do not. For example, New Jersey might raise its minimum wage while Pennsylvania does not. As a result, the cities and counties in Pennsylvania that border New Jersey can be used as a control group. It is not a perfect control group, but it's close. Because of the superior design of matching studies, we should have more confidence in their results. Of course, a matching study that was poorly done would be inferior to a fixed effect study that was well done. There continues to be debate on the pros and cons of each of these techniques, as well as debate about the quality of studies that have been done using each technique.

There are those who are attempting to reduce poverty from low wages by introducing legislation to substantially increase the minimum wage without simultaneously introducing legislation to increase employment. For these individuals, the employment effects of the minimum wage are highly important. If employment does not fall, then the passage of such legislation substantially improves the living conditions of the working poor and near poor, and rest of society receives the associated benefits. If, on the other hand, increases in the minimum wage result in decreases in employment, then the benefits of minimum wage legislation for the working poor become less and may end up helping some while injuring others.

For those pushing for a substantial increase the minimum wage, it is tempting to point to the matching studies and say that this significant rise in the minimum wage has no effect on employment, but they can't really do that. The studies that exist were made with relatively small changes in the minimum wage. We can't extrapolate from results based on small changes to predict what happens with a large one. We just don't know whether the effects of a higher cost of employment and the effects of a greater aggregate demand are both linear.[61]

What do we mean by linear? An example of linear would be if the minimum wage goes up by 10%, 20%, and 30%, and employment then falls by 2%, 4%, and 6% because of the higher cost of production. If we know that all the effects are linear, we can extrapolate from a small change in the minimum wage to a large one. A change that is three times as big will have an effect that is three times as great. However, we don't know whether these effects are linear. In fact, we should strongly expect that they are not. However, as we will later see, this does not in any material fashion affect the heterodox solution to poverty.

Market Power

For jobs that pay wages and salaries above the minimum wage, firms must decide how much to pay workers. There are several factors the firm must consider. In this section, we'll look at one of them—market power, which is the relative strength of the employer versus the employee. For our discussion, we will divide firms into those with unions and those without.

Firms with Unions

If a firm's workforce is unionized, then wages, benefits, and certain workplace procedures are determined by formal negotiations. How large an increase in wages and benefits workers receive in any contract depends, in part, on the relative power of the employer and the union when they are bargaining.

The ultimate threat that the union has in negotiations is a strike. A strike is an attempt to shut down the production of goods and services by walking off the job. Often the firm's countermove is to try to keep production going, at least to some extent, by using supervisors and by hiring temporary or sometimes permanent replacement workers. These individuals are usually referred to as "scabs" by the union. The strike boils down to a contest of who can inflict and absorb more economic damage. The more the union can reduce production, the more injurious it is for the firm. On the other hand, workers who aren't working aren't receiving any income except for what they might get from the union's strike fund and any temporary work they can find.

The side that suffers the most damage is the one that gives in the most when the strike is settled and an agreement is reached. In general, the longer the strike goes on, the worse it tends to be for the workers as their loss in pay starts to mount up and the replacement workers get better at production. The level of unemployment often plays a role in the final outcome. The higher the unemployment rate is, the easier it is for firms to find replacement workers, and the harder it is for strikers to find temporary work.

Neither side likes to go to strike because at least in the short run, both sides suffer financial setbacks. Most negotiations therefore end in a settlement without a strike. However, the level of unemployment still plays a role in the ultimate wage settlement. When unemployment is high, the firm can be more aggressive in its bargaining demands. When unemployment is low, the union can be more aggressive.

Unsurprisingly, unionized workers receive more in wages and benefits than similar non-union workers. Additionally, increases in union wages often drag up non-union wages. When I was young, I worked in a town that had a US Steel plant—a union firm. Every time US Steel raised their wages, the local non-union DuPont facility raised their wages by approximately the same amount. The professed reason for DuPont mimicking US Steel's wage policy was to attempt to keep their employees from forming a union. Why would workers go through the trouble and expense of unionizing if they are already getting essentially union wages?

As we discussed earlier, the percentage of the workforce that is unionized in the US has declined significantly since the 1950s. In addition, the unions that still exist appear to be far less powerful than they were fifty or sixty years ago. Therefore, the effect of unions on determining the wage structure in the US is far less than it was at one time.

Firms Without Unions

Non-union firms who don't compete with union firms to attract workers must choose how much to pay their workers. Firms without unions are more constrained than we might think.

The first thing to realize is that while most workers are compelled to seek employment because they don't have any other way to make a living, Worker A is not required to work for Employer Z. Worker A can apply for work with any employer that is looking for the skills they possess. If a firm pays too little, it has few workers to choose from. These workers might also be of low quality, and the turnover rate may be high. As the firm increases its wage, the pool of workers it can attract becomes larger and of higher quality, and the turnover rate goes down.

As we discussed earlier, there are some firms who want to have a large pool of high-quality workers to choose from. Normally, they also want to have low turnover rates. To have both, these firms have to pay high wages. On the other hand, there are firms who just need bodies to fill their positions. The required skill level is low, and it can be filled by just about anyone. These firms are going to pay relatively low wages.

A number of factors affect the wage structure of a firm. However, regardless of firm type, the level of unemployment plays a role. The level of wages is always affected by the degree of market power possessed by the employer versus the employee. The more workers a firm has to choose from, the more power they have to keep wages low. The more job offers workers have to choose from, the higher the wages they command as employers compete for workers. As the level of unemployment goes down, firms have fewer potential employees to choose from, and potential employees will have more potential employers to choose from.

If all else is equal, lower unemployment means higher wages. Firms with internal labor markets are unlikely to react to temporary changes in unemployment. However, if unemployment becomes persistently high or low, then changes in market power gradually affect wage structures. Low unemployment is helpful to workers because it decreases their chances of unemployment and raises wage.

For firms, lower unemployment has two effects— one lowers profits, and the other raises them. The lower unemployment is, the higher wages are, and profits fall. However, the lower unemployment is, the stronger the economy is, so sales and profits rise. Businesses like to see an economy that is strong enough for sales to be good but not so strong that it pushes up wages.

The reason for putting so much emphasis on the effect of unemployment on wages is that part of the heterodox solution to poverty is for the government to increase employment until it reaches full employment. While this reduces poverty, it also shifts the balance of power in labor markets. The heterodox solution to poverty thus helps out not just the poor but almost all wage and salary earners. Wages will rise throughout the economy, and profits will most likely fall. In the past, this solution to poverty has been opposed by the business community and the mass media that they own. We should expect the same in the future.

References

Card, David and Alan Kruger. 1995. *Myth and Measurement: The New Economics of the Minimum Wage*. Princeton, NJ: Princeton University Press.

Cooper, David. 2015. "Raising the Minimum Wage to $12 by 2020 Would Lift Wages for 35 Million American Workers." Washington D.C.: Economic Policy Institute.

Doeringer, Peter and Michael Piore. 1971. *Internal Labor Markets and Manpower Analysis*. Lexington MA: D.C. Heath and Co.

Dworak-Fisher, Keenan, Maury Gittleman, and Thomas Moehrle. 2014. "Trends in Employment-Based Health Insurance: Evidence from the National Compensation Survey." *Monthly Labor Review*, October: 1–19.

Edwards, Richard. 1979. Contested Terrain: The Transformation of the Workplace in the Twentieth Century. USA: Basic Books.

Finley, Klint. 2018. "A California Ruling Threatens the Gig Economy." *Wired*. May 2.

Harrison, Bennett. 1994. *Lean and Mean: The Changing Landscape of Corporate Power in the Age of Flexibility*. USA: Basic Books.

Katz, Lawrence and Alan Krueger. 2016. "The Rise and Nature of Alternative Work Arrangements in the United States, 1995–2015." Princeton University Working Paper.

Kuehn, Daniel. 2014. "The Importance of Study Design in the Minimum-Wage Debate." Washington D.C.: Economic Policy Institute

Neumark, D. and W. Wascher. 1992. "The Effects of Minimum and Subminimum Wages: Panel Data on State Minimum Wage Laws." *Industrial and Labor Relations Review* 46, (1): 55–81.

Sundararajan, Arun. 2016. "The 'gig economy' is coming. What will it mean for work?" *The Guardian*. July 26.

Veblen, Thorstein. 1899. *The Theory of the Leisure Class: An Economic Study of Institutions*. New York: B.W. Huebsch.

Weil, David. 2014. *The Fissured Workplace: Why Work Became So Bad for So Many and What Can Be Done to Improve It*. Cambridge, MA: Harvard University Press.

Wolff, Edward. 2009. *Poverty and Income Distribution*, 2nd ed. Chichester, West Sussex, UK: Wiley Blackwell.

❖ 6

Heterodox Solutions to Poverty

As we discussed in Chapter 2, economists discover the causes and solutions to social problems by working in alternative universes — models. The focus of this chapter is to discuss the causes and solutions to poverty from the heterodox perspective in order to understand how these causes and solutions are derived from using heterodox models.

Heterodox Causes of Poverty

For the sake of simplicity, we will talk about two reasons for poverty — poverty due to unemployment and poverty due to low wages. Of course, poverty can be a blend of these two — working part-time *and* for low wages. However, by making this distinction, we can focus on the causes and solutions to each separately.

Poverty Due to Unemployment

To determine the heterodox causes and solutions to poverty due to unemployment, we need to know which of the heterodox model we should use. So far, we have encounter three models:

1. The Simple Keynesian Model.
2. The Business Cycle Model.
3. The Segmented Labor Market Model.

Which one is best for determining why there is poverty due to unemployment? Two of the models deal with the level of employment. However, the simple Keynesian model is only an introductory model. It can explain the effect of certain factors on employment or unemployment. For example, an increase in the animal spirits increases investment, which increases aggregate demand, which increases employment and decreases unemployment. However, this model can't make predictions about what should happen over time to employment and unemployment. For that, we need a more complex model. The simple Keynesian model is built into our more complex business cycle model. [62] It is the business cycle model that we use to discover the causes and solutions to poverty due to unemployment.

As we saw in Chapter 4, the basic result of the heterodox business cycle model is that there is always or almost always some level of under- and unemployment in a capitalist economy. Assuming that some other force — a hurdle — doesn't bring the expansion to an end beforehand, then according to the Basic Mechanism of the business cycle model, as the expansion approaches full employment, inventories of raw materials and the number of unemployed workers declines. At some point, this causes raw material prices and wages to rise. In addition to these rising costs, firms may also be using more of their least efficient capital as the expansion progresses — further increasing their costs.

Eventually, the costs of production rise faster than revenues. As a result, profits start to fall. As profits fall, the optimism of businesspeople, the animal spirit, starts to decline and firms' purchases of new plant and equipment starts to fall. If this is widespread, it causes a general decline in aggregate demand, and the economy fall into recession. Generally, this happens before full employment is reached.

This effect of rising production costs on investment is often amplified by the Federal Reserve increasing interest rates and by banks raising their standards of creditworthiness. According to the heterodox theory of business cycles, in capitalist societies, there are always or almost always more people looking for jobs than there are jobs available. Those who end up unemployed or underemployed long enough end up in poverty. [63] We will discuss the complete package of heterodox solutions in a few pages, but clearly the solution to poverty due to unemployment is to increase the number of jobs.

Poverty Due to Low Wages

For determining the causes of poverty due to low wages we use the heterodox segmented labor market model. In stark contrast to the orthodox model that we will meet later, in this model, a worker wage depends on the *job* that they have, not on their productivity.

It might seem like it should be the reverse because those who are the best educated and the most productive have the highest chance of landing a well-paying job in the primary labor market. However, their relatively higher paid is primarily due to the job they have and not due to their higher productivity. Two individuals with the same education, same experience, and same productivity can have very difference wages if one gets a job in the primary labor market and the other gets a job in the secondary labor market.

According to dual labor market model, jobs can be divided into two segments — the primary labor market, where jobs have good wages and good benefits, and the secondary labor market, where jobs have low wages and little or no benefits. However, what is it about jobs in the primary sector that forces firms to build internal labor markets and to follow a high-wage/high-benefit strategy? There are two possible reasons:

1. These jobs may be in firms that are so large that owners and upper management cannot monitor the performance of their employees. As a result, they build structures that allow for continuous monitoring and performance reviews by supervisors. In addition, they provide monetary incentives to make sure that employees work hard.

2. These jobs may require a large amount of firm-specific skills or on-the-job training, which in many cases goes on for years. To reduce turnover, the firm forms an internal labor market and pays high wage.

What is it about jobs in the secondary market that makes firm follow a low-wage/low-productivity strategy? These are the opposite of the primary sector jobs. There is little in the way of firm-specific skills or on-the-job training. The employees who hold these jobs can be replaced easily, and there are plenty of individual available during most time periods to replace them. Therefore, there is no need for the firm to try to reduce turnover by paying these workers a good wage. Furthermore, these firms, which are sometimes franchises, are often small, and the owners can easily monitor the performance of their employees. In those circumstances, there is no need for forming internal labor markets or giving laborers higher pay to incentivize them to work hard. Because of the nature of these jobs, employers do not need to pay much more than the bare minimum.

While the majority of the jobs are in the primary labor market, there are still many jobs in the secondary labor market. Moreover, the portion of all employment in this low-wage segment appears to be growing.

In the heterodox model, the cause of poverty from low wages is that a certain portion of jobs pay low wages and have little or no benefits. For households whose primary source of income comes from employment in the secondary labor market, it is highly likely that these households are either poor or near poor. To overcome this problem, the heterodox solution needs to have some government program or programs to increase the wages of low wage workers.

Adding together the heterodox causes of poverty due to unemployment and poverty due to low wages we can summarize the heterodox view as a "blame the system explanation," which claims that the system simple doesn't provide enough well-paying jobs for everyone to pull themselves out of poverty. The sociologist Marc Rich's (2011) metaphor about capitalism being like a game of musical chairs essentially sums up the heterodox position:

> In class, I often use the analogy of musical chairs. . . . Picture a game with ten players but only eight chairs. When the music stops, who's most likely to be left standing? It will be those who are at a disadvantage in terms of competing for the available chairs (less agility, reduced speed, a bad position when the music stops, and so on). However, given that the game is structured in a way such that two players are bound to lose, these individual attributes only explain who loses, not why there are losers in the first place. Ultimately, there are simply not enough chairs for those playing the game.
>
> The critical mistake that's been made in the past is that we've equated the question of who loses at the game with the question why the game inevitably produces losers. They are, in fact, distinct and separate questions. So, while characteristics such as deficiencies in skills or education or being in a single parent family help to explain who's at a heightened risk of encountering poverty, the fact that poverty exists in the first-place results not from these characteristics, but from a failure of the economic and political structures to provide enough decent opportunities and support for the whole of society. (p. 19)

Changing the Characteristics of the Poor

Because solutions based on orthodox economics have dominated public discourse on poverty, there has been much discussion of changing the characteristics of the poor as the road to solving the problem of poverty. Before moving on to what we will call "the basic solution," it's worth spending a moment discussing the effects of changing the characteristics of the poor in the heterodox model.

In the heterodox model, people are poor because they are unemployed, underemployed, or employed at low-wage jobs. However, who tends to end up in poverty? What are their characteristics, and will changing those characteristics be a part of the heterodox solution to poverty?

Those who end up in poverty either end up in the lower end of the secondary market or are unemployed. For some, they are in and out of employment. Earlier, we discussed the characteristics of those who are consistently in the back of the queue and as a result don't get jobs in the primary sector: [64]

- People with little education

- People with a poor education

- People with little work experience

- People with no connections

- People who have an anti-social attitude

- People with an unstable work history

- People with inflexible schedules

- Minorities and women if an employer is prejudiced[65] or believes their current workforce is prejudiced[66]

- People who don't live near or don't have access to primary sector employment

Some of those characteristics can be changed. People can get more education, dress more appropriately, work on improving their resume-writing skills, and so on. By doing so, they can move out of poverty by moving up the list and getting a better job. According to the heterodox model, however, this does not reduce poverty. It just changes who is in poverty.

Handler and Hasenfeld (1997) have a useful metaphor about income distribution being like a strangely shaped hotel where the income people receive depends on which room they're in. We might call this Hotel America, which is depicted in figure 1. The rooms on the bottom floor have the lowest incomes. Rooms on the second floor have the next lowest incomes, and so on. Changing the characteristics of the people shuffles who gets what rooms, but it has no effect on poverty because it doesn't affect the number of jobs or their wages. The number of rooms on the bottom floors is still the same, as is the height of those floors.

For this reason, federal training programs have no effect on poverty. If Worker A receives training and lands a primary sector job, it means that Worker B — who otherwise would have received that job — now replaces Worker A in the secondary market. These training programs only affect who gets which rooms and the characteristics of those in each room. If we want to reduce poverty, we need to either structurally reshape Hotel America to have fewer rooms on the bottom, or we need to raise the level of the bottom rooms. According to the heterodox theory, attempting to discover a solution to poverty by studying and changing the characteristics of the poor is a waste of time and money.

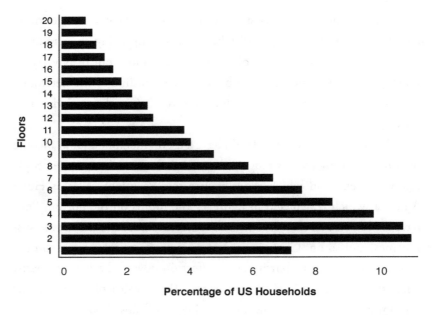

Figure 1. The rooms in Hotel America. The shape of this hotel reflects the actual distribution of household income in the US for those with incomes below $200,000 (94% of households). The first floor represents the number of households with incomes from 0 to $10,000. The second floor represents the number of households with incomes from $10,001 to $20,000, and so on.

Heterodox Solutions to Poverty

In the heterodox model, poverty is the natural result of the operation of the capitalist social system. The same system that makes some people incredibly wealthy also makes a large number of people poor. We present the heterodox solutions to poverty in several layers. The first layer is what we call "the basic solution." It comes directly from the heterodox business cycle and segmented labor market models.

The next layer looks at the real world and finds that there are special circumstances that if unaddressed will result in the basic solution being unable to eliminate all poverty. To offset these problems, we add a couple of pieces to the basic solution.

The last layer looks a little deeper into the business cycle model and realizes that the basic solution may eliminate excess capacity in certain labor markets. If true, this would prevent some parts of the economy from being able to grow during an expansion. We present two plans for reestablishing excess capacity into the economy when the basic solution is being used.

The Basic Solution

The Basic Solution is similar but not identical to those suggested by other heterodox economists (Wray 1997, 2012; Papadimitriou 1999; Minsky 2013). All of these rely heavily on the federal government playing the role of employer of last resort.

Solutions to Poverty Due to Unemployment

In the heterodox model, poverty due to unemployment is caused by a persistent lack of employment — not enough jobs and not enough full-time jobs. Thus, the solution is to increase the number of jobs through the following provisions:

1. Use stimulus policies to increase aggregate demand — ideally, so that the economy operates at or near full employment. The policies to achieve this are an increase in federal government spending, a lowering of taxes, and a decrease in interest rates. There is obviously a limit as to how much we can lower taxes or lower interest rates. Therefore, if we are going to stimulate the economy, then as a practical matter, it must be primarily by increasing government spending.

2. Achieve an increase in aggregate demand by making taxes more progressive. Because the poor and middle class have a higher MPC than the rich, redistributing income through a change in the tax code increases consumption and thus increases aggregate demand.

3. Use federal public service employment (PSE) programs as the employer of last resort. The government can directly employ anyone who can't get a job in the private sector.

4. Dispense a sufficient level of cash payment to individuals who are temporarily or permanently unable to participate in the labor market.

The first three provisions attempt to eliminate poverty by increasing the number of jobs. The fact that the economy then operates at or near full employment also increases the bargaining power of all workers because individual workers have more potential employers to choose from, and individual employers have fewer potential employees. These policies not only help the poor but benefit most wage and salary earners. The fourth provision is for those who are disabled and can't work and those with small children who can't or shouldn't work.[67]

Before moving on to poverty due to low wages, we should briefly discuss PSE programs because they play such an important role in the heterodox solution. With PSE programs, the government hires the unemployed for projects that serve the public and their communities. The goal is not to compete with private industry or other governmental agencies.

The US has only briefly used PSE programs. During the Great Depression, the Civil Works Administration (CWA) employed 4 million workers at its peak. However, the CWA lasted for less than four months (1933–34). Other, smaller programs during the Great Depression can also be viewed as PSEs—the Civilian Conservation Corp, which provided jobs in the national forests, and the Public Works Administration, which put people to work building roads, bridges, schools, and cities.[68] In the 1970s, PSE programs were part of the Comprehensive Employment and Training Act (CETA). This was also true in the late 1970s and early 1980s with the Youth Incentive Entitlement Pilot Projects. In every case, PSE programs encountered intense opposition from the business community, and that opposition resulted in the demise of these programs.

Solutions for Poverty Due to Low Wages

Poverty due to low wages is caused by secondary market jobs paying wages that are too low. The solution is to increase the wages of those jobs. This can be accomplished by dramatically increasing the minimum wage and then indexing it to increases in inflation and productivity.

There are other ways of increasing the take home wages of low wage workers. Liberal orthodox economists generally prefer using the Earned Income Tax Credit (EITC). One reason they prefer the EITC is the claim that an increase in the minimum wage will increase unemployment. However, even if this is true, it isn't a problem for the heterodox solution, because simultaneously with the increase in the minimum wage, the heterodox solution has programs to increase employment.

Success Depends on the Model Being Correct

As we discussed earlier, according to the heterodox business cycle model, the reason for poverty due to unemployment is a lack of jobs. There are always people who are without work. The solution is for the government to increase the number of jobs using the programs discussed above. The success of these programs critically depends on the business cycle model being correct—that there are always or almost always more people looking for work than there are jobs available. If the business cycle model is wrong and the economy naturally achieves full employment on a regular basis, then not only will the heterodox solutions be ineffective, but as we will see in Chapter 12, they will damage the economy. Whether the heterodox theory of business cycles is correct, then, is crucial to whether the heterodox solution to poverty from unemployment is effective.

The heterodox solution to poverty due to low wages is a significant increase the minimum wage. This is critically dependent on the heterodox segmented labor markets model. In this model, each job has a wage attached to it. Jobs in the primary labor market have good wages and benefits attached to them because of the natural of those jobs. Employers in the primary sector believe that by pursuing a high-wage/high-productivity strategy they can lower their cost of production. Employers in the secondary market believe that because their jobs are fundamentally different from those in the primary sector, a low-wage/low-productivity strategy lowers their cost of production. If the wage is attached to the job, then to eliminate poverty due to low wages, we need to elevate the wages on those low-wage jobs. Significantly increasing the minimum wage will produce that result.

If the heterodox theory is wrong and wages are not simply attached to the job but are based on the individual's productivity, then raising the minimum wage may not result in a decline in poverty. In fact, the result will be mass layoffs as the wage becomes much higher than the laborer's productivity, and firms will be forced to lay off workers to keep from losing mone. Whether the heterodox segmented market model is correct, then, is crucial to whether the heterodox solution to poverty from low wages is effective.

Special Considerations

The basic solution is based on the heterodox business cycle and segmented market models. However, as we move from our models and look at the real world, we see two problems that need to be explicitly addressed to have a truly effective anti-poverty program—geographic isolation and labor law violations.

Geographic Isolation

If unemployment is the same in all parts of the country, and if the percentage of good jobs is the same everywhere, then poverty rates will be relatively the same everywhere. However, poverty is *not* evenly spread throughout the country. Certain areas have persistently higher levels of poverty.

One area that gets a lot of attention in the poverty literature is inner-city black poverty. In his research of the black inner-city sections of

Chicago, the famous sociologist William Julius Wilson (1996) highlights problems of economic isolation that have blighted many inner cities. His work suggests that the inner city and other economically isolated areas may need special attention if poverty in these areas is going to be eliminated.

According to Wilson, well-paying blue-collar jobs started leaving the inner city of Chicago in the late 1950s. This caused a significant rise in unemployment and poverty in the black inner city, resulting in an increase in crime. Once housing discrimination lessened, individuals with good jobs tended to leave the area, further reducing the percentage of non-poor individuals in the black inner city. Local small businesses also tended to relocate elsewhere, further reducing jobs and increasing poverty. This led to more increases in violence and crime. The fear of violence kept new businesses from coming in and deterred non-inner-city residents from visiting. The result was a downward spiral. The black inner city became more and more isolated, largely cut off from the rest of society, which was only blocks away.

Many inner-city residents have developed patterns of social inter-action, behavior, and dress that make it difficult to get jobs outside the inner city, even if they can find reliable transportation to these jobs. In these regions, poverty rates are high, and those who are in poverty are often long-term poor. Simply increasing aggregate demand and the minimum wage will not fully reverse the problems of the inner city. PSE programs specifically targeting the inner city are necessary to turn the downward spiral around.

There are other areas of the country where we see economic isolation, too, such as Native American reservations and parts of Appalachia. These areas also need targeted PSE programs if poverty is to be eliminated.

Labor Law Violations

Our discussion of the corporate restructuring of employment raised two other concerns that must be addressed in proposals to eliminate poverty. The first is the tendency to spin off employment from the core to the periphery. The second is an increase in labor law violations, including wage theft and forced unpaid work, that has accompanied these changes.

In his book, Weil (2014) has a lengthy section that spells out in detail suggested legal changes to help low-wage workers who have been spun off into the periphery. Based on his work, we make two additions to the basic heterodox solution to poverty:

- Change the definition of what constitutes an employee to make it more difficult to have employees be independent contractors. In addition, other changes should be made to make the core corporation more responsible for the workforce employed by their subcontractors.

- Substantially increase funding for the enforcement of labor laws.

The reason for the second suggestion is that, since the Carter Administration, the amount of money in inflation-corrected dollars that has been allocated for enforcement of labor laws has stayed essentially constant. Since then, however, the number of businesses and the complexity of business relationships has increased substantially. As a result, the probability of being investigated for a labor law violation has gone down, and when the chance of being caught goes down, the cost for violating the law also goes down. Not surprisingly, this has resulted in the number of firms violating the law to go up. Moreover, significantly increasing the minimum wage gives small contractors an even greater incentive to violate labor laws. It is no good increasing the minimum wage if employers are just going to steal it back from their workers.

Providing Excess Capacity

Our basic solution may cause a problem that makes it incompatible with a real capitalist economy. One key to eliminating poverty without relying on massive welfare expenditures is to devise a system that allows everyone to have a job while at the same time maintaining the feature of excess capacity. We should remember that the economy is always in one phase or another of the business cycle, always expanding or contracting. Most of the time it is expanding, so excess capacity must exist to allow the economy to expand.

We can argue that for capitalism to operate, there must be a reserve army of the unemployed, a marginalized segment of the population that can always be drawn upon as needed during an expansion. For capitalism to exist, a portion of the population must necessarily be poor. As a result, the basic solution can't be implemented because it eliminates excess capacity in some labor markets, making it incompatible with a real capitalist economic system.

This position assumes that to provide excess capacity in labor markets we must have people who are either unemployment or under employed. However, this isn't necessarily true. Thus, if we are to truly eliminated poverty, we need a plan that will allow the government to move the economy to or near full employment while maintaining excess capacity in labor markets. Below are two plans that can achieve this goal.

The Two-Tiered Minimum Wage

The two-tiered minimum wage achieves excess capacity in a full-employment economy by encouraging workers who are employed in PSE programs to move to private sector employment as the economy expands. The first step in building the two-tiered minimum wage is to recognize that even when unemployment is low, the current system already contains a large amount of excess capacity for expanding college-educated jobs:

> Hecker (1992) found that "roughly 1 in 10 college graduates were employed in jobs previously held by high school graduates at the beginning of the 1970s and this ratio gradually crept to roughly 2 in 10 by the end of the decade...." Based on research by Pryor and Schaffer (1997), "high-school jobs might reasonably be defined as those in which the average education level of

a jobholder in 1971–72 was 13 or fewer years. If so, the proportion of all prime-age, college-educated workers who held jobs that traditionally employed high-school graduates rose from 22.1% in 1971 to 34% by 1995." (Gray and Chapman 1999)

In general, these college graduates are not unemployed. They are simply working jobs that don't require a college education while searching for jobs that do. This is the "reserve army of the over educated."[69] When a large primary sector firm wishes to expand its marketing department and needs some college-educated English majors, for example, the fact that the unemployment rate among English majors is low doesn't mean that there are no English majors to be had. The firm just needs to puts out a job announcement, and those college-educated English majors who are currently working as bartenders and baristas will apply. There is plenty of excess capacity for college-educated workers even when the unemployment rate among college graduates is low. The question is how to produce this same result for the lower end of the wage spectrum — employed individuals who can be hired by the private sector firms as the economy expands.

One way to accomplish this is to develop a two-tiered minimum wage, a minimum wage for the private sector and a different minimum wage for PSE programs. For this to work, the minimum wage in the private sector must be high enough that public-sector workers will take a private-sector job if it is offered. People often get off track by thinking that a two-tiered minimum wage means one minimum wage for primary sector jobs and another for secondary sector jobs, or they think that it means one minimum wage for educated workers and another for non-educated workers. Both of those ideas are wrong. We are looking at workers with relatively the same skill set and the same basic education. The private sector minimum wage is for jobs and workers at firms like McDonald's, and the PSE minimum wage is for those who, at the moment, can't get a job at McDonald's.

After guaranteeing that everyone who wants a job can have a job through public service employment, the second step is to set the minimum wage for PSE at a level that lifts most households out of poverty. In 2016, for full-time employment, the wage that lifts a family of three out poverty was approximately $9.50 per hour. For this example, then, let's set the PSE minimum wage at $9.50 per hour.

The third step is to set a private sector minimum wage at a level that is attractive to those working for a minimum wage in PSE, such as $15 per hour.

We can now combine this two-tiered minimum wage with the basic solution. Let's assume that as part of its anti-poverty program, the government increases aggregate demand by increasing government spending so the level of unemployment reaches 6%. Six percent may not be the percent that actually works best for society, but we'll use it for this example.

To reach full employment, the reminder of the unemployed are hired into PSE programs. It would be tempting to say that PSE programs would have hire 6% of the labor force. However, this is not true. In a dynamic economy where people are always entering or leaving the labor market, where firms are being born and are dying, and where workers leave one job to take another, the unemployment rate is never zero. There are always unemployed people looking for work, at the same time as firms have job opening and are looking for workers.

In this situation, then, full employment can be thought of as occurring when the number of job seekers equals the number of job openings. To figure out how many workers must be hired by PSE programs, we need to know how many job vacancies there are when the unemployment rate is 6%. Based on recent data from the Labor Department's JOLTS survey, when the unemployment rate is 6%, the job vacancy rate has been between 2.4% and 3.2% of the labor force. The number of people looking for work in excess of the number of job vacancies is thus 2.8 to 3.6% of the labor force—or 6.0% minus 2.4% to 3.2%.[70] Therefore, we should expect in our example that approximately 2.8% to 3.6% of the labor force will have PSE jobs.

As the economy expands, firms in the secondary market need to hire additional laborers and advertise their openings. Those who are working for the PSE minimum wage of $9.50 per hour should be more than happy to take a private sector minimum wage job at say $15.00 per hour. Thus, people are pulled out of PSE into higher paying private sector jobs. This can happen in two ways:

1. As the economy expands, businesses that hire minimum-wage workers need to hire additional workers. They hire minimum wage workers from PSE programs.

2. As the economy expands, businesses that need college-educated workers hire college graduates who are working at Starbucks or other similar jobs. Starbucks now has a job opening and hires someone from a PSE program. We can envision situations where a new position for a college-educated worker sets off a chain of upward mobility for several workers.

As the economy expands, then, the excess capacity necessary for the economy to expand comes from the "reserve army of the overeducated" and from those working in public service employment. As the economy continues to expand, the number of workers in PSE programs continues to decline. If we reach full employment in the traditional sense, PSE programs have no workers. This solution thus achieves the elimination or near-elimination of absolute poverty within a capitalist economy while providing businesses with the excess capacity they require, and it does so without depending on welfare benefits.

Government Spending

Another way to build excess capacity into the economic system is to vary the level of non-PSE government spending over the business cycle. This can be done with or without the two-tiered minimum wage. In our discussion of the two-tiered minimum wage, we assume that government spending is such that the economy has an unemployment rate of 6% without PSE programs. Let's assume the same starting point in this equation:

$$AD = C + I + G + NX = 6\% \text{ unemployment (6.1)}$$

In the two-tiered minimum wage discussion, we implicitly assume that the level of non-PSE government spending stays constant as the private sector expands. However, we can provide more room for the private sector to expand if G decreases when C and I increase:

$$AD = C\uparrow + I\uparrow + G\downarrow + NX = 6\% \text{ unemployment (6.2)}$$

This is not as easy as it looks on paper. The public expects and depends on most government programs to continue into the future. Just because the economy is expanding, we can't close the local community college or fire department. Citizens depend on their ongoing existence. This is true of many other government programs, too. However, because in this plan we are using government spending to increase aggregate demand to a certain level, programs that are used to increase government spending can also be designed so they can be reduced when the economy expands to the point where the unemployment rate without PSE is below 6%.

Equation 6.2 contains another oversimplification. It implies that, if aggregate demand increases by $500 billion due to increases in consumption and investment, we can simultaneously—and with precision—reduce government spending by $500 billion. None of that is possible. The decrease in government spending has to come later. Furthermore, in operating this policy, we don't want to reduce government spending by a greater amount than the combined increase in consumption and investment. That will cause the overall level of aggregate demand to fall, which could trigger a decline in the animal spirits.

Therefore, the goal in running this policy is to "lean against the wind," to reduce government spending by some percentage of the perceived increase in consumption and investment spending. For example, if we believe that consumption and investment are increasing at $600 billion per year, then we reduce government spending by $300 billion. In this way, we provide the excess capacity that allows the private sector to expand by freeing up resources that are being used in the government sector while, at the same time, maintaining a fully employed society.

The Second-Best Solution

All of the above solutions will no doubt run into fierce political opposition from the business community. David Weil, who has experience attempting to get legislation through Congress as President Obama's Wage and Hour Administrator in the US Department of Labor, states:

> [Joseph] Stiglitz points to the intensifying role played by the very top of economic elites in affecting political outcomes over the past three decades. The point can certainly be made in regard to legislation affecting the workplace. Passage of legislation to improve protections against a variety of workplace problems has been vexing, to put it mildly. One element that has been consistent in efforts to pass such laws has been the adamant and fierce opposition from the business community. Each new workplace proposal is denounced as undermining market functions and ultimately hurting rather than helping working people. (p. 209)

If this is true for legislation affecting the workplace, it will certainly be true of policies aimed at reaching full employment or significantly increasing the minimum wage.

If the primary solution is thus politically untenable, it is worth talking about what might be the second-best solution. This second-best solution involves greatly increasing government handouts to the point where no one is poor. This can be done either through increasing payments in the current array of programs or through a negative income tax. A negative income tax means that if people's income is below a certain level, the government pays them money. The further people are below that level, the more the government pays them.[71]

The use of government support programs is considered an inferior solution for a number of reasons. First, those being supported suffer negative psychological effects. People who are working feel like they have a purpose, that they are being productive, and that what they have they earned. People who are working can feel good about what they have done. People who are being supported don't have that sense of accomplishment or self-worth. In the long term, this can have damaging psychological effects.

Second, these programs generate resentment from those who are working and paying taxes. As a result, support programs tend to be divisive, pitting those who are working and paying taxes against those who are not working and being supported.

Finally, in a system that is, in effect, paying people not to work, there are fewer goods and services produced than if these individuals are working. The standard of living of the average person is thus lower.

We can anticipate that our second-best solution will also encounter intense resistance. However, in a society in which the system doesn't provide enough jobs for all its citizens — where a proportion of the population must live in poverty so that others can prosper — it is morally irresponsible for those who benefit from society not to pay those who don't.

Unfortunately, the widespread belief that poverty is not the fault of the system but of the poor themselves allows for the continuous blaming and denigrating of the poor. This belief is based on the orthodox economic models that we will study in the next chapters.

References

Doeringer, Peter and Michael Piore. 1971. *Internal Labor Markets and Manpower Analysis*. Lexington, MA: D.C. Heath and Co.

Gray, Jerry and Richard Chapman. 1999. "Conflicting Signals: The Labor Market for College-Educated Workers." *Journal of Economic Issues* 33, (3): 51–62.

Handler, Joel and Yeheskel Hasenfeld. 1997. *We the Poor People: Work, Poverty, & Welfare*. New Haven, CT: Yale University Press.

Minsky, Hyman. 2013. *Ending Poverty: Jobs, Not Welfare*. Annandale-on-Hudson, NY: Levy Economics Institute.

Papadimitriou, Dimitri. 1999. "Full Employment Has Not Been Achieved. Full Employment Policy: Theory and Practice." Public Policy Brief No. 53. Annandale-on-Hudson, NY: Levy Economics Institute

Rich, Mark. 2011. "Rethinking American Poverty." *Contexts*, Spring: 16-21

Weil, David. 2014. *The Fissured Workplace: Why Work Became So Bad for So Many and What Can Be Done to Improve It*. Cambridge, MA: Harvard University Press

Wilson, William J. 1996. *When Work Disappears: The World of the New Urban Poor*. New York: Alfred A. Knopf Inc.

Wray, L. Randall. 1997. "Government as Employer of Last Resort: Full Employment without Inflation." Working Paper No. 213. Annandale-on-Hudson, NY: Levy Economics Institute

Wray, L. Randall. 2012. *Modern Money Theory: A Primer on Macroeconomics for Sovereign Monetary Systems*. London: Palgrave Macmillan

❖ 7

Scarcity and Choice

Before studying the orthodox theory of labor markets, it is useful to understand the basic starting point and tools of orthodox analysis. According to orthodox economists, society's fundamental economic problem is scarcity. If we add up all the goods and services that we can produce and compare that to all the goods and services that people would like to have, the goods and services we can produce will be far less than the goods and services people would like to have.[72]

As a society, then, we are forced to make choices. At a minimum, we must decide which goods and services to produce, who receives the scarce resources to produce these goods and services, and who receives the goods and services. According to orthodox theory, those decisions are primarily made through the market.

To help us understand how this works, we will develop some basic tools in this chapter: the production possibilities frontier, opportunity costs, supply and demand analysis, and marginal analysis. For the most part, we will develop these ideas as if we are orthodox economists.

The Production Possibilities Frontier

Before looking at how decisions are made in product markets, we'll start with an often used and handy visual tool for illustrating scarcity and choice, the production possibilities frontier (PPF). We will look at how this works at an individual level and then at a societal level.

Individual Production Possibilities Frontier

Let's start by considering a simplified, individual situation. Leaky Blacktooth is headed down to his local neighborhood pub, Pour Red's, to socialize and have some beer. Assume that Leaky has $8.00, no access to additional funds, and can't run a tab. Furthermore, assume that Red's only serves two beers, Budweiser for $2.00 a pint and Pray for Snow (PFS) for $4.00 a pint.

As Leaky hobbles down to Red's, he considers his options. If he spends all his resources on Budweisers, he can have four pints. If spends all his money on PFS, he can have two. He can also split his money and have two pints of Budweiser and one of PFS. However, Leaky's choices are even greater. Assume that Pour Red's is an unusual pub that serves any size drink we wish. Mr. Blacktooth could thus order 2.6512 pints of Budweiser and 0.6744 pints of PFS. As figure 1 illustrates, Pour Red's Pub offers a linear continuum of possible choices of Budweiser and PFS.

That linear continuum—also known as a line—is Leaky's personal PPF. It shows all the combinations of Buds and PFSs that Leaky can obtain if he uses all of his resources.

While walking to the pub, Leaky thinks that it would be nice to have four pints of Budweiser (point A), but as he sits down at the bar, he thinks it might be nice to have a pint of PFS. What does it cost Leaky to have the PFS (point B)? Choosing point B costs Leaky two pints of Budweiser. If Leaky uses all $8.00 of his resources, he must make a choice. If

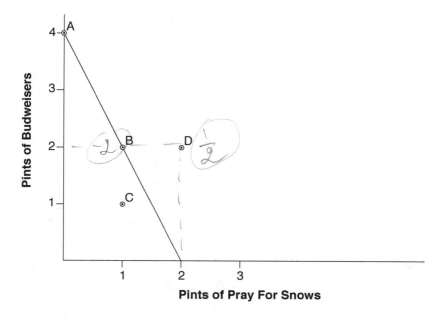

Figure 1. Leaky Blacktooth's production possibilities frontier.

he wants more of one good, PFS, he must take resources away from the other good, Budweiser, and use them to obtain the PFS.

Notice that the slope of the PPF is 2 — to be technical, it's actually −2. The absolute value of the slope expresses the opportunity cost of obtaining one more unit of the good on the *x*-axis. The inverse of that value, 1/2, is the opportunity cost of obtaining one more unit of the good on the *y*-axis.

When orthodox economists use the word "cost," they are usually referring to the concept of "opportunity cost." The opportunity cost of deciding to do *X* is what we have to give up in order to do *X*. Part of that cost is not doing our next best alternative. Opportunity costs take into account *all* the costs that a decision-maker feels, not just the out-of-pocket costs.

In our example of Leaky Blacktooth, there is no difference between out-of-pocket costs and opportunity costs because all the costs are out-of-pocket costs. However, if we ask what the opportunity cost is of going to college full time, the distinction between the two concepts becomes clearer. All students face the same out-of-pocket costs for tuition, materials, and books. Students also face out-of-pocket costs for transportation and housing if these costs would be lower if the student was not going to school.

There are also costs that are not out of pocket. For most students, the next best alternative to going to college full time is to get a job, so one of the biggest opportunity costs of going to college is the cost of foregone wages. This cost will differ from student to student depending on their job possibilities. Because they are studying hard, especially for their economics class, there are also the social costs of time away from friends and family. There are psychological costs associated with taking exams and writing papers. The true cost of going to college, then, is not just the out-of-pocket costs but the full range of opportunity costs.

With this in mind, let's return to Leaky and his choices. Leaky can choose point C, one pint of Budweiser and one of PFS, but in that case, he hasn't used all of his resources. Mr. Blacktooth doesn't have to make a choice, at least not in the way orthodox economists use the word. He can have another Budweiser without giving up his PFS. Any point below and to the left of the PPF is a point of unused resources. All these points are part of the feasible set, but they are considered inefficient because all the resources have not been used.

Leaky might really want to have two pints of Budweiser and two more of PFS (point D), but point D is not feasible. It requires more resources than Leaky has. Any point above and to the right of the PPF is not feasible due to a lack of resources, and only more resources will allow us to reach these points.

A Societal PPF

Let's now look at a PPF that represents society as a whole. Resources in this example are no longer just money but the total amount of labor, physical capital, and managerial talent in society. In addition, to be on the societal PPF, it takes more than just the full employment of all resources — they must also be used efficiently. While it is unclear what the full and efficient employment of raw materials means, the availability of raw materials certainly affects the total production of goods and services.

One of the downsides of graphs is that they are only two-dimensional, so we can only represent two goods with the *x*- and *y*-axis. Orthodox economists often use the example of "guns and butter" — the choice between military and consumer good production, which was a particular favorite during the cold war. Another useful PPF is to show the tradeoff between a high current standard of living and having a faster rate of growth in the future. Figure 2, for example, illustrates the choice between producing capital goods and producing consumption goods.

If we dedicate all our resources to the production of consumer goods, we are on point A. If we produce no consumption goods and use all our resource to produce capital goods, we would be at point B, which would be a problem because if we produced zero consumption goods, everyone would starve. The points between A and B on the PPF are where society has divided its resources between the production of capital goods and consumption goods.

In this example, the PPF is not linear. This is because the resources are not equally productive in each sector. If we start at point B, producing only capital goods, and then transfer some resources to the production of consumption goods, it is most efficient to transfer those resources that are best at producing consumption goods. The loss of capital goods for every additional unit of consumption goods produced is thus the lowest amount possible. The opportunity cost is the smallest, so the slope of the PPF is the flattest possible.

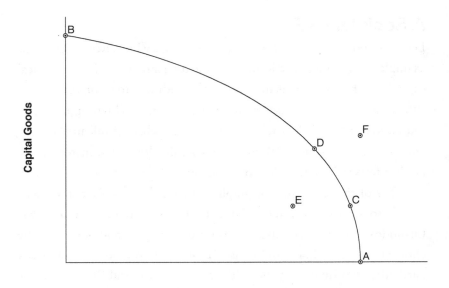

Figure 2. Society's production possibilities frontier.

As we attempt to produce even more consumption goods, we have to use resources that are slightly less efficient at producing consumption goods. The loss in capital goods is thus greater, the opportunity cost is slightly larger, and the slope of the PPF is steeper. As society attempts to produce more consumption goods, the slope of the PPF becomes steeper, giving it the shape we see in figure 2.

As the construction of PPF shows, society doesn't automatically face a scarcity problem. Society only faces scarcity when it is on the PPF. Let's assume that all resources are being used and used efficiently. Let us further assume that we are at point C, with a large amount of consumption goods being produced but not much in the way of capital goods. Given the current technology, point C represents a high standard of living. Let's further assume that the level of capital goods production is just large enough to replace the capital that wears out each year. The nation's capital stock is therefore neither increasing nor decreasing. For the sake of simplicity, let's also assume that neither technology nor the nation's population is changing. As a result, the standard of living stays the same year after year.

In this case, the only way to increase the standard of living in the future is to increase the production of capital goods in the present, but we can only do that by convincing members of society to accept a lower standard of living in the present. In other words, to move from point C to point D, we must reduce our standard of living in order to free up resources that we can then transfer to the capital goods sector. Therefore, if we wish to produce more of one good when facing scarcity, we must reduce the production of some other good or goods. Society must make a choice, and sometimes the choices are hard. During World War II, for example, a period in which everyone or almost everyone agrees that the nation faced scarcity, citizens repaired, reused, and did without many goods so that as many resources as possible could be used in the war effort.

When society is not using all its resources, or when it is using them inefficiently, then while some households may face scarcity, society as a whole does not. If the nation is at point E, the question it must answer in order to produce more capital goods is not how to free up resources but how to overcome the institutional problems that are preventing the full employment of resources or how to overcome the inefficient use of resources. To go from point E to point D requires the employment of unemployed resources and the efficient use of all resources.

The possibility that the nation could become stuck below the PPF is damaging to the entire orthodox perspective. As we will see, market forces not only make the choices for society but in the orthodox theory, they also ensure that any time the nation is below the PPF, society is ultimately driven back to the PPF, as if by an invisible hand.

Just as we saw in Leaky's simplified PPF, any points outside the PPF are unattainable. In real world, however, the PPF is not stationary. Over time, the capital stocks normally grow, the technology embedded in the capital stock normally improves, the labor force normally grows, and the educational level of the labor forces normally improves. As a result, while point F is not feasible now, it may be in the future as the PPF shifts out over time.

At a societal level, the operation of the labor and capital markets guarantees that in the long run we are always on the PPF and that periods below the PPF are only temporary. Before demonstrating how the markets for labor and capital produce this result, however, we need to first learn how markets work in general.

Demand

A market is place where buyers and sellers of a good or an asset meet. In the olden days it was a physical location. Now days the world is much larger and more complicated. Instead of a place, a market is often a set of institutional arrangements that allow buyers and sellers to interact with one another.

Markets can and do have several different forms. Orthodox economists prefer supply-and-demand markets. While there are markets for other items like labor, capital, financial assets, and loanable funds, for now we will use the market for goods and services to illustrate the basic principles of supply-and-demand markets. But before studying supply-and-demand markets we need to address how decisions are reached in orthodox theory.

Orthodox microeconomics is the study of how individual households, firms, and workers make decisions when their choices are constrained. A question that is often asked is how do these decision makers make their decisions? In orthodox economics, it is assumed that decision-makers make optimal decisions and that they have all the information necessary to make optimal decision — as the following section from Baumol and Blinder's orthodox introductory textbook (2016) illustrates:

Often, when the required information is scarce and the necessary research and calculations are costly and difficult, the decision maker will settle on the first possibility that he can "live with"—a choice that promises to yield results that are not too bad and that seem fairly safe. The decision maker may be willing to choose this course even though he recognizes that there might be other options that are better but are unknown to him. This way of deciding is call "satisficing."

In this book, we will assume that decision makers seek to do better than mere satisficing. Rather, we will assume that they seek to reach decisions that are optimal—decisions that do better in achieving the decision makers' goals than any other possible choice. We will assume that the required information is available to the decision makers, and we will study the procedures that enable them to determine the optimal choices. (p. 42)

In almost all instances, orthodox economists assume that consumers, firms and workers possess perfect knowledge.

We will start with the concept of demand, and we'll use a fictitious product, MacBurgers, to illustrate how demand works. Let's assume that we live in a small town with one MacBurger store. Further, let's assume that it is near lunchtime. What factors will affect the number of Mac-Burgers sold? A typical list generated by students might include the following:

- Quality of MacBurgers
- Price of MacBurgers
- Location of the MacBurger stand
- Price and availability of other lunch options
- Income of households in town
- Consumer preferences
- Number of people in the town

Typically, orthodox economists draw graphs of demand. Graphs are only two-dimensional, so if the quantity demanded is on the *x*-axis, only one factor can be on the *y*-axis. Price is the factor that is almost always chosen by orthodox economists, so we will put the price of a MacBurger on the *y*-axis.

To make the development of the demand curve easier, we assume that there is sufficient supply to meet whatever is demanded. Later, when we develop the idea of supply, we will assume that there is always sufficient demand to purchase all that is supplied. When both curves have been developed, we will then drop these assumptions and allow both surpluses and shortages to exist.

To have the type of demand curve envisioned in orthodox supply-and-demand analysis, one major domain assumption must hold true—the market must contain many small buyers. Each buyer must be so small that the buyer's actions don't affect price. Most markets meet this condition, so it is rarely an issue. The classic example of when it is not met is when producers sell their goods to Walmart. Walmart often purchases such a large percentage of a firm's product that it has the ability to affect—dictate—the price. But for our illustration, we will assume that there are no Walmarts, that all the buyers of our MacBurgers are small and powerless.

Change in the Quantity Demanded

In order to draw a graph of the relationship between the price of a Mac-Burger and the quantity of MacBurgers demanded, we must make the assumption that none of the other variables that effect the number of MacBurgers sold can change. After all, we can't isolate the effect of a price change on the quantity demanded if household income is changing at the same time. That would be like attempting to discover why a car won't start by simultaneously replacing the battery, fuel pump, and spark plugs. If it then starts, that's great, but we won't know why it didn't start

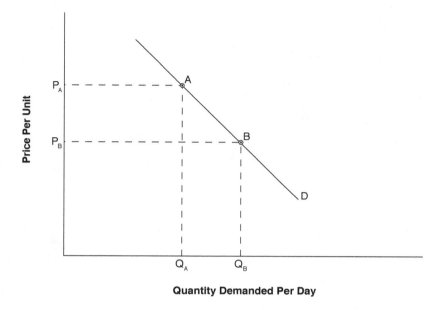

Figure 3. The demand curve.

earlier. If we change one factor at a time, however, we can see the effect of that factor.

Orthodox economists, like the general public, believe there is a strong and unambiguous relationship between the price of a good and the quantity sold. The lower the price, the greater the quantity demanded and vice versa. The demand curve, as figure 3 illustrates, is thus downward sloping.

The quantity of the product sold per day is on the *x*-axis. The unit price of one MacBurger is on the *y*-axis. At point A in figure 3, the price of a MacBurger is P_A, and the amount sold is Q_A. If we lower the price of a MacBurger to price P_B, then the amount sold increases to Q_B, point B. This movement along the demand curve, from point A to point B, is known as *a change in the quantity demanded.*

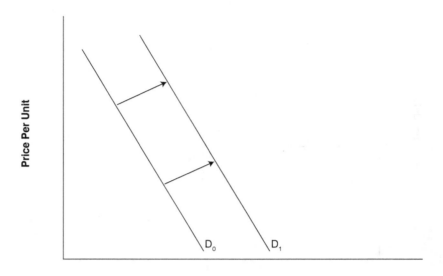

Figure 4. A shift up in the demand curve.

Change in Demand

So far, we have assumed that all the other factors that affect demand don't change. What happens if they do? The demand curve shifts. If the quality of MacBurgers improves, for example, and if all households understand that the quality of MacBurgers has improved, then the amount of Mac-Burgers demanded increases at each and every price level. The result is a shift up in the demand curve, as shown in figure 4.

A shift in the demand curve is known as *a change in demand*. Not only does an increase in the quality of the burger make the demand curve shift up, but so does an increase in the population of the town, a more convenient location, or a change in consumer preference towards eating more burgers. As figure 5 shows, a change in the opposite direction causes the demand curve to shift down.

Our list of possible factors includes the price and availability of other lunch options, which are substitutes in consumption. If Burger Queen

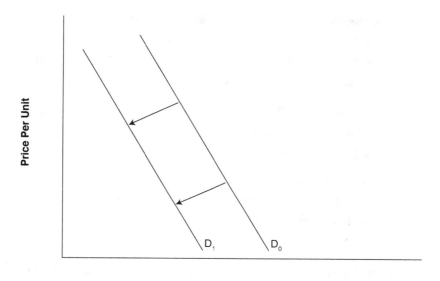

Figure 5. A shift down in the demand curve.

lowers the price of its Whooper, what happens to the demand for Mac-Burgers? For some patrons, there is nothing like the taste of a MacBurger, so they always purchase a MacBurger. For many, though, these products are close substitutes for one another. If the price of a Whooper goes down, they switch from MacBurgers to Whoopers, and the demand for MacBurgers falls like the demand curve in figure 5. There are other lunch options besides burgers, too, including tacos, wraps, and peanut butter sandwiches from home. The closer the substitute is to the original, the more consumers look at these goods as interchangeable, and the price change of a substitute has a bigger impact on demand. The shift in the demand curve is then larger.

What happens if household incomes rise? Will people buy more or fewer MacBurgers? The answer may not seem clear-cut, and that's because it isn't. For some households, as their income increases, they buy more MacBurgers. Others reduce their purchasing of burgers and use the extra income to purchase steaks or halibut at a nicer restaurant.

When looking at a market, what matters is not the action of each and every household but the actions of consumers as a group. In studying the reaction of markets to increases in income, economist have divided goods into two groups, normal and inferior goods:

1. Normal goods: The demand for these goods and services goes up as household incomes increase, and the demand for these goods and services goes down as household incomes decrease.

2. Inferior goods: The demand for these goods and services goes down as household incomes increase, and the demand for these goods and services goes up as household incomes decrease.

As the name indicates, most goods are normal. Many people find it surprising that the demand for inferior goods booms during recessions. It also tends to surprise students that a good could be normal at some income levels and inferior at others. MacBurgers are an excellent example. At low- to medium-income levels, as family incomes increase, they most likely go out to eat more often, but they go to lower-end eateries like our MacBurger store. MacBurgers are thus a normal good. However, when family income reaches a higher level, they still tend to eat out more, but now they go to fancier restaurants. For the individual, the demand for MacBurgers is thus likely to be normal at low- and medium-income levels but inferior at high-income levels.

Supply

To have the type of supply curve envisioned in orthodox supply-and-demand analysis, two major domain assumption must hold true.

First, many small firms must exist, and no firm can be large enough to affect price. For the college textbook market, for example, three large corporations sell over 70% of all college textbooks, so we can't use a supply-and-demand model to analyze price and output in the college textbook market.

The second domain assumption is that goods must be homogenous. A carrot is a carrot is a carrot, in other words, and it's difficult to tell which farm produced it. Carrots are thus homogenous. On the other hand, the Ford F-150 and Chevy Silverado are similar but not homogenous. We can thus use a supply-and-demand model to analyze the price and quantity sold of carrots but not of Ford F-150s and Chevy Silverados.

While most markets have demand curves like those discussed earlier, few markets have a supply curve. In advanced capitalist countries, most markets are dominated by a few large firms, and those that aren't often have products or services that are not homogenous. However, orthodox economists believe that most markets can be modeled as supply-and-demand markets. Because our goal here is to understand the basics of orthodox economic analysis, we will focus our attention on developing the supply curve and on markets where we can use supply-and-demand analysis.

Markets only have a supply curve when a large number of small, powerless firms produce the exact same product. While agricultural goods are often used as examples, there are some difficulties using them for developing supply.[73] Instead, let's start our discussion of supply by using a fictitious good, the widget. We assume that the typical supply curve is upward sloping like figure 6 illustrates. Remember, though, that the supply curve is not the amount of goods produced by a single firm but the sum of all goods produced by *all* firms in the expansive widget industry. That is why all the goods must be homogenous in order to be added together and displayed on the same axis.

Change in the Quantity Supplied

Figure 6 shows us that at $2.00 per unit, firms produce 10,000 widgets per day. At $2.50 per unit, they produce 13,000 widgets per day. The graph shows that these firms are capable of producing 13,000 widgets per day, but they refuse to do so if the price is $2.00 a unit. Why? A good

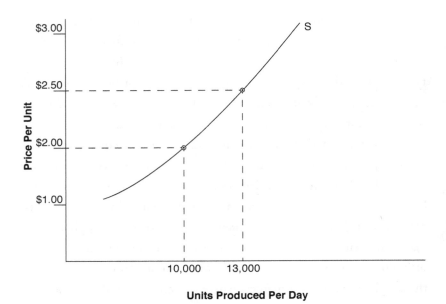

Figure 6. The supply curve.

starting point for answering a question of this type is to ask why firms are in business. They're in business to make a profit. Firms will do something if they expect to make a profit, and they won't do it if they expect to lose money. As we saw earlier, profits are defined as:

Profits = Total Revenue (TR) – Total Cost (TC) (7.1)

However, for firms that produce at a combined rate of 10,000 widgets per day, the question isn't whether these firms make profits by expanding production. The question is whether their profits will increase or decrease. To answer this question, we need to define two new terms — marginal revenue (MR) and marginal cost (MC).

Marginal Revenue is the change in total revenue with a change in output:

MR=ΔTR/ΔQ (7.2)

Marginal Cost is the change in total cost with a change in output:

$$MC = \Delta TC / \Delta Q \quad (7.3)$$

If a firm considers expanding output and MR > MC, then profits will rise, and the firm should expand. If a firm considers expanding output and MR < MC, then profits will fall, and the firm should not expand.

In our example, the price is $2.00 per unit whether firms sell one or one hundred thousand widgets. The MR from selling one more widget is always two dollars. But what is the MC? At the moment, we don't know. What we know is that at production rates of 0 to 10,000 units per day, the marginal cost is less than $2.00 per widget. We know this because firms are only willing to produce more output if MR > MC. Because firms are willing to expand output from 0 to 10,000, the MC must be less than MR, which is at $2.00.

What is the MC for output greater than 10,000 units per day? We don't know exactly, but it must be greater than $2.00 per unit. Because firms are unwilling to expand output beyond 10,000 units, MC > MR = $2.00. If the price increases to $2.50, output increases to 13,000 units per day, so the MC must be between $2.00 and $2.50 when output is between 10,000 and 13,000 widgets per day. The MC must be greater than $2.50 for outputs above 13,000 widgets per day.

Is there a curve in figure 6 that is below $2.00 from zero to 10,000 units a day, between $2.00 and $2.50 when output is between 10,000 and 13,000 units per day, and is greater than $2.50 when output is greater than 13,000 unit per day? Yes — it's the supply curve. The supply curve is the sum of all the firm MC curves for the industry.

Knowing that piece of information allows us to figure out some of the factors that will shift the supply curve. As with the demand curve, a movement along the supply curve is known as *a change in the quantity supplied.*

Change in Supply

A shift in the supply curve is known as *a change in supply*. We know that anything that causes marginal cost to change will also cause the supply curve to shift. The following is a list of factors that will cause the supply curve to shift. The first six factors cause marginal cost to change. The last two factors don't directly affect marginal cost, but they do cause the supply curve to shift for other reasons.

1. Wages
2. Raw material costs
3. Intermediate good costs
4. Transportation costs
5. Debt costs
6. Technology
7. Price of a substitute in production
8. Weather

For the first five factors, if a change in a factor increases costs, then marginal cost rises, making all firms less profitable at each and every output level. As a result, the switch from MR > MC to MR < MC occurs at a lower output level, and firms supply less product to the market, as figure 7 illustrates. A shift down in the supply curve is a shift to the left, or as some like to think, a shift towards the northwest. If a factor changes that lowers costs, the curve shifts to the right or to the southeast.

A shift up or down in the supply curve doesn't look up or down to most people. If these visual cues are confusing, don't attempt to memorize which is which. To get the direction of the shift correct, we pick a price, such as P_A in figure 7, and locate the output level associated with that price on the original supply curve, such as Q_0. Then, if MC increases, then we know that the firm supplies less at that same price,

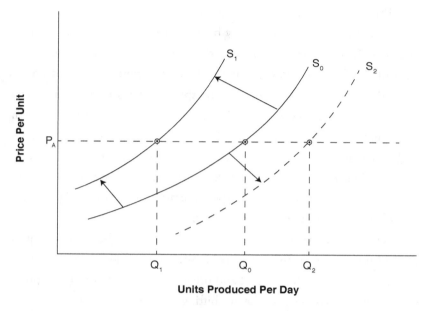

Figure 7. Shifts up and down in the supply curve.

P_A. To get the shift correct, choose a quantity that is less, Q_1, and draw a new supply curve through that point — one that is roughly parallel to the original supply curve.

If marginal costs fall, we do the opposite by finding a point of greater quantity at price P_A, Q_2. If we approach supply curve shifts in this mechanical fashion, we get the direction of the shift correct every time.

The last three factors on our list above need a little extra explanation.

First, we assume that firms never adopt new technology that makes their production process less efficient and thus costlier. Therefore, a change in technology only results in an increase in supply — a shift to the right or southeast.

Second, a change in the weather normally has to do with the output of agriculture goods. Good weather results in more output, and bad weather results in less. However, the terms "good" and "bad" refer to what is good or bad for the crop, not for people. Rainy weather can be good for crops, for example, but most people think of it as bad weather.

Third, while not restricted to agriculture goods, a change in the price of a substitute in production may be easier to explain using agriculture goods as the example. Let's assume that Sean McDonald, former president of the farmer's union Local 17 of EIEIO, grows two crops on his land, rice, and soybeans. Last year, he split his fields fifty-fifty between the two crops. However, events in other parts of the world make Mr. McDonald and the other farmers believe that rice prices will be much higher six months from now, when their rice crops will be ready for harvest, than they were last year. So how will Sean and other farmers divide their fields? Because they expect the price of rice to be higher, they will plant more rice and fewer soybeans.

Let's assume that we are economists working for the Department of Agriculture and that we are interested in the supply of soybeans. As a result of the actions of old McDonald and other farmers in identical situations, the supply of soybeans goes down, shifting the curve to the northwest. As the price of a substitute in production (rice) goes up, then, the supply of the good we are interested in (soybeans) goes down, and vice versa.

Disequilibrium and Equilibrium

Now that we have developed the supply-and-demand curves, let's put them together and perform some basic supply-and-demand analysis. We start by analyzing disequilibrium situations and seeing how market forces automatically push these markets to an equilibrium position.

Shortage

Assume that the diagram in figure 8 represents the supply and demand for bread. If the price is P_0, how much bread will households want to purchase? To find that amount, we draw a line from P_0 to the demand curve. Where it intersects the demand curve, we go down to the x-axis (Q_D), as in figure 9.

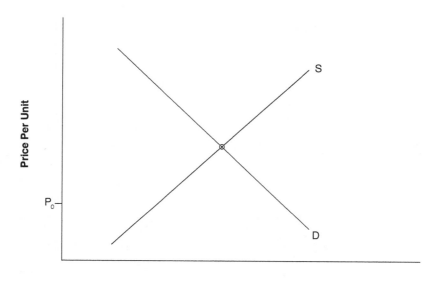

Figure 8. The supply and demand curves for bread.

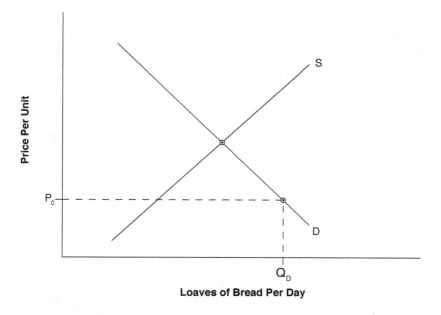

Figure 9. The quantity demanded of bread at the price P_0.

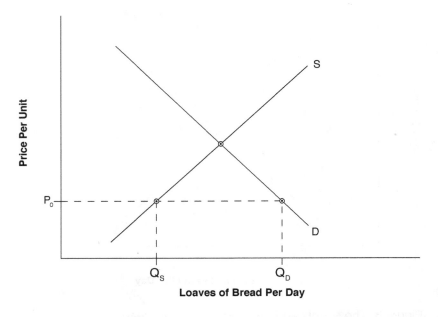

Figure 10. The quantity supplied and demanded of bread at the price P_0.

At price P_0, how much bread will firms supply to the market? To find that value, we draw a line from P_0 over to the supply curve. Where it intersects the supply curve, we go down to the x-axis (Q_S), as in figure 10.

Is P_0 the equilibrium price? No. There is a shortage in the market, and the size of the shortage is the distance between Q_D and Q_S:

$$\text{Shortage} = Q_D - Q_S \text{ (7.4)}$$

In the real world, how would we know that a shortage exists? Let's assume a firm sells bread. Every Sunday morning, the firm stocks a week's worth of bread on the shelves. If by Wednesday all the bread is gone and for the rest of the week customers keep coming into the store asking for bread, then we know a shortage exists. Customers clearly want to purchase more bread than there is bread available.

If faced with a shortage, what do firms do? Firms want to increase their profits. They are currently selling all the bread they have, and there

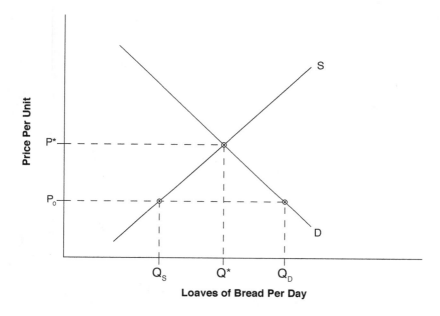

Figure 11. Market forces move the bread market from a shortage to equilibrium.

are customers left over. If they raise the price, some of their customers will seek alternatives. However, as long as there are enough customers to buy all the bread, their profits will rise. Therefore, firms increase their prices. This causes the quantity of bread demanded to fall, a movement along the demand curve from the southeast to the northwest. It also causes the quantity supplied to rise because it is now profitable to produce additional units of bread, a movement along the supply curve from the southwest to the northeast. Both actions cause the shortage to shrink. However, as long as a shortage exists, firms have an incentive to keep raising prices. This process continues until the shortage disappears and the quantity demanded equals the quantity supplied. That price is called the market clearing or equilibrium price (P*), as shown in figure 11.

There are two concepts of equilibrium. One is known as a Walrasian equilibrium. This is where the market clears and there is neither a surplus nor a shortage. The other is known as a Marshallian equilibrium. This

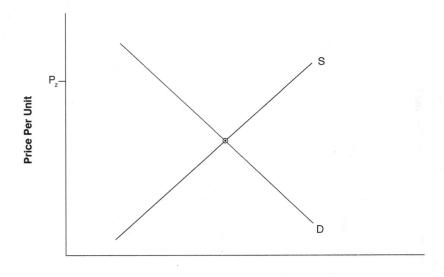

Loaves of Bread Per Day

Figure 12. The supply and demand curves for bread.

is where the market comes to a point of rest and there is no tendency for change. The equilibrium in figure 11 is both a Walrasian and Marshallian equilibrium. This is true for most equilibriums within orthodox economics. However, in Chapter 8, we will soon encounter a situation where we have Marshallian equilibrium but not Walrasian equilibrium. Market forces will drive us to a point of rest where there is no tendency for change, but a surplus of labor still exists.

Surplus

What happens if we start at price P_z in figure 12? How much bread will households purchase? How much bread will firms supply?

To find out, we draw a line from P_z to the demand curve to find Q_D and then to the supply curve to find Q_S.

Figure 13 shows us that there's a surplus. The size of the surplus is the distance between Q_S and Q_D:

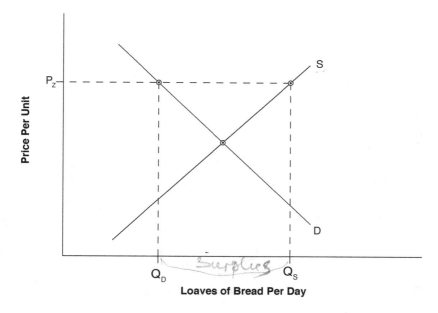

Figure 13. The quantity supplied and demanded of bread at the price P_z.

$$\text{Surplus} = Q_S - Q_D \ (7.5)$$

In the real world, how can we spot a surplus? Using the bread example, if the firm stocks its shelves on Sunday and if on the following Sunday there is still bread on them, the firm has a surplus.

When faced with a surplus, what do firms do and why? If the firm never sells a good, it receives nothing. However, it still costs the firm something to produce the good. Fearing large losses from unsold goods, a firm reduces its price to sell more goods. However, all firms face the same pressures, and a price war may begin, with each firm attempting to under-price the other. As a result of the lower prices, the quantity demanded by consumers increases, and the quantity supplied by firms decreases. This process continues until the surplus goes to zero and the market reaches equilibrium at a price of P^*, as shown in figure 14 on the next page.

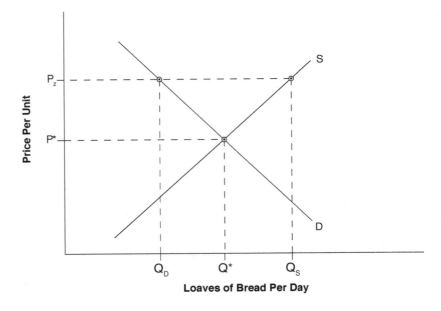

Figure 14. Market forces move the bread market from a surplus to equilibrium.

Shifts in Supply and Demand

One of the questions that supply-and-demand analysis can answer is what effect any particular change will have on the price and quantity sold of some good or service. For example, let's assume we are interested in the corn market and that corn is a normal good. In addition, assume that several large financial firms have collapsed because risky investments in the housing industry went bad, and that has plunged the economy into recession.

What will happen in the corn market? With a recession, household incomes fall. As figure 15 shows, because corn is a normal good, the demand for corn also falls.

At first, the price stays at the original P_O, but as demand declines, a surplus occurs at that price. Soon market forces exert themselves, and the price of corn declines. The decline in corn prices continues until the new

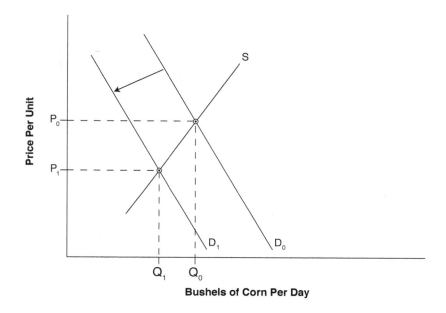

Figure 15. The effect on the price and quantity of corn sold from a decrease in demand.

equilibrium is reached at a price of P_1. At that price, the quantity sold is Q_1. Comparing the beginning equilibrium point with the new one, we see the recession's impact on the corn market is a lower price and a lower quantity sold.

Let's consider another example. Assume that a war breaks out between Saudi Arabia and Iran. Both are large producers of oil, and the war disrupts oil production in both countries. What effect will this have on the corn market? A reduction in oil production results in increased fuel prices. Corn must be trucked to market, and tractors and harvesters also run on either gasoline or diesel. Therefore, a war in the Middle East causes the cost of producing corn to increase. As figure 16 on the next page illustrates, this results in a decrease in supply, a shift in the supply curve to the northwest.

At first, the price stays at the original P_O. As supply declines, a shortage occurs at that price. Soon market forces exert themselves, and

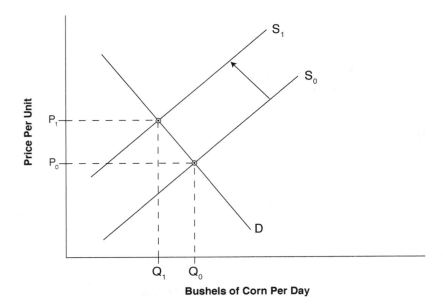

Bushels of Corn Per Day

Figure 16. The effect on the price and quantity of corn sold from a decrease in supply.

the price of corn increases. The increase in corn prices continues until the new equilibrium is reached at a price of P_1 and at a quantity sold of Q_1. Comparing the beginning equilibrium point with the new one, we see that the effect of the war on the corn market is an increase in the price of corn and a decrease in the quantity sold.

Supply and demand curves can each shift in two directions, up and down. As figure 17 shows, this means that there are four possible combinations of changes in price and quantity sold that can occur if a factor of supply or demand changes. We have already addressed two of these, a demand shift down and a supply shift down.

It is common to ask what the effect will be of a given change in the price and quantity sold of some good or service. If we remember which factors shift the curves and in which direction, we can find the answers to those questions.

	Price	Quantity Sold
Demand Shifts Up	Up	Up
Demand Shifts Down	Down	Down
Supply Shifts Up	Down	Up
Supply Shifts Down	Up	Down

Figure 17. The four possible outcomes from a shift in either supply or demand.

Price Floors

To improve and stabilize farm incomes, the government has instituted price floors at various times and for various crops. A price floor is where the government intervenes in the market to ensure that the price doesn't fall below a certain value. How does this work? The following explanation is simpler than the real world because it doesn't contain all the institutional details, but it is close enough to the real world to give us the basic idea.

Let's say that the government sets a price floor of $8.00 per bushel for corn in the spring. When corn is harvested and comes to market, we can encounter two situations—either the price of corn is at or above the price floor or it is below the price floor. If it is at or above the price floor, the government does nothing. The price floor is completely irrelevant, but farmers are happy. However, suppose that the price of corn is below the price floor, say at $6.00 per bushel. What will the government do then? How will their actions affect the welfare of farmers, consumers, and taxpayers?

Looking at figure 18 on the next page, we see that at a price of $8.00 per bushel, consumers purchase eight million bushels of corn per day. However, at $8.00 per bushel, farmers bring eleven million bushels of corn per day to market. At $8.00 per bushel, we will have a surplus of three million bushels per day.

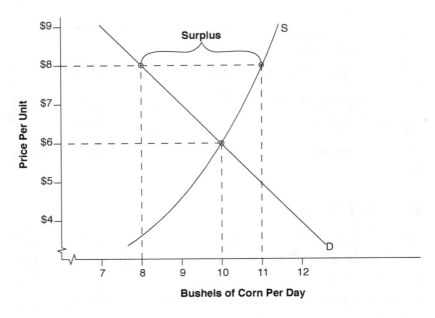

Figure 18. At the price floor of eight dollars a surplus will occur in the corn market.

If the government does nothing, market forces will drive the price of corn down to $6.00 per bushel. In order to keep the price at $8.00 per bushel, the government buys up the surplus. In essence, they must become an added consumer, driving demand up to the point where the market price is $8.00 per bushel, as we see in figure 19.

How does the price floor affect the welfare of farmers, consumers and taxpayers? If the price floor did not exist, farmers would receive $60 million dollars per day—the equilibrium price of $6.00 per bushel times the equilibrium output of ten million bushels per day. With the price floor, they receive $88 million per day—the price floor ($8.00) times the amount farmers produce when they believe the price will be $8.00, which is eleven million bushels per day. The price floor clearly succeeds in making farmers better off.

For the consumer, the price of corn is $6.00 per bushel without the price floor. With the price floor, the price is $8.00 per bushel. Consumers

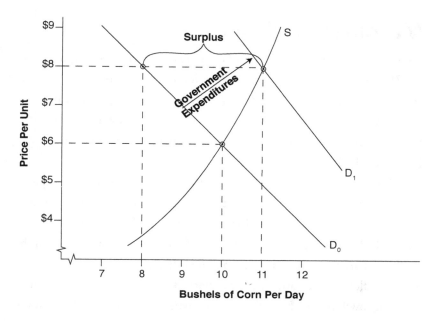

Figure 19. In order to maintain the price floor, the government purchases the surplus.

are clearly worse off—unless they are also corn farmers—because the price of anything that contains corn is now higher.

In order to maintain the price floor of $8.00 per bushel, the government buys up the surplus. In this example, the government spends $24 million per day to buy three million bushels at $8.00 per bushel. Taxpayers are worse off, too, because they pay higher taxes to support the program. The price floor thus results in a transfer of income from consumers and taxpayers, who are often one and the same, to corn farmers. However, as a society we may believe that supporting corn farmers is a good idea, and that the cost of doing so is worth it.

Marginal Analysis

One of the most important tools of orthodox economics is marginal analysis.[74] It occurs in many places and at all levels of economics. Memorizing each situation can be overwhelming. However, defining, calculating, and using marginals follows a consistent pattern, so if we understand the basic pattern, then performing marginal analysis becomes easier. We can break marginal analysis down into four steps.

The first step is defining the marginal. Each marginal has two parts, a change in one item divided by the change in another ($\Delta X / \Delta Y$). The Greek letter delta (Δ) stands for "a change in." Thus, "ΔX" means "a change in X." The top part of the fraction (ΔX) is always the change in the total of whatever name is on the marginal. If we use a term called "marginal cowflop," for example, the top part of that marginal is the change in "total cowflop." We have already met marginal revenue (MR), and the top part is the change in total revenue.

The bottom part of the fraction (ΔY) is a little trickier, but normally you can figure it out by the surrounding discussion. In our earlier discussion of marginal revenue, we considered how much extra revenue a firm receives from producing and selling one more unit of output. The bottom part of MR is the change in the quantity produced and sold by the firm. This is otherwise known as a change in output (ΔQ). The definitions of these marginals are themselves mathematical formulas.

The second step is to take the definition — that is, the formula — and calculate the marginal. Let's say, for example, that we want to calculate a marginal cost schedule from the total cost schedule in figure 20. In the following total cost schedule, we assume that even if the firm doesn't produce any output, it still has to buy \$20 worth of capital.

The formula for marginal cost is the change in total cost divided by the change in output:

$$MC = \Delta TC / \Delta Q \ (7.6)$$

Quantity (Q)	Total Cost (TC)
0	$20
1	$24
2	$30
3	$39
4	$51
5	$67

Figure 20. The total cost schedule.

Quantity (Q)	Total Cost (TC)	Marginal Cost (MC)
0	$20	0
1	$24	$4
2	$30	$6
3	$39	$9
4	$51	$12
5	$67	$16

Figure 21. Calculating the marginal cost schedule from the total cost schedule.

To calculate the marginal cost of producing the first unit of output, we first consider by how much costs change:

$$\Delta TC = \$24 - \$20 = \$4.00 \ (7.7)$$

Then we compute how much output changes:

$$\Delta Q = 1 - 0 = 1 \ (7.8)$$

As figure 21 shows us, the marginal cost of producing the first unit is

$$MC = \$4.00 \ / \ 1 = \$4.00 \ (7.9)$$

Then we perform the same three calculations for the second unit:

$$\Delta TC = \$30 - \$24 = \$6.00 \ (7.10)$$
$$\Delta Q = 2 - 1 = 1 \ (7.11)$$
$$MC = \$6.00 \ / \ 1 = \$6.00 \ (7.12)$$

We can do the same for the third unit:

$$\Delta TC = \$39 - \$30 = \$9.00 \ (7.13)$$
$$\Delta Q = 3 - 2 = 1 \ (7.14)$$
$$MC = \$9.00 \ / \ 1 = \$9.00 \ (7.15)$$

We can keep going with this same pattern for as many units as we wish.

The third step is to know the decision rule that is associated with the marginal we plan to use. Each marginal has an associated decision rule that is used to answer a particular question. When we used marginal cost earlier, for example, the question was how much output the firm should produce. The decision rule for that question is that the firm should continue to increase production as long as $MR \geq MC$.

We skipped the situation of $MR = MC$, by the way. In that case, an increase in production neither increases nor decreases the firm's profit. The firm is indifferent as to whether to produce that last unit of output or not. Normally decision rules are set up assuming that firms will produce that last unit. That is why the decision rules are generally set up as $MR \geq MC$ rather than as $MR > MC$. Logically, however, they can be set up either way.

The fourth step is to take the decision rule and apply it to the marginals that we calculated in the second step to produce the needed answer. For example, let's say we want to ask about the profit maximizing level of output for a firm whose marginal costs we calculated in the second step. Our decision rule is that the firm should expand output as long as $MR \geq MC$. If the $MR = \$15.00$ for all units of output sold, then the firm should produce four units of output, as shown in figure 22. For the first four units of output, $MR > MC$, but for the fifth unit, $MR < MC$.

Once we have these four steps down, using marginal analysis becomes manageable. Figure 23 presents some typical marginals that a student might encounter in an introductory class and breaks the analysis into the

Q	TC	MC	MR	Decision Rule
0	$20			
1	$24	$4	$15	MR > MC
2	$30	$6	$15	MR > MC
3	$39	$9	$15	MR > MC
4	$51	$12	$15	MR > MC
5	$67	$16	$15	MR < MC

Figure 22. Apply the decision rule to obtain the profit maximizing level of output.

Marginal	Top Part	Bottom Part	Decision Rule	Question to Answer
Marginal Revenue (MR)	Δ Total Revenue (ΔTR)	Δ in Output (ΔQ)	MR ≥ MC	How much output should the firm produce?
Marginal Cost (MC)	Δ Total Cost (ΔTC)	Δ in Output (ΔQ)	MR ≥ MC	How much output should the firm produce?
Marginal Utility (MU)	Δ Total Utility (ΔTU)	Δ in Total Goods Pur-chased (ΔQ)	MU ≥ P	How much of Good X should the family purchase?
Marginal Disutility (MDU)	Δ Total Disutility (ΔTDU)	Δ in Hours Worked (ΔHW)	W ≥ MDU	How many hours should a laborer work?
Marginal Product of Labor (MP$_L$)	Δ Total Product of Labor (TPL)	Δ in Hours Worked (ΔHW)	We need another piece of info. That information will be intro-duced in the next chapter.	

Figure 23. Marginals like these often appear in introductory classes.

four steps.

These last two marginals, along with a third one built from the MP$_L$, will be used in the next chapter.

References

Baumol, William, and Alan Blinder. 2016. *Economics: Principles and Policy*, 13th Edition. Mason, OH: South-Western, Cengage Learning.

Veblen, Thorstein. 1899. *The Theory of the Leisure Class: An Economic Study of Institutions*. New York: B.W. Huebsch.

❖ 8

The Orthodox Model of Labor Markets

In the orthodox perspective, wages and employment are determined by the forces of supply and demand. The two most important results of this model for the study of poverty are the following:

1. Everyone who wants a job at the going wage can get a job.
2. Workers are paid the value of what they produce, there is no exploitation.[75]

In the last chapter, we studied the supply-and-demand curves of the product market. The underlying theories upon which the labor supply and labor demand curves rest are quite different from those of the product market. The next order of business is to understand these theories before using orthodox labor supply and demand model to analyze poverty. Both the decisions by firms as to how much labor to hire and the decisions by households as to how much labor to supply are based on marginal analysis. As we tell the stories that lie behind labor demand and supply, we will incorporate our four-step approach to doing marginal analysis.

The Demand for Labor

The demand for labor and capital are derived demands. Employers don't purchase conveyor belts to decorate their front lawns. They purchase capital and labor because they believe those two factors can be used, along with raw materials and intermediate goods, to produce goods and services that they can sell to the public. It's the employer's expectation that they can use laborers to produce profits that underlies labor demand.

For the moment, let's assume that there are no other costs but labor costs. This is unrealistic, but it helps to set up the main argument in this section. The revenue generated by workers equals the number of goods or services they produce (Q) times the selling price (P). The revenue going to the employer from hiring a worker is Q × P. If it costs less to hire the worker than Q × P, the firm makes a profit. To keep it simple, we assume the only cost to hire a worker is the wage rate (W). Thus, the firm hires the worker if (Q × P) ≥ W, and it does not hire the worker if (Q × P) < W.

However, what if a firm wants to hire more than one worker? Will the amount of output produced by the second worker be the same as the first? According to the orthodox model, the answer is no. At first, as a firm hires more workers, it experiences efficiency gains as the additional output from adding an additional worker goes up. Eventually, as the firm hires more and more workers, the firm experiences diminishing returns. The additional output from adding additional workers goes down.

Because workers do not each produce the same amount of output, the Q in our equation Q × P must be replaced with a schedule of Qs — a Q for the first worker, a separate Q for the second worker, and so on. That schedule is known as the marginal product of labor schedule (MP_L), and it must be calculated from the total product of labor schedule. In figure 1, schedule A is the total product of labor for Saint Chuck's Football Factory. It shows the number of footballs produced per day by different quantities of labor. The marginal product of labor is defined by this formula (step 1):

$$MP_L = \Delta TP_L / \Delta L \quad (8.1)$$

Schedule A	
Workers (L)	**Total Product of Labor (=TP$_L$)**
0	0
1	8
2	18
3	26
4	32
5	36
6	39

Schedule B	
Workers (L)	**Marginal Product of Labor (MP$_L$)**
0	0
1	8
2	10
3	8
4	6
5	4
6	3

Figure 1. The total and marginal product of labor schedules.

The MP$_L$ for Saint Chuck's Football Factory is schedule B, and it shows the additional output the firm receives from adding an additional worker. Let's calculate the first few numbers of the MP$_L$ (step 2). Looking at schedule A, the total product of labor schedule when there are zero workers is zero output, no footballs. When Chuck hires one worker, output increases to eight footballs per day.

The MP$_L$ for the first worker is eight units of output, the change in the total product equals eight, and the change in the number of laborers equals one. In this example, the change in the number of laborers is always one. When the Chuck hires the second worker, output increases to eighteen footballs. The second worker has added ten units of output to production (18 − 8), and the MP$_L$ of the second worker is therefore ten. For the third worker, the total number of footballs produced increases to twenty-six, and the MP$_L$ is eight (26 − 18) / (3 − 2). Schedule B (MP$_L$) has the expected shape. When Saint Chuck hires the first few workers, production becomes more efficient. MP$_L$ increases. After that period, however, Chuck faces diminishing returns — MP$_L$ falls.

What is important to the firm, however, is how much additional revenue it receives. As the firm adds workers, it increases the total amount of output

Schedule B					Schedule C
L	**MP$_L$**				**Value of Marginal Product of Labor (VMP$_L$)**
0	0	×	× $15	=	$0
1	8	×	× $15	=	$120
2	10	×	× $15	=	$150
3	8	×	× $15	=	$120
4	6	×	× $15	=	$90
5	4	×	× $15	=	$60
6	3	×	× $15	=	$45

Figure 2. The marginal product of labor and the value of the marginal product of labor schedules.

it produces. To sell the increased output, is the firm forced to lower its price? The answer depends on what percentage of the market's total output this firm produces. If the increase in output doesn't seriously increase the total output in this market, then the firm's expansion has little or no effect on price. On the other hand, if the firm's output makes up a large share of market, then any attempt to expand output causes the firm to reduce its price.

While the answer to this question is important for some types of labor market analysis, it isn't for our examination of poverty. Capitalist economies tend to be dominated by giant corporations, but the math is simpler if we assume the firm is small and that there are a large number of small firms in the industry. This is exactly what we assume, so when the firm expands its output, the price of the product stays constant.

To find out how much revenue each new worker brings to the firm, we multiply the MP$_L$ schedule times the price of the product (P). The resulting schedule is called the value of the marginal product of labor (VMP$_L$) (step 1):

$$VMP_L = MP_L \times P \ (8.2)$$

Assuming the price of a football produced by Saint Chuck's Football Factory is $15.00, we can calculate Saint Chuck's VMP$_L$ schedule in

Schedule C

L	VMP$_L$	Wage	Decision Rule
0	$0		
1	$120	$100	VMP$_L$ > Wage
2	$150	$100	VMP$_L$ > Wage
3	$120	$100	VMP$_L$ > Wage
4	$90	$100	VMP$_L$ < Wage
5	$60	$100	VMP$_L$ < Wage
6	$45	$100	VMP$_L$ < Wage

Figure 3. Using the decision rule to determine how many laborers the firm should hire.

schedule C of figure 2 (step 2). Because there are two parts, output and price, that determine how much revenue the worker brings into the firm, we in essence have two step ones and two step twos in our process for doing the marginal analysis.

The basic rule, then, is that firms hire new workers if the new workers produce more revenue than it costs to hire them. Therefore, the decision rule is that the firm should continue to hire laborers as long as VMP$_L$ ≥ W (step 3). If the wage is $100 per day, how many workers should Saint Chuck hire? Appling the decision rule (step 4), he should hire the first worker because the first worker brings $120 per day into the firm, and it only costs the firm $100 to hire that person. He should hire the second and third workers, too. However, Chuck should not hire the fourth worker. The fourth worker only brings in $90 per day, and it costs Chuck $100 per day to hire the worker, so the firm loses $10 per day. Figure 3 illustrates how the decision rule is to continue hiring laborers as long as the VMP$_L$ ≥ W.

The downward sloping part of the VMP$_L$ schedule is the firm's labor demand curve. Adding all the firm labor demand curves to together, we get the market labor demand curve. Given the wage, the labor demand

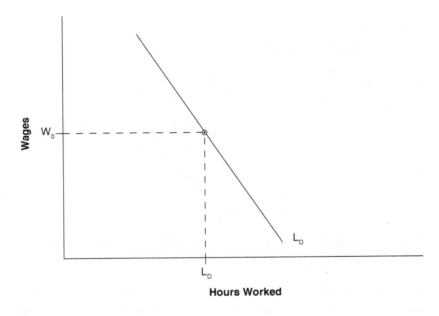

Figure 4. The labor demand curve.

curve tells us how many laborers firms wish to employ. Labor market diagrams can be set up with either number of laborers or number of hours worked on the *x*-axis.

I find it easier to develop the labor demand curve using the number of laborers. On the other hand, others find it easier to develop the labor supply curve using the number of hours worked. Students also find it easier to understand labor demand and labor supply if I do it that way. However, to be consistent with the labor supply and in order to account for people who work part-time, the *x*-axis in figure 4 is the hours worked per week. In a labor demand diagram, the *y*-axis is measured in dollars and is traditionally labeled as the wage rate (W). However, because the *y*-axis is in dollars, we can also read VMP_L from it. After all, we graphed the VMP_L curve by plotting the dollar value of VMP_L associated with each laborer. In figure 4, when the wage rate is W_0, employers offer to hire L_D hours of work.

Let's now drop the assumption that all costs other than labor costs

Hours Worked	Schedule D Total Disutility (TDU$_L$)	Schedule E Marginal Disutility (MDU$_L$)	
0	$0		$0
1	$5	5-0 =	$5
2	$11	11-5	$6
3	$18.50	18.5-4	$7.50
4	$28	28-18.5	$9.50
5	$40	40-28	$12
6	$55	55-40	$15
7	$74	74-55	$19
8	$98	98-74	$24
9	$128	128-98 =	$30

Figure 5. The total and marginal disutility schedules.

are zero. What changes? Our decision rule ($VMP_L \geq W$) continues to give us the profit-maximizing or loss-minimizing level of labor to hire. Unfortunately, if we only have information on the VMP_L and W, we can't tell whether the firm actually makes profits or takes losses. However, if the firm is not making a profit, it will minimize its losses by following the decision rule, $VMP_L \geq W$. For this firm, there is no level of employment that makes the firm a profit. If this lack of profits continues, then the firm eventually drops out of the market and is not part of the market labor demand curve.

The Supply of Labor

In the orthodox model, workers not only choose whether or not to work but also how many hours they work. This model assumes that work is painful and people are willing to pay money to avoid this displeasure. This assumption is the result of two other assumed factors: First, work itself is unpleasant. Second, if not working, workers will do something enjoyable.

The model further assumes that as workers work more, the displeasure caused by working increases. Orthodox economists refer to displeasure caused by work as disutility. In figure 5 on the previous page, schedule D is the total disutility schedule (TDU_L) for Downhill Doug, who, as the name suggests, would rather be skiing. However, in order to determine how many hours old Downhill will work we need to know his marginal disutility schedule, marginal disutility is defined as this formula (step 1):

$$MDU_L = \Delta TDU_L \ / \ \Delta HW \ (8.3)$$

Schedule E is Downhill's marginal disutility schedule (step 2). Notice that the MDU_L schedule has the expected shape of ever-increasing marginal disabilities. This means that when graphed, the curve is positively sloped.

To determine how many hours Downhill Doug chooses to work, we need the decision rule (step 3), which is workers offer their services as long as the wage rate is greater than or equal to the displeasure caused by work ($W \geq MDU_{L)}$.

Applying the decision rule (step 4), if the wage rate is $10 per hour, the displeasure from working the first hour is $5.[76] Because the wage Downhill receives is greater than the displeasure of work, he works the first hour. Downhill feels $6 of displeasure if he works a second hour, but because the wage rate is still greater, he works the second hour. He also works the third and the fourth hours. However, Downhill doesn't work the fifth hour because he suffers $12 of displeasure and receives only $10. Therefore, if the wage rate is $10, Doug will choose to work four hours. If the wage rate is $20 dollars, he will work seven hours.

The marginal disutility schedule is thus the individual labor supply

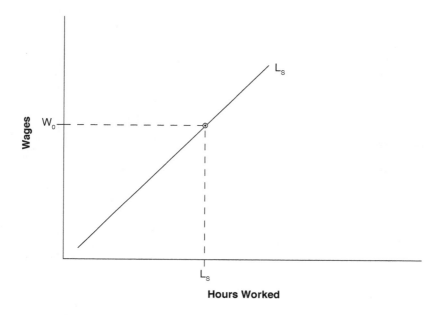

Figure 6. The labor supply curve.

curve. To obtain the market labor supply curve, we add up all the individual labor supply curves. In figure 6, the x-axis is the total number of hours laborers want to work, and the y-axis is the wage rate and marginal disutility of labor. When the wage rate is W_0, workers offer L_S hours of work to employers.

Disequilibrium in the Labor Market

If employment and wages are determined by supply and demand, then labor markets must naturally gravitate towards equilibrium. In this section, we investigate the mechanisms by which the labor markets return to equilibrium when there is a shortage or a surplus of labor.

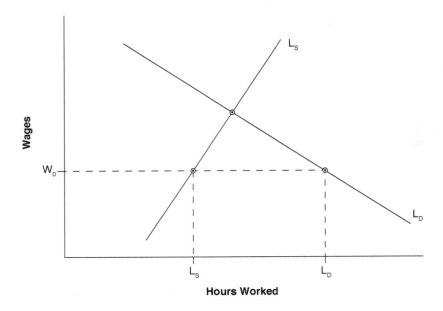

Figure 7. A shortage of labor.

Shortage of Labor

Figure 7 illustrates a labor shortage. At the current wage of W_0, the demand for labor (L_D) is much greater than the supply of labor (L_S). The size of the shortage will equal to $L_D - L_S$.

When a shortage occurs, some firms are unable to hire as much labor as they wish because not enough laborers are offering their services. These firms are missing out on the profit they could make if there were available laborers. The solution to this problem is for firms to bid workers away from other firms by offering a higher wage. This causes the wage rate to rise. As wages go up, the number of hours laborers are willing to work goes up, and the quantity of labor supplied increases.[77] At the same time, some firms can no longer use this labor profitably, so the quantity of labor demanded thus goes down. As we can see in figure 8, the size of the shortage goes down as the wage rate goes up to W_1.

As long as there is a shortage, however, at least some firms have an incen-

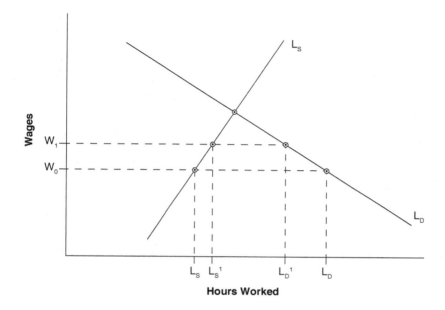

Figure 8. As wages rise, the shortage of labor becomes smaller.

tive to bid up wages, so wages continue to increase until they reach W*, where there is no longer a shortage, as shown in figure 9 on the next page.

At the equilibrium wage W*, all laborers who want to work at that wage have a job and are working exactly the number of hours they wish to work. All firms that wish to hire laborers at that wage can hire workers and for exactly the number of hours they wish to hire them. This is often referred to as full employment.

You should note that, as wages go up, those firms that can no longer use the laborers profitably drop out of the bidding. Only those who can still profitably use them remain. Therefore, by using the market, laborers go to those firms that can most profitably use them. If we define the most efficient use of resources as equal to the most profitable use of resources, as orthodox economists implicitly do, then by using the market labor, capital and other resources naturally flow to their most efficient uses, to their highest valued users. In this model, the market not only produces full employment of resources but also the most efficient use of resources.

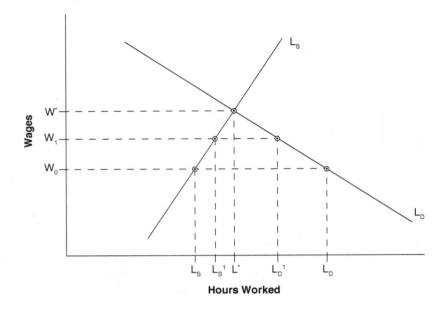

Figure 9. Market forces move the labor market from shortage to equilibrium.

Surplus of Labor

Figure 10 illustrates a labor surplus, which is commonly known as unemployment. At the current wage of W_z, the supply of labor (L_S) is greater than the demand for labor (L_D). The size of the surplus is equal to $L_S - L_D$.

When a surplus occurs, there are more people looking for work than there are jobs. People who depend on having a job in order to earn a living are without work. Orthodox economists cite two mechanisms by which labor markets return to equilibrium. The first mechanism is initiated by firms attempting to lower their costs of production. The second is initiated by unemployed workers who are desperate for a job.

With the first mechanism, a firm sees that more people are applying for jobs than there are job openings and realizes that it can lower its cost of production by lowering the wage rate. Doing so causes some workers to quit, but if the firm replaces them with unemployed workers, it lowers its

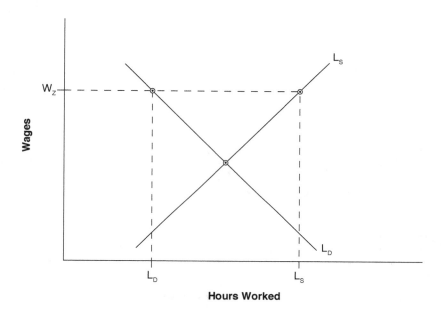

Figure 10. A surplus of labor.

cost of production by lowering wages. As wages go down, firms hire more workers, and workers supply fewer hours. The quantity of labor demand increases, while the quantity of labor supply decreases. Both cause the surplus of labor to shrink. However, as long as a surplus exists, firms have an incentive to continue to lower their wages. Wages continue to decline until the equilibrium wage is reached, W* in figure 11 on the next page.

In the second mechanism, unemployed workers wish to work for the wage of W_Z. However, if they never get a job, their income is zero. It is far better to have a job and be paid a lower wage than to have no job at all. Therefore, the unemployed workers, desperate for jobs, offer to work for firms at a wage that is below what firms are currently paying their employees. This is known as underbidding. A firm may accept such an offer and replace one of its current workers with the underbidding, unemployed worker. The firm may also give its current employees an opportunity to match the underbidder's offer. Either way, wages fall. As long as unemployment exists, the unemployed have an incentive to

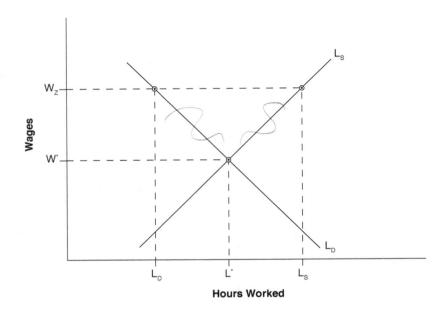

Figure 11. Market forces move the labor market from surplus to equilibrium.

underbid the employed. Once again, as we see in figure 11, this continues until we return to equilibrium.

The Invisible Hand

In the orthodox model, regardless of the current situation, labor markets always return to equilibrium in the long run.[78] At equilibrium, all workers who want a job at the going wage have a job. Furthermore, workers choose the amount hours they work. The market forces that drive the economy back to equilibrium or full employment are more important to orthodox theory than we might first suppose.

The answer to the question of how the market guarantees that over the long run we are always on the PPF is that the market forces we've just described always drive the economy back to full employment, back to the full and efficient utilization of resources, as shown in figure 12. Therefore,

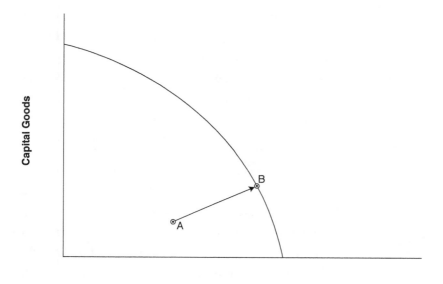

Figure 12. Market forces drive the economy back to the PPF, a point of scarcity.

orthodox economists theorize that without the aid of government, the economy naturally produces the best of all possible results on its own, as if guided by an invisible hand. Whether or not these market forces actually operate is thus critical for the entire foundation of orthodox theory.

For the general public, one of the most well-known ideas in economics is Adam Smith's (1776) invisible hand:

> As every individual…endeavors as much as he can both to employ his capital in the support of domestic industry, and so to direct that industry that its produce may be of the greatest value; every individual necessarily labors to render the annual revenue of the society as great as he can. He generally, indeed, neither intends to promote the public interest, nor knows how much he is promoting it. By preferring the support of domestic to that of foreign industry, he intends only his own security; and by

directing that industry in such a manner as its produce may be of the greatest value, he intends only his own gain, and he is in this, as in many other cases, led by an invisible hand to promote an end which was no part of his intention.... By pursuing his own interest he frequently promotes that of the society more effectually than when he really intends to promote it. (p. 423)

The idea is that everyone following their own self-interest automatically generates the best outcome for society. A natural corollary to the invisible hand is that the best policy for a nation to follow is one of laissez-faire ("allow to do"). This concept suggests that no matter how well-intentioned, government interference into economic affairs only causes the economy to perform worse. If the invisible hand produces the best of all possible results, then doing something different must produce inferior results. It is thus best for all if we minimize government involvement into the economy and allow people pursuing self-interest to reign supreme.

In this chapter, we have seen how the orthodox model of labor markets produces this result. Without any help from the government, the economy naturally gravitates to an equilibrium position where everyone who wants a job at the going wage has a job and where all laborers are most efficiently used.

While Smith's idea of the invisible hand is more in keeping with conservative orthodox economists, we find the invisible hand presented favorably in orthodox textbooks regardless of the author's perspective. However, the idea that the economy naturally gravitates to best and most fair results did not originate with Smith. In fact, it was expressed by a number of authors as far back as a hundred years before Smith (Routh 1989).

However, we should be suspicious of the motives of these early economists and the idea that if left alone, the economy will naturally generate the best of all possible outcomes. Very few people in the 1600s and 1700s could read and write. These authors came from the upper crust of society. Did they have the best interest of farmers and workers in mind when they wrote?

Let's look at their view of rent paid by farmers to landlords. William

Petty, who among other things was large landowner, "regarded rent as the surplus over what was necessary to maintain the cultivator." Richard Cantillon agreed that the "overplus of the Land is at the disposition of the Owner" (qtd. in Routh p. 91). While Smith had a low opinion of landlords, here is what he considered "the natural rent" of land to be:

> Rent . . . is naturally the highest which the tenant can afford to pay in the actual circumstances of the land. . . . The landlord endeavors to leave him no greater share of the produce than what is sufficient to keep up the stock from which he furnishes the seed, pays the labor, and purchases and maintains the cattle and other instruments of husbandry, together with the ordinary profits of farming stock in the neighborhood. This is evidently the smallest share with which the tenant can content himself without being a loser, and landlord seldom means to leave him anymore. (p. 144)

The farmer does all the work, and the landlord does nothing except allow the farmer to work the land. What is so natural and fair about a landlord who takes every bit of produce above that which is necessary to keep the farmer and his family alive?

While early economic theories stated that the economy naturally produce harmonious results under certain conditions, some of the early economists also saw situations in which the natural operation of the economy did not produces harmonious results. We see this from Smith himself:

> The price of monopoly is upon every occasion the highest which can be got. The natural price, or the price of free competition, on the contrary, is the lowest which can be taken. . . . The one is upon every occasion the highest which can be squeezed out of the buyers. . . . The other is the lowest which the sellers can commonly afford to take, and at the same time continue their business. (p. 61)

Smith's theory of the invisible hand comes from the assumption that the world is made up of numerous powerless small firms engaged in what he calls "free competition" and what we now call "perfect competition." In that situation, the price is as low as possible and thus good for the consumer. But if a firm has the market power of a monopoly, then the price will be as high as possible and thus bad for the consumer. The existence of power is the death knell of the invisible hand and laissez-faire policy. When it comes to renting, landlords have the majority of the power, and farmers have little. The farmer needs to farm the land to survive. Thus, the landlord can charge as high a rent as possible, everything above what is necessary for the farmer to survive. When there are more people who wish to farm the land than there is land to farm, landlords are in a position of power, and they can charge as much as possible.

Today, a few very large corporations dominate most areas of economic activity. They have power in the marketplace. Moreover, their ability to make large political contributions gives them a certain amount of power over governmental affairs when it comes to the writing and enforcement of laws or the appointment of industry-friendly heads of federal and state agencies. We should be suspicious of those who advocate for a laissez-faire policy and the invisible hand in the modern world. Economists who build models that assume firms are small and powerless—while the real world is dominated by large corporations—appear to be working for the interests of large corporations.

In the modern world, the only entity powerful enough to prevent large corporations from taking advantage of average citizens is the government. Therefore, a theory that suggests we should have as little government intervention as possible also suggests that we remove the only force that is capable of protecting the average citizens from the actions of large corporations. As students of economics, one of the most important aspects of the real world—one of the main features we should look for in choosing which model to use—is whether people interact as equals or whether one player is in a more powerful position than the others.

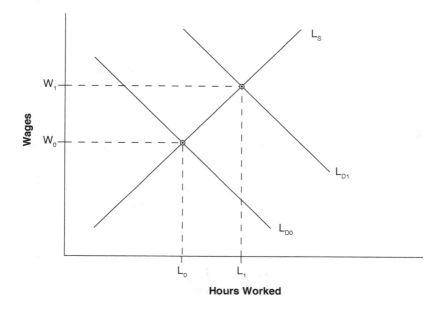

Figure 13. A shift up in the labor demand curve.

Shifts in Labor Supply and Demand

One of the questions that supply and demand labor market analysis can answer is what effect any particular change will have on wages and employment. Let's say, for example, that computer applications now make every worker in the sawmill industry more productive. According to the orthodox model, what happens to the wages and employment of sawmill workers? If workers become more productive, their MP_L increases, and so does their VMP_L. The demand for labor thus shifts up, as shown in figure 13.

At first, the wage stays at the original W_O, but as demand increases, a shortage occurs. Market forces exert themselves, and the wage of sawmill workers increases. The increase in wages continues until the new equilibrium is reached at a wage of W_1 and an employment level of L_1. Comparing the beginning equilibrium point with the new one, we see that an increase in technology causes both wages and employment to increase.

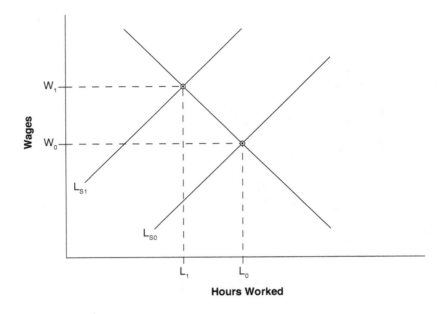

Figure 14. A shift down in the labor supply curve.

Let's see another example. Assume that the US is hit by the bubonic plague and that its effects are similar to what happened in Europe in 1348–49 when a quarter to a third of the population died. Due to advancements in medicine, the bubonic plague would have relatively little effect now, but for the sake of this example, play along and assume that a quarter of the population dies. According to the orthodox supply and demand model for labor, what effect does this have on wages and employment?

With fewer laborers, the supply of labor decreases, as shown in figure 14. At first, the wage stays at the original W_0, but as supply declines, a shortage occurs. Soon market forces exert themselves, and wages increase. The increase in wages continues until the new equilibrium is reached at a wage of W_1 and an employment level of L_1. Comparing the beginning equilibrium point with the new one, we see that the effect of the bubonic plague is to increase wages and decrease employment.

Minimum Wage

What is the effect of the minimum wage in the orthodox model? Using labor supply and demand curves, we see that the minimum wage distorts the market. However, to analyze the effect of the minimum wage we must look at two situations: first, where all employment is covered by the minimum wage, and second, where some jobs are covered, and some jobs are not. We'll see when we examine the second situation, there is a division amongst orthodox economists as to what exactly happens.

In the US, the minimum wage has been in existence since 1938. However, to make our job of analyzing the effects of the minimum wage on employment easier, we assume at the beginning that there is no minimum wage. We then compare that situation to one where there is a minimum wage.

Employment Effects of the Minimum Wage

In our first situation, let's assume we are observing a local labor market where the low wage jobs are covered by the minimum wages. If there is no minimum wage, then labor markets clear with a wage of W^* and a level of employment of L^*, as shown above in figure 15. The minimum wage is a wage below which employers are not allowed to pay. It's a price floor for wages. We assume that for certain types of labor when a minimum wage law is enacted that the minimum wage is higher than the equilibrium wage ($W_{MIN} > W^*$). As a result, the minimum wage causes unemployment, as the demand for labor is less than the supply of labor. As figure 15 shows, the amount of unemployment, which is the size of the surplus, is $L_S - L_D$.

In our second situation, the minimum wage does not cover all employees. Low-skilled employment exists in two sectors: the covered sector where employers must pay at least the minimum wage, and the uncovered sector, where employers are not required to pay the minimum

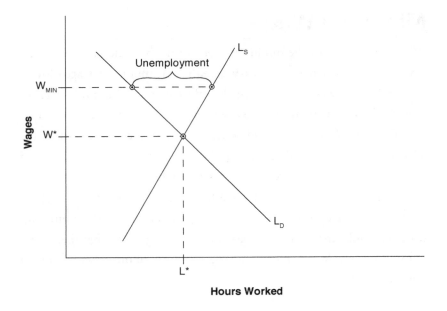

Figure 15. The employment effects of the minimum wage when there is only a covered sector.

wage. Before there was a minimum wage, wages in the uncovered sector would have been the same as wages in the covered sector (W*). Once the minimum wage is instituted, those working in the covered sector have a higher wage, but some workers are now unemployed. What happens to those unemployed workers? Do they take jobs in the uncovered sector, or do they stay unemployed and look for work in the covered sector? Orthodox economists don't agree on the answer to this question.

Full-Employment and Natural-Rate Economists

Full-employment orthodox economists assume that all the unemployed move to the uncovered sector, shifting the labor supply curve out or to the southeast in the uncovered sector. This depresses wages below W*, as shown in figure 16. As the unemployed leave the covered sector, this shifts the

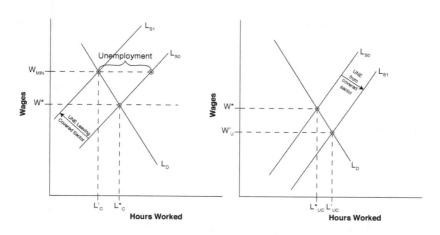

Figure 16a (left). Employment effects of a minimum wage on the covered sector.

Figure 16b (right). Employment effects of a minimum wage on the uncovered sector.

labor supply curve in the covered sector down or to the northwest, reestablishing full employment in both sectors, as shown in figure 16a.

Natural-rate orthodox economists believe that because the turnover rate in minimum wage jobs is high, some unemployed people will not look for work in the uncovered sector. Instead, they will stay unemployed and continue to seek employment in the higher-paying covered sector. The result of the minimum wage is thus to cause a certain level of unemployment. It also causes a depression of wages in the uncovered sector, but this depression is not as large as predicted by the full-employment economists because the shift in the labor supply curve is not as great. However, a worker can always take a job in the uncovered sector and continue to look for work in the covered sector, though perhaps not looking with the same intensity.

The difference between these two sets of orthodox economists is whether they believe people take jobs in the uncovered sector and continue to look for work in the covered sector or whether they believe that at least some people forgo employment in the uncovered sector and search full-time for a job in the covered sector. For these latter economists, the minimum wage causes unemployment, and for the former, it does not.

For both groups, when a recession strikes, unemployment increases, and market forces swing into action, driving wages down and the economy towards full employment. For the first group, the economy returns to full employment. For the second group, the decline in unemployment stops short of full employment. The point where the decline in unemployment stops is referred to as the "natural rate of unemployment," or the "natural rate" for short. The natural rate is a Marshallian equilibrium, a point of rest with no tendency for change, but it is not a Walrasian equilibrium because the market doesn't clear. There is a surplus of labor.

Those who take the natural-rate position believe that the existence of labor unions also results in a natural rate of unemployment above the full employment rate of unemployment.[79] The analysis of labor unions is exactly the same as for the minimum wage. Unions cause wages to be above the equilibrium level, leading to unemployment. There is a non-union sector that the unemployed can look for work in. However, because wages are higher for unionized employers, some stay unemployed and search for jobs in the union sector rather than take a job in the non-union sector.

We should be suspicious of the claim that higher union wages lead to unemployment. The key point in the argument that the minimum wage leads to unemployment is that the turnover rate in minimum wage jobs is high. With a high turnover rate, it may make sense to remain unemployed and look full-time for a minimum-wage job because the probability of finding a minimum-wage job in a short amount of time is relativity high. However, the turnover rate with union jobs is low. The chances are small that someone would choose to stay unemployed — potentially for a long time — when non-union jobs are readily available.

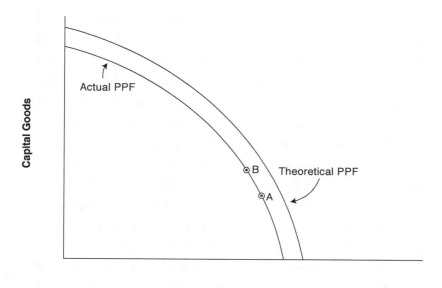

Figure 17. The natural rate of unemployment and the dual PPFs.

The Natural Rate

The viewpoint of natural-rate economists potentially calls into question the idea of scarcity. If the economy does not reach full employment, as the natural rate economists claim, does that mean that society is inside the PPF and therefore doesn't face scarcity? The answer from natural rate economists is no. It is as if, in their theory, there are two PPFs, one real and the other theoretical. Given that there are unions and that there is a minimum wage, they theorize that market forces reduce unemployment as far as it can be accomplished—to the natural rate. At that point, no more reductions in unemployment can be squeezed out of the economy. In order to produce more capital goods, resources must be taken out of the production of consumption goods and transferred to the production of capital goods, as shown in figure 17. Society is thus on its PPF. It faces scarcity.

There is also a theoretical PPF. If society eliminates the minimum wage, unions, and any other laws or programs that encourage indolence, then market forces will reduce unemployment to the true natural rate, the full-employment unemployment rate. Society will then be on a higher PPF, and the total production of goods and services will be greater, as shown in figure 17. Because the standard of living for the average person is higher, society is better off eliminating the minimum wage, unions, and so on. This is certainly a message corporate CEOs would love the natural-rate economists to spread far and wide.

According to natural rate economists, there is a third reason why the natural rate of unemployment is above the full-employment unemployment rate, and it comes under the heading of efficiency wage theory. It works with a slightly different mechanism. In this theory, market forces push wages down towards the equilibrium level during a recession, but there comes a point where market forces cease to operate. Firms voluntarily stop reducing wages on efficiency grounds. Even though involuntary unemployment exists, firms do not lower wages because they fear a reduction in profits. However, as we will see later, there are some serious problems with the way the ideas that underlie the efficiency wage theory are modeled.

References

Routh, Guy. 1989. *The Origin of Economic Ideas,* 2nd Edition. Dobbs
    Ferry, NY: Sheridan House
Smith, Adam. 1776, 1937. *An Inquiry into the Nature and Causes of the
    Wealth of Nations.* New York, NY: The Modern Library

❖ 9

Orthodox Solutions to Poverty

As we discussed in Chapter 2, economists discover the causes and solutions to social problems by working in models. To determine the orthodox solutions to poverty that is caused by unemployment and low wages, we need to know which orthodox model we should use. The answer to this question should be easy. We have encountered only one orthodox model that deals with labor markets: the orthodox supply-and-demand labor market model, as in figure 1.

Because employment is on the x-axis and wages are on y-axis, we can discuss both poverty due to unemployment and poverty due to low wages with the same model.

When analyzing poverty from the orthodox perspective, we must consider the two major results of the orthodox theory of labor markets:

- In the long-run, everyone who wants a job, at the going wage, can get a job.

- Workers are paid the value of what they produce — there is no exploitation.

223

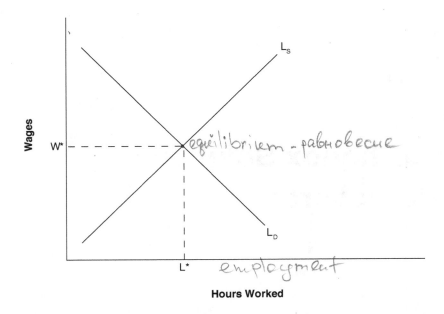

Figure 1. The orthodox supply-and-demand labor market model.

Because market forces always work to push labor markets to equilibrium, it should be clear how the orthodox supply-and-demand labor market produces the first result. How the second result naturally emerges from a supply-and-demand labor market model will not be explained until the next chapter. For the moment, you will just have to believe me that this result is a feature of the orthodox supply-and-demand labor market model.

These two results leave orthodox economists with few options for explaining why poverty exists and particularly for why long-term poverty exists. If anyone who wants a job can get a job at the going wage, and if the wage equals the person's productivity, then why is *anyone* in poverty? It is no wonder that the orthodox economics profession has attempted, as best it can, to ignore the existence of poverty. Orthodox introductory economics textbooks devote almost as many pages to price ceilings and price floors, which have relatively minor negative impacts, as they do to poverty, which causes major social problems.

Explaining poverty's existence is a challenge for orthodox economists. Outside of a temporary recession, the possibilities are all limited to some deficiency in the poor themselves:

- Too lazy to get a job

- Poor work habits

- Behavior patterns that are so disturbing, that firms are afraid to hire them

- Lack of intelligence

- Limited skills due to low-quality schooling or not trying in school

- Good skills but for a type of employment that no longer exists

- A single parent with insufficient skills or an inflexible schedule

- A disability that prevents work

- A poor work history that makes firms unwilling to hire them

Because these causes of poverty are the result of shortcomings in the poor themselves, the orthodox solutions necessarily work to change these characteristics of the poor. However, conservatives and liberals have different assumptions about human nature, and as a result, they also have different methods for motivating the poor to change.

Conservative Causes and Solutions

Conservatives take a negative view of human nature and the poor. For the most part, they assume that the poor are poor because they are lazy, short-sighted, and self-indulgent. Because African Americans and Latinx Americans have much higher poverty rates than whites and Asians, the conservative position implies that African Americans and Latinx Americans are naturally lazier than whites and Asians.

This puts conservative economists in a precarious position. On one hand, they wish to distance themselves from the racist[80] implications of their theory. On the other hand, they tend to focus on inner-city poverty, which is predominately a poverty of African Americans. Conservatives seem to enjoy walking this knife-edge, denying that they and their theories are racist while talking about poverty in terms of race.

There is a second and even more important part to the conservative approach. According to conservatives, government safety net programs give the poor an *incentive* to be lazy. According to conservatives, what allows people to not work, or to not put much effort into work when they have jobs, or to develop anti-social behaviors is the fact that they can get the income and services they need to survive from government aid programs. For conservatives the solution is clear, eliminating all these programs will eliminate most if not all poverty. Without the aid from government safety net programs, the poor will be unable to support themselves and will therefore be forced to get jobs. To get jobs, they must discard any trace of an anti-social lifestyle. They must also work hard to keep their jobs. In poverty-stricken neighborhoods, a new role-model blossoms — the hard-working adult. This creates an upward spiral in blighted inner-city neighborhoods. The solution to poverty from the conservative perspective is, in other words, tough love, eliminating all or nearly all government assistance programs for the poor and unemployed.

Poverty Due to Unemployment

The conservative explanation of the causes and solutions to poverty due to unemployment and low wages are similar. However, because their solutions depend on the orthodox model in different ways, it is worth separating the two.

The conservative solution to poverty due to unemployment depends critically on the orthodox model. When we eliminate government assistance programs, it is imperative that the poor are able to find jobs. If they

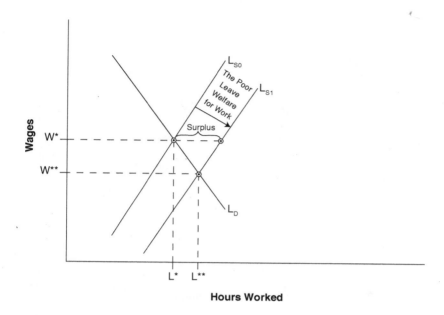

Figure 2. In the conservative orthodox perspective, the supply of labor increases with the elimination of welfare.

can't, they face starvation. However, in the supply-and-demand labor market model, jobs automatically appear. As we see in figure 2, when these safety net programs are eliminated the poor, in order to replace the income from these programs, must join the labor force and look for work. This causes the labor supply curve to shift out to the southeast. At the original equilibrium wage (W*), there is now a surplus of labor (L_S > L_D). Market forces then drive wages down to the new equilibrium wage (W**). At the new equilibrium, everyone who wants a job at the going wage has a job. All former welfare recipients are absorbed into the labor force, so poverty from unemployment is eliminated.

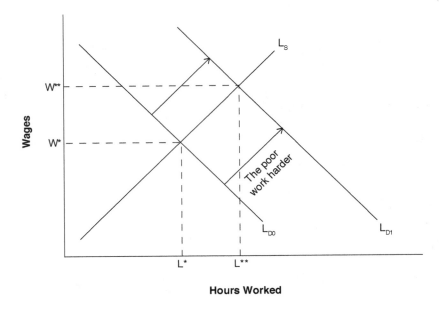

Figure 3. In the conservative orthodox perspective, the demand for labor increases as the poor work harder.

Poverty Due to Low Wages

The conservative solution to poverty from low wages rests on the second result of the orthodox model, that an individual's wage rate is equal to the value of what that individual produces (W=VMP$_L$). Some current anti-poverty programs assist members of the working poor and near poor. Without these assistance programs to augment their earned income, these workers would have to rely purely on what they earn. If their wages are insufficient, then according to the conservative approach, they must work harder, either at the job site or at acquiring new skills.

According to the orthodox model, if they work harder at the job site and produce more, then their marginal product of labor (MP$_L$) increases. If their MP$_L$ increases, then so does the value of the marginal product of labor (VMP$_L$ = MP$_L$ x P). In the orthodox model, the demand curve is just the downward sloping portion of the VMP$_L$ curve. As we see in figure 3, as the working poor work harder at the job site the demand curve will rise. At the original equilibrium wage (W*), there is now a shortage of labor ($L_D > L_S$). Market forces then drive wages up to the new equilibrium wage (W**).

By the same token, if the poor work harder at acquiring more skills, they become more productive and their wages rise. This occurs either by the individual now having the skills to get a job in the high-wage labor market or by being more productive in the low-wage labor market. Either way, their wage increases. In this way, the elimination of government assistance programs spurs the working poor and near poor to develop the toughness and moral fiber necessary to increase their wages to the point where poverty due to low wages is eliminated.

Thus, we can see how within the orthodox model the conservative solution eliminates both poverty due to low wages and poverty due to unemployment. However, it should also be clear that if the orthodox model of labor markets is incorrect, then the conservative solution will fail, and that failure could be catastrophic. Determining which model can most accurately predict and explain real world events thus becomes vital for determining the correct policies for eliminating poverty.

Liberal Causes and Solutions

Liberals have a positive view of human nature and a somewhat positive view of the poor. Liberals assume that the poor are, with a few exceptions, like the rest of us. They are hard-working people who wish to provide the best for themselves and their families. However, for one reason or another, the poor find themselves in an unfortunate position. As a caring society, we should thus help those among us who are in need. If the poor can be given the proper assistance, they will be able to pull themselves back onto their feet and rejoin mainstream society.

From the liberal perspective, people are thus in poverty for these possible reasons:

1. Limited skills due to low-quality schooling or not trying in school

2. Good skills but for a type of employment that no longer exists

3. Single parent with insufficient skills or an inflexible schedule

4. Disability that prevents work

5. Un- or underemployed due to a recession

According to liberals, there are numerous reasons for people being unable to earn incomes above the poverty level. As a result, there needs to be a series of assistance programs, each one tailored to directly deal with a particular problem. However, liberals don't agree on what programs the government should use to eliminate poverty.

In addition, liberals also believe that it is unfair to punish the children of the poor for the mistakes, bad judgments, or unfortunate circumstances of their parents. Therefore, they are also in favor of programs that provide critical services to the children of the poor, such as health care and education.

As we discussed earlier, conservative orthodox economists tend to have much more in common with one another than liberals. Liberal orthodox economists generally believe that there is a need for government intervention when markets fail or clear slowly. However, liberals don't generally agree on the extent of market failures or on how effective certain government programs have been. Therefore, the breadth and depth of government involvement that they advocate varies widely. The difference between the solutions to poverty proposed by Edmund Phelps[81] (1997) and Bradley Schiller (2008), for example, is quite large.

For the purposes of this book, we define a liberal orthodox economist as one who believes that efforts to eliminate[82] poverty should contain, in addition to unemployment insurance, some mixture of items from each of the first three categories:

1. A variety of different programs aimed at individuals who are temporarily or permanently unable to participate in the labor market.

2. Programs to increase the income of the working poor and near poor, such as Supplemental Nutrition Assistance Program (SNAP, formally known as food stamps), employer subsidies, earned income tax credit (EITC), or an increase in the minimum wage.

3. Programs to increase the productivity of the poor, including programs to improve the quantity and quality of education, and job training programs.[83]

There are also some liberal orthodox economists who believe that labor markets clear so slowly that their solutions contain a fourth category:

4. Programs to increase employment through a public service employment program or by increasing aggregate demand via increases in government spending, as discussed in the heterodox solutions.

In the future, liberal orthodox economists may add a fifth category. The provisions that we laid out as part of a heterodox solution—legal changes to make shifting work from the core to the periphery more expensive and the provision of greater funding for the enforcement of labor laws—are based on relatively recent writings of the liberal orthodox economist David Weil.

Poverty Due to Unemployment

For liberal economists there are a number of reasons why workers might be in poverty due to unemployment: a recession, their company moves overseas or goes out of business, they're disabled, their education and skills aren't sufficient to get a job, or they're divorced and don't have the skills or the flexibility of schedule due to child care to get a job.

For each reason, liberal economists have suggested a government program or programs to deal with the situation. The last two reasons, which deal with a lack of education and skills, are also reasons why an individual could be in poverty due to low wages and we will deal with these two in the next section.

Poverty Due to Low Wages

For liberal orthodox economists, the cause of poverty due to low wages is because poor individuals have low productivity (a low VMP_L). How do we know their VMP_L is low? We observe that their wages are low. It's a circular argument that depends on the wage rate (W) always equaling the VMP_L, the second result of the orthodox model. It's not based on any data, just based on the model. Liberals suggest two broad programs to address poverty due to low wages. Both of their suggestions are rooted in the operation of the orthodox model of labor markets:

1. Increase the income going to the poor by using government programs to increase the take-home wages of low-wage workers.

2. Increase the productivity of the poor by improving education and by providing job-training programs.

Increasing Take-Home Pay

The first liberal orthodox solution for poverty due to low wages is to increase the take-home pay of low-wage workers. Liberal orthodox economists tend to suggest one of two government programs — increases in the minimum wage or increases in the earned income tax credit (EITC). In general, liberals tend to favor increasing the EITC. While both programs increase the take-home wages of the poor, they have different effects on the economy.

First, the cost of these programs falls on different groups. The cost of increasing the minimum wage falls directly on employers. Employers may attempt to pass these costs on the consumers, but competitive pressures may make that impossible. To the extent that employers are able to pass on some or all the costs, the consumers of goods and services produced by minimum wage workers indirectly pay part or all of the costs of increasing the minimum wage. If firms can't pass on the costs, then the employers of minimum wage workers pay all the costs. Given the intense opposition to increases in the minimum wage from the business community, we should expect that employers can't pass all the cost on the customers.

An increase in the size of the EITC is a reduction in taxes on low-wage workers. The cost of this plan falls on taxpayers in the form of either higher taxes or an increase in the budget deficits and the national debt. An increase in the national debt means that the interest payments on the debt become larger. This leads either to an ever-larger national debt or to reduced expenditures on other government programs, most of which benefit the general public. Clearly, the business community prefers taxpayers to pay for this solution to poverty. They thus prefer an increase in the EITC rather than an increase in the minimum wage.

According to orthodox theory, the two plans also have different employment effects. As we saw earlier, when there is no uncovered sector, an increase in the minimum wage increases unemployment. In addition, in markets where there are both covered and uncovered sectors, if natural rate economists are correct, then an increase in the minimum wage increases unemployment.

Contrast that with the employment effects of an increase in the EITC. An increase in the EITC increases the after-tax wages of the poor. This causes an increase in the supply of labor. An increase in labor supply results in an increase in employment, and a decrease in wages paid by employers. Figures 2 and 4 show the results of an increase in the supply of labor. It is probably these employment effects along with who pays the costs that makes most liberal orthodox economists favor the increasing EITC over an increase in the minimum wage.

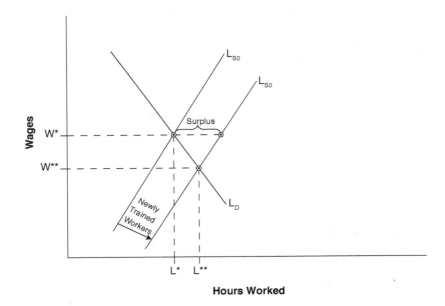

Figure 4. In the liberal orthodox perspective, training programs increase the labor supply in higher wage markets.

Education and Job Training Programs

The second liberal solution is to increase the productivity of the poor by improvement in education and providing job training programs. This solution is based on both of the two main results of the orthodox supply-and-demand labor market model. The explanations of how increases in education and job training work to reduce poverty are the same. For the sake of simplicity, we'll focus on training programs. If successful, these training programs can do one of two things: move an individual from a low-wage labor market to a high-wage market, or make a worker in the low-wage market more productive.

If the training moves workers from a low-wage market to a high-wage market, then it is imperative that the newly trained workers are able to find jobs in the high-wage labor market. In the orthodox model, this is indeed what happens. As we see in figure 4, the training programs

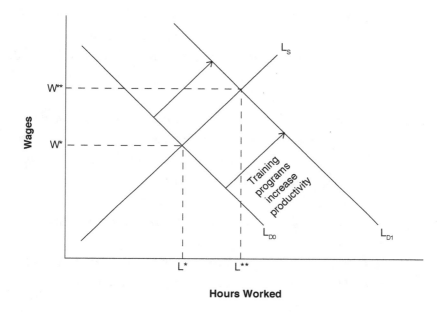

Figure 5. In the liberal orthodox perspective, training programs increase productivity and as a result increases the demand for labor in low wage markets.

increase the supply of labor in the high-wage market. At first, there is a surplus of labor at W*. However, market forces bring us back to equilibrium at a lower wage (W**). All those who want a job at the going wage (W**) have a job. The market absorbs all the new, higher-skilled workers.

In the second case, training programs make workers in the low-wage market more productive. In this case, the workers' MP_L increases, and thus their VMP_L also increases. As we saw earlier, when the VMP_L increases, the labor demand curve shifts up. As we see in figure 5, this results in an increase in wages.

If education and training programs can successfully increase the productivity of the poor, then poverty due to low wages can be eliminated. Not only are the poor employed in jobs that use their newly acquired skills, but their pay is now higher because their productivity is now higher ($VMP_L = W$). It should be clear from the above how the liberal solutions for eliminating poverty due to low wages are derived from the working of the orthodox model. It should also be clear that if the orthodox model of labor markets is incorrect, then the liberal solutions will most likely fail.

References

Danziger, Sheldon and Peter Gottschalk. 1995. *American Unequal.* Cambridge, MA: Harvard University Press.

Phelps, Edmund. 1997. *Rewarding Work: How to Restore Participation and Self-Support to Free Enterprise.* Cambridge, MA: Harvard University Press.

Schiller, Bradley. 2008. *The Economics of Poverty and Discrimination,* 10th ed. Upper Saddle River, NJ: Pearson Prentice Hall.

Weil, David. 2014. *The Fissured Workplace: Why Work Became So Bad for So Many and What Can Be done to Improve It.* Cambridge, MA: Harvard University Press.

❖ 10

Questionable Assumptions

As we have seen, there are two major results of the orthodox model that are essential to orthodox solutions to poverty:

1. Everyone who wants a job at the going wage can get a job.
2. Workers are paid the value of what they produce, so there is no exploitation.

However, these two results depend heavily on questionable assumptions. In this chapter, we explore how without these assumptions the orthodox supply and demand labor market model can't produce those results.

Questioning the First Result

When unemployment exists in the orthodox model, there are two mechanisms that drive the economy to either full employment or the natural rate of unemployment.

First, as firms see more people applying for jobs than there are job openings, they realize that they can lower the cost of production by lowering the wage rate. Doing so causes some workers to quit, but if firms replace them with unemployed workers, then they lower the cost of production. As wages go down, the surplus of labor shrinks, but as long as unemployment exists, firms have an incentive to continue to lower their wages. Wages will continue to decline until the equilibrium wage is reached.

Second, as unemployed workers become desperate for work, they offer to work for wages below what a firm is currently paying. The firm then accepts the offer and replaces current workers or gives current workers an opportunity to match the underbidders' wage offers. Either way, wages fall. As long as unemployment exists, the unemployed have an incentive to underbid the employed. Once again, this continues until the equilibrium wage is reached.

Assumptions

The orthodox supply-and-demand labor market model and two clearing mechanisms depend on questionable assumptions that are rarely emphasized when the model is presented. Below are three of the assumptions:

1. Workers never learn skills on the job. They are no more productive on their second, third, or fiftieth day than they are on their first day.

2. Changes in the wage rate do not affect how hard people work.

3. Productivity is individual and not dependent on the speed or skill of other workers.

Without either of the first two assumptions, it is highly unlikely that these two orthodox mechanisms could ever clear labor markets in the real world. We'll take a closer look at these assumptions, starting with the first.

Never Learning Skills on the Job

This first assumption guarantees that the unemployed worker and the employed worker are equally as productive and thus perfectly interchangeable. In the orthodox model, the fact that unemployed and employed people can be interchanged without any loss in productivity is key for both clearing mechanisms. If the firm accepts the bid of an unemployed worker and replaces a current worker, productivity is unaffected in the orthodox model. If the firm lowers its wage and current employees quit and are replaced by unemployed workers, the productivity of the firm is again unaffected, and lower wages increase profits.

However, if current employees do learn skills on the job, then they are more productive than unemployed workers, and the two will *not* be interchangeable. Because the current employee is more productive, the firm must look at each worker's unit labor cost (ULC) to determine whom they should hire.

Looking at the first mechanism, you can see firms are reluctant to lower wages for two reasons. First, if decreasing wages causes skilled workers to quit, they have to be replaced with unskilled, unemployed workers. Second, the act of lowering wages risks demoralizing their workforce, which can result in a decline in work effort.

Looking at the second mechanism, you can see firms only accept the wage offers of unemployed workers if they are low enough to offset their lower productivity. This may require a sizable underbid—one too great for unemployed workers to make. However, this is not the largest problem facing real-world firms. A firm that accepts an underbid and replaces some of its current workers risks demoralizing its entire labor force. This almost assuredly would result in a decline in work effort and an increase in turnover. For firms whose workers learn skills on the job, this would be devastating to productivity. It is no wonder that actual cases of underbidding by individual workers are almost never observed in the United States.

If laborers learn skills on the job, then we *cannot* draw a supply-and-demand labor market graph because the employed and unemployed have different productivities. It would be like putting apples and toasters on the same product market graph. It can't be done. The *x*-axis can only represent the quantities of one type of labor at a time. Just as we need two separate graphs to represent apples and toasters, we need two separate graphs to present the employed and unemployed. Standard supply-and-demand analysis, with its tendency towards equilibrium, vanishes. Firms still demand labor, and households still supply it. High unemployment still reduces workers' bargaining power. However, we can't draw a supply-and-demand labor market graph.

We can assume that with all jobs, there are skills to be learned. Even taking bags of celery off a pallet and dumping the contents onto a conveyer belt has skills that need to be learned. However, learning those skills doesn't take long. With many jobs in the secondary market, the time it takes to become efficient at the job is relatively short, so employers aren't as worried about turnover. With these jobs, the orthodox assumption about skill acquisition is still inaccurate, but this inaccuracy may not be significant enough to make their analysis incorrect.

With jobs where skill development takes a long time or where the employers have long job ladders, however, the orthodox concept of the market forces working to drive wages down when involuntary unemployment exists either disappears or is very weak. Firms are reluctant to lower wages for these jobs, and they refuse to take underbids for fear of demoralizing their workers and creating a turnover. If we look at labor markets where jobs require a reasonable amount of on the job training, which Doeringer and Piore (1971) characterize as most jobs, the chances that market forces will drive wages down to clear the market is either remote or nonexistent depending on the number of skills learned on the job.

Changes in the Wage Rate

Eliminating this assumption also results in a model where wages are not likely to fall sufficiently to clear the market.

If the work effort of employees is a positive function of their wage rate, then as a firm lowers its wage rate, output per worker falls. Because both output and wages fall, the question is whether unit labor costs rise or fall as the firm lowers its wages. If the ULC rises at any point in the process of lowering wages, then the firm stops lowering its wage. Even if the initial wage decreases don't have a large effect on work effort and the ULC falls, reducing wages likely results in a serious decline in work effort. As the economy approaches full employment, the cost of being fired for underperformance declines because it is easy to find another job.

In a world organized into supply-and-demand labor markets, work effort is likely to decline significantly as the economy approaches full employment, which causes ULC to increase.[84] If the firm believes this to be true, then it stops lowering wages regardless of how much unemployment exists. The market mechanism thus ceases to function, and labor markets do not clear.

If this second assumption doesn't hold, but the first assumption does, then you could draw a supply-and-demand labor market graph. However, the labor demand curve could have a very curious shape. It would be much steeper, and part of the curve could be positively sloped like a supply curve. Even if the best model for labor markets is a supply-and-demand model, it is entirely possible that, once we add the assumption that work effort is a positive function of wage, supply and demand might not intersect and that the model might not produce an equilibrium wage and employment.

Finally, when we look at work effort more broadly, we see that all the concerns raised by Edwards (1979) around management's ability or inability to monitor the pace of work and the quality of production are wholly absent from supply-and-demand labor market analysis. It is simply assumed in the orthodox model that all laborers work at a pace that makes the owners happy and that all laborers know how to produce the product.

Productivity

Most members of the public believe that both of the first two assumptions are false. However, if this third assumption that productivity is *not* purely individual is also false, then the effects of the first two assumptions are amplified.

In a time of high unemployment, firms are always tempted to lower wages. However, if they lower wages, firms run the risk of losing some of their current employees and having to replace them with less efficient new employees. It then becomes a question of what happens to the ULC. How do the costs saved by lowering wages compare to lost productivity? A firm's willingness to lower its wage depends on how much of a decline in output will result from the decline in work effort and the increase in skilled workers quitting.

This loss in productivity is magnified if output depends on a team effort. If output is purely individual, then new, unskilled employees only slow themselves down. However, if production is the result of teamwork, then the unskilled employees slow everyone else down, too, making the decline in productivity that much larger. Firms whose output is the result of a team effort are thus going to be more reluctant to lower wages than firms whose output is purely a result of individual effort.

Most jobs have some element of teamwork in them. Clearly, assembly line work is a team effort. In many cases, office workers are dependent on information generated by others, and others dependent on information generated by them. To be effective, even a salesperson in the field is dependent on an efficiently operating support staff in the home office.

Internal Labor Markets

This chapter contains some strong criticism of the orthodox sup-ply-and-demand labor market model. We conclude that if the orthodox model assumes that workers *do* learn skills on the job, that work effort *is* a function of wages, and that output is often the result of a team effort, then the result of this model is that market forces cease to operate.

Such a model must conclude that ultimately, in the presence of unemployment, wages will not drop to clear the market. If that is the case, it destroys the foundations of orthodox micro- and macroeco-nomics because market forces will not drive the economy to full employ-ment or some natural rate of unemployment. As a result, increases in government spending can be used to lower the unemployment rate and reduce poverty.

However, in making these criticisms, we have allowed orthodox economists to play on their own "home court." We have implicitly assumed, as a starting point, that labor markets can best be described as supply-and-demand markets. However, the majority of jobs in the US are, in fact, part of internal labor markets. Most laborers work for firms with complex sets of wages and work relationships that seek to maximize work effort and reduce turnover. In internal labor markets, firms struc-ture the work environment to minimize unit labor costs in the long run. Edward Wolff's (2009) characterization of internal labor markets puts relative positions of the two type models in context:

> [There] is a relatively rigid wage structure, which does not respond or change much in relation to changes in outside con-ditions such as unemployment and shifting wage rates. Internal consistency in the wage structure is therefore considered more important than external consistency. (p. 320)

Supply and demand don't play a role in internal labor markets, except to the extent that the level of unemployment impacts the bar-gaining position of workers and employers. Therefore, the biggest criticism of orthodox labor market theory is that the main feature of the US labor markets—internal labor markets—is wholly absent from their analysis. Orthodox economists concentrate their efforts almost exclusively on supply-and-demand labor markets, which make up a minority of labor markets in the US.

Efficiency Wage Theory

In developing their supply-and-demand models of labor markets, orthodox economists have assumed away many of the most important features of real-world labor markets. Have orthodox economists ever seriously addressed these deficiencies in their models? Yes and no. There is a branch of labor and macroeconomics known broadly as "efficiency wage theory" that addresses firm-specific skill learning, the effect of wages on work effort, and control issues. Efficiency wage theory has had an impact on orthodox economics but not a significant impact.

This lack of a significant effect is mainly because an efficient wage theory uses simplistic equilibrium models. If we model these features in a more complex, realistic fashion, it removes the key ingredient in orthodox theory—scarcity. It also destroys the results that orthodox models were created to produce. However, we will take a moment to see how orthodox economists have addressed these concerns and how their models produce firms that pay an optimal wage rather than form internal labor markets.

According to the orthodox supply-and-demand labor market model, any measured unemployment must in the long run either be the result of workers being between jobs[85] or workers who are voluntarily unemployed—holding out for a better wage when they could have a job at the current wage. However, according to some orthodox economists, generally of the liberal variety, historical data doesn't appear to line up with the standard labor market theory.[86]

In the 1970s and 1980s, several economists attempted to explain this data with orthodox equilibrium models that assume that either the firm is maximizing profit and minimizing costs or the worker and household are maximizing their well-being. A number of these studies were collected in a now-famous book by Akerlof and Yellen (1986), *Efficiency Wage Models of the Labor Market*. In this book, the researchers do not attempt to revolutionize orthodox economics. They attempt to find equilibrium models that better explain the data. In pursuing this research, they potentially open a Pandora's box, but because of the self-censoring nature of orthodox economists, this has not become a serious problem.

Efficiency Wage Models

Some of these efficiency wage models touch upon the three points we emphasize, that worker productivity is a function of wages, management's imperfect ability to monitor work performance, and firm-specific training. In every case, the result of these orthodox models is that at some point, market forces cease to work to clear the market and that there is an optimal wage that is above the market-clearing wage.

Robert Solow's (1986) model includes work effort as a positive function of the wage rate. As expected, this model shows that firms voluntarily pay wages above the market-clearing wages. They do so because of the increased work effort that results from the higher wage minimizes the firm's ULC.

In the beginning of their "shirking model" article, Shapiro and Stiglitz (1986) acknowledge that at full employment, workers have little incentive to work hard:

> The intuition behind our result is simple. Under the conventional competitive paradigm, in which all workers receive the market wage and there is no unemployment, the worst that can happen to a worker who shirks on the job is that he is fired. Since he can immediately be rehired, however, he pays no penalty for his misdemeanor. With imperfect monitoring and full employment, therefore, workers will choose to shirk. (p. 45)

In their model, there are two states of the world. The first is that the workers do their duty and put in a full day of work. The second is that the workers are slackers who will be fired if their poor performance is ever discovered. At the market-clearing wage, there is no penalty for being a slacker, so all workers shirk their responsibilities. If the firm pays a wage above the market-clearing wage, however, there *is* a cost for under-performing. Once again, even in the presences of a substantial amount of unemployment, the firm voluntarily pays a wage above the market clearing wage.[87]

In Steve Salop's (1986) model, new employees receive training upon being hired and become more productive and thus more valuable. If employees quit, the firm loses its investment. The firm, therefore, has an incentive to pay a wage that is higher than the market-clearing wage to reduce turnover. Again, the key is for the firm to find the "optimal wage" that minimizes ULC.

In the orthodox model, the market coordinates decisions that determine what goods are produced, which firms produce them, and who receives these goods. Any time there is disequilibrium, a surplus or shortage, the price in that market—that is, the price for the goods and services market, interest rates for the loanable funds market, and the wage rate for the labor market—adjusts to bring the economy back to equilibrium, eliminating the surplus or shortage.

Wage adjustments play an important role in driving the economy back to the PPF when a recession occurs. With the efficiency wage models, wages do not adjust to clear the market. The market forces expressed in our two mechanisms stop functioning. The question is, what have orthodox economists done with this information. Have they used it to revolutionize the view of orthodox economists, or have they found a way to reestablish the old theory within the context of the efficiency wage theory?

Reaction from Orthodox Economists

We might be able to guess how this problem has been resolved. In her discussion of the famous heterodox Harvard economist John Kenneth Galbraith, Diana Coyle (2007) encapsulates the basic thinking of the orthodox economics profession:

> Yet, despite his Harvard professorship and public acclaim, many economists don't think Galbraith counted as an economist.... By contrast many of us spurn Galbraith because he wasn't a modeler.... The combination of rational maximizers and the equilibrium concept, in theories tested against a counterfactual and refined by comparison with the data, makes economics incredibly powerful. For all that its practitioners criticize us, the other social sciences don't have anything remotely approaching the flexibility and strength of the economic method nor the capacity of economic models to be honed and tested empirically. As Paul Krugman once put it: "'The clarity and power of economic analysis can spoil you: once you have a taste of what it means to have a really insightful model, you tend to be inhibited about looser speculations." That's why Paul Ormerod, for all his sharp criticism of the mainstream, is an economist but John Kenneth Galbraith wasn't. (p. 231, 252-53)

Orthodox economists know that if they want to be part of the orthodox economics fraternity, they must use models that are based on individual maximization and that produce equilibrium. Internal labor market models don't produce equilibrium wages or a natural rate of unemployment, and neither do heterodox business cycle models. Orthodox economists know that using either of those models would be committing professional suicide.

Within orthodoxy, then, there has been no debate on which way to take the new information from the efficient wage theory. Those who would use it to revolutionize the discipline would have to stop believing in equilibrium, so in the view of other orthodox economists, they would cease to be economists. As a result, there would be no reason to read or discuss their work. Even the extremely well-known and accomplished Dr. Galbraith was ignored by the orthodox economics profession for the last thirty to forty years of his life.

For orthodox economists who wished to stay relevant in their chosen field, the way forward was clear. The information had to be taken in a safe direction. It needed to be incorporated into the old equilibrium theory. That was accomplished by wrapping the efficiency wage theory into Edmund Phelps' (1967) idea of the natural rate of unemployment. Market forces presumably work to eliminate any surplus of labor until the wage reaches the efficient wage. At that point, market forces cease to work, and we arrive at the natural rate of unemployment.

The old theory said that market forces drive the economy to full employment. The new theory says that market forces drive the economy to the natural rate, where a certain level of involuntary unemployment still exists. In both concepts, however, this is as low as unemployment can go. No efforts by the government and no increase in government spending can lower the unemployment rate in the long run. The only impact such actions have is to increase inflation.

Using the concept of the natural rate of unemployment,[88] the efficiency wage theory has been made safe. Orthodox economists can now point to the fact that they have models that consider that work effort is a function of wages, that workers need to learn firm specific skills, and that firms have issues controlling the work effort of their employees. They can also show that these factors make no material difference to the outcome of their theories. Thus, for the purpose of educating new economists, these concerns can be forgotten—except to briefly mention them for a page or two in a 900-page textbook.

Simplistic Models

The fact that workers learn skills on the job and that major corporations have control issues can only be resolved by firms building complex internal labor markets. Internal labor markets eliminate supply-and-demand analysis altogether. The fact that work effort is a function of wages also mangles the shape of the labor demand curve.

How can orthodox economists consider these deviations from the orthodox theory and still avoid concluding that a large number of firms need to form internal labor markets? They can do this by using extremely simple equilibrium models that differ dramatically from the real world. In addition, they never attempt to place two variations in the same model at the same time. The model of Shapiro and Stiglitz and the model of Salop are excellent examples of how simplistic design eliminates the need for firms to develop internal labor markets.

In the Shapiro and Stiglitz's model, there are only two states of the world — workers either do their duty or they are slackers. Given these two simple states, the firm only needs to find the optimal wage that reduces slacking to the point at which the firm minimizes its ULC. In the real world, however, there are infinite levels of work effort. There is no optimal wage. Under real-world conditions, firms can further lower their ULC if they build a structure to control work effort, an internal labor market. We know that firms can do better by building internal labor markets because that is what firms have actually done. If they had been better off finding an optimal wage, they would have done that instead.

In Salop's model, we see another simple design that allows the firm to find an optimal wage rather than build an internal labor market. In this model, new employees receive training upon being hired and become more productive. After the initial training, however, employees never learn anything more, and all workers are paid the same wage. Again, the solution to the model is to find the optimal wage. In a more complicated model where employees are always acquiring additional skills through on-the-job training and firms have long employment ladders, the solution to retention problems is not finding the optimal wage. The solution is developing an internal labor market.

While orthodox economists may use efficiency wage models to show that their theory has addressed concerns about their models being built on unrealistic assumptions, the concerns remain. Taking complex matters and addressing them with simplistic, one-dimensional models is insufficient. It's like putting a Band-Aid on a machete wound. Efficiency wage models can't shield orthodox supply-and-demand labor market models from the criticism that their results depend on highly unrealistic assumptions.

Questioning the Second Result

By now, it should be clear how the unrealistic assumptions of the orthodox supply and demand labor market model are necessary to generate the first result. However, based on what we have covered so far, it is not obvious why the orthodox model generates the second result, that workers are paid the value of what they produce.

As we will see, producing a model that generates this result is a clear case of building a model in order to produce the desired result. For a supply-and-demand labor market model to generate this result, it must have a highly unrealistic—and imaginative—hidden assumption. We will look at the hidden assumption first and then at how this model uses it to produce the desired result.

The Assumption of Play-Doh Capital

If workers are paid a wage that equals the dollar value of what they produce, then all workers receive a fair wage. Workers who are below the poverty line because of low wages thus have no one to blame but themselves. If they are more productive, their wages will be higher. However, this result is created by an assumption that was introduced into the model

L	VMP$_L$
0	0
1	$120
2	$150
3	$120
4	$ 90
5	$ 60
6	$ 45

VMP$_L$ - Value of the Marginal Product of Labor

Figure 1. The VMP$_L$ schedule for Saint Chuck's football factory.

by the famous US economist J.B. Clark.

Providing some context may help us understand how this assumption generates the second result. Figure 1 presents the VMP$_L$ schedule for Saint Chuck's football factory from earlier in the book.

If the wage rate is $90 per day, Saint Chuck hires four workers. It appears that, while the fourth worker is paid a wage equal to their VMP$_L$ ($90), the first, second, and third workers are exploited. They too receive a wage of $90, but their VMP$_L$ exceeds $90. These workers don't receive the full value of what they have created. Saint Chuck has stolen a part of their wages for himself.[89]

However, according to orthodox theory, the above paragraph is incorrect. The correct interpretation of the VMP$_L$ schedule goes like this: When Chuck hires three workers, the VMP$_L$ for each one of them is $120. When the fourth worker is added, not only does the VMP$_L$ of the fourth worker fall to $90, but the VMP$_L$ for each of the other three workers also falls to $90. How is this possible? It is the result of Clark's imaginative assumption.

Over the years, various names have been given to this assumption, but the assumption of Play-Doh capital provides the best imagery. Imagine a preschool table with a pile of Play-Doh on it. Each day, the Play-Doh is evenly divided so that each child has the same amount to play with. The amount of Play-Doh each child receives depends on how many children come to preschool. Fewer children means a larger portion of Play-Doh for each child, and more children means a smaller portion for each.

Clark assumes that capital has the same properties as the Play-Doh at our preschool. Each day, the company's capital magically changes so that every employee works with exactly the same amount of capital. Factories and conveyor belts change their size and shape to accommodate whatever number of workers the firm hires. Or, as Joan Robinson put it, if a ditch-digging crew of ten people with ten shovels adds an eleventh person, their ten shovels will magically change into eleven smaller shovels. In this way, because all workers are assumed to be homogenous and each worker has the same amount of capital, the VMP_L is the same for all workers. The labor demand curve, which equals the VMP_L, not only assumes there is always 100% capacity utilization of capital, but also that capital magically changes each time the firm adds or subtracts a laborer.[90]

This assumption produces a second interesting and counter-intuitive result. If a firm increases the size of its capital stock, then both wages and employment increase. This is because increasing capital equipment gives each worker more capital to work with and thereby increases the productivity of each worker. The entire labor demand curve thus shifts up, increasing employment and wages. In the orthodox model, then, there is no such thing as labor-saving capital equipment. There is no reason for workers to fear being replaced by a machine.[91]

In the orthodox model, the interaction of labor supply and demand at the market level sets the wage rate. Every firm hires labor up to the point where VMP_L = W. Because all firms are assumed to possess capital that magically changes, every worker is paid the value of what they produce (VMP_L), and hence there is no exploitation. This is also true for owners of capital, the managers of companies, and so on. All participants within the economy receive an income equal to the value of what they or the money they loaned contributes to output. According to orthodox theory, if a person's income is high, it is because that person is productive. If somebody's income is low, it is because that person is not productive. The poor, therefore, are in poverty due to their own shortcomings.

With this in mind, the solution to poverty is clear. The poor need to increase their productivity either by working harder or by acquiring more skills. If they do that, then they will earn the higher wages that higher productivity brings. With perhaps the exception of providing the poor with the opportunity to improve their skills, this theory shows that no other sacrifices need be made by the rest of society.

We can see why the rich have been willing to finance the dissemination of the orthodox theory. However, this result can't be produced without Clark's assumption. If actual pieces of capital equipment in the real world don't magically change their size and shape as the number of workers or the amount of capital changes, then the result, that workers are paid the value of what they produce, will not occur in the real world. Even within the orthodox model, without Clark's assumption, most workers will be exploited by their employers — paid less than the value of what they produce. That's not the message that the business community wants the public to hear.

Testing the Second Result

In our chapter on modeling, we establish that just because a model has unrealistic assumptions, that isn't enough to disqualify the model from further consideration. However, those unrealistic assumptions do point to where the model should be tested to determine if it can mimic the actions of the real world.

In this chapter, we've seen that, when it comes to poverty, the orthodox theory of labor markets produces two main results that are dependent on assumptions that appear to vary dramatically from what is true in the real world. Because these two results are highly dependent on questionable assumptions, we should be suspicious of the notion that

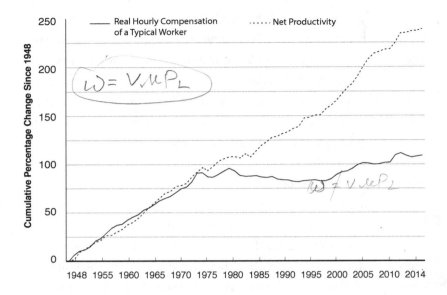

Figure 2. Net productivity and real hourly compensation of a typical worker. (Economic Policy Institute)

these two results actually occur. We also have three areas that are ready for testing:

1. Do wages fall when there is a surplus of labor?

2. Do labor markets clear in the long run or converge to the natural rate?

3. Do wages change with changes in productivity?

We will test the first two areas later when we test the heterodox and orthodox models simultaneously. Both models make definite predictions about whether wages will fall during a recession and whether labor markets tend to clear or converge to the natural rate, so it makes sense to test them together. The heterodox model makes no claims about the third area, the relationship between wages and productivity, so no test we run will disprove the heterodox theory on this point. However, we can test whether the orthodox model predicts correctly.

As figure 2 shows, after increasing at relatively the same rate for twenty-five years, net productivity and real compensation of the typical worker have diverged over the last forty years. The divergence is dramatic. The only way that this data would not disprove the second result is if there was something wrong with the measures of productivity and real compensation.

Bivens and Mishel (2015) argue convincingly that given the data, these are the best measures of productivity and real compensation available. However, to be definitive proof that $VMP_L \neq W$, we need a measure of VMP_L, which means we need a measure of MP_L:

$$VMP_L = MP_L \times P \ (10.1)$$

In other words, we need to be able to separate the growth in productivity of labor from the growth in productivity for the economy as a whole. We don't have that measure, and we probably never will.

Some suggest that labor productivity grew across the entire income spectrum from 1948 to 1973 and that the growth rate in labor productivity stagnated after 1973 for the typical worker while growing rapidly for those at the top of the income spectrum. This implies that those factors that increase productivity—better and more capital, increased education, and having more experience—stopped increasing for the typical worker but increased dramatically for workers in the upper ten percent. According to Bivens and Mishel, the data we have doesn't support this idea:

> Further, about 40 percent of all measure productivity growth in the post-1979 period was due simply to 'capital deepening'— workers having more and better capital equipment to undertake production. This capital-deepening seems widespread across most workers in the economy." Furthermore, "the BLS measure of 'labor quality,' reflecting changes in experience and education levels, grew more quickly each year between 1973 and 2014 (0.33 percent) than it did from 1947 to 1973 (0.27 percent)

(Fernald 2014). This improvement in labor quality did not occur just for the top 20 percent of the workforce.

The data in figure 1 cannot be viewed as definitive proof that wages are not determined by a worker's productivity. There is no direct measure of labor productivity. We only have indirect measures. However, because net productivity and real compensation moved closely together for twenty-five years and then diverged dramatically, we have indirect evidence that wages are not determined by productivity. We shouldn't be surprised by these finding given the magical assumption needed to produce the theoretical result that $VMP_L = W$.

However, there is more evidence. While there are not many studies on the microeconomic level, the Federal Reserve Bank of Kansas City published a study by Drabenstott, Henry, and Mitchell in 1999 on the meat-packing industry entitled "Where Have All the Packing Plants Gone? The New Meat Geography in Rural America." The study states:

> The puzzle is compounded by the fact that productivity in the meat industry generally held steady or edged up even as wages fell. The LRD contains data on value-added per worker, a broad proxy for the productivity of workers. In the Midwest metropolitan meat packing plants, for example, value-added per worker "climbed" from roughly $60,000 to $66,000 from 1982 to 1992, even as wages "dropped" 44%. (p. 71)

In the orthodox model, the profit motive gives firms an incentive to continue hiring labor until the value of the marginal product of labor equals the wage rate ($VMP_L \geq W$). In the orthodox model, wages thus change with productivity. The normal expectation is that worker productivity raises over time, as the data on value added per worker shows. While the value added per worker may not be a perfect proxy for worker productivity, we can be sure that worker productivity in the meat industry didn't fall by 44% between 1982 and 1992. Therefore, at least for the Midwest meat packaging industry, $VMP_L \neq W$. In fact, it isn't even close.

Joseph Stiglitz (2013) raises other excellent points in his book, *The Price of Inequality*. How can there be a link between productivity and wages when there are jobs where one is paid now but the consequences of one's work will not be known for years to come? Furthermore, how can we measure productivity when so much of what people do depends on the technology they have inherited from others? Stiglitz discusses these questions in this way:

> We began the last chapter by explaining how those at the top have often sought to justify their income and wealth, and how "marginal productivity theory," the notion that those who got more did so because they had made a greater contribution to society, had become the prevailing doctrine, at least in economics. But, we noted that the crisis had cast doubt on this theory. Those who perfected the new skills of predatory lending, who helped create derivatives, described by the billionaire Warren Buffett as "financial weapons of mass destruction," or who devised the reckless new mortgages that brought about the subprime mortgage crisis, walked away with millions, sometimes hundreds of millions, of dollars.
>
> But even before that, it was clear that the link between pay and societal contribution was, at best, weak. As we noted earlier, the great scientists who have made discoveries that provided the basis of our modern society have typically reaped for themselves no more than a small fraction of what they have contributed, and received a mere pittance compared with the rewards reaped by the financial wizards who brought the world to the brink of ruin.
>
> But there is a deeper philosophical point: One can't really separate out any individual's contributions from those of others. Even in the context of technological change, most inventions entail the synthesis of preexisting elements rather than invention de novo. Today, at least in many critical sectors, a large fraction of all advances depends on basic research funded by the government.

Gar Alperovitz and Lew Daly concluded in 2009 that "if much of what we have comes to us as the free gift of many generations of historical contribution, there is a profound question as to how much can reasonably be said to be *earned* by any one person, now or in the future." So too, the success of any business person depends not just on this "inherited" technology but on the institutional setting (the rule of law), the existence of a well-educated workforce, and the availability of good infrastructure (transportation and communications). (p. 97–98)

Removing the second result, that workers are paid the value of what they produce, can be done without mortally wounding the orthodox theory of labor markets. However, it would require orthodox economists to admit that capitalism is fundamentally an unfair social system in which workers are systematically paid less than what they produce and owners get more than they deserve. However, as Galbraith observes, because of the tremendous increases in the standard of living, the indictment of "exploiting labor" no longer has the explosive, system-changing potential that it had in the days of Clark. However, removing the second result does severely damage both the liberal and conservative solutions to poverty due to low wages. Increased education and training will no longer guarantee an increase in wages, and neither will working harder at the job site.

The first result, however, is the more important result—not only for the orthodox theory of labor markets but for orthodox theory in general. Both the orthodox micro- and macroeconomics theories will crumble to dust if you remove the assumption of a supply-and-demand labor market that always clears or converges to the natural rate in the long run. There is no feature that is more important, and therefore there should be no assumption in economics that has been more thoroughly and systematically tested than the assumption that labor markets clear or converge to the natural rate. Orthodox economists have been rather uninterested in testing this assumption, and for good reason, as we will see.

References

Akerlof, George, and Janet Yellen. 1986. "Introductions." In *Efficiency Wage Models of the Labor Market*. Edited by George Akerlof and Janet Yellen. Cambridge, UK: Cambridge University Press, 1-21.

Bivens, Josh and Lawrence Mishel. 2015. "Understanding the Historic Divergence Between Productivity and a Typical Worker's Pay." *Economic Policy Institute*. September 2.

Clark, John Bates. 1899, 1956. *The Distribution of Wealth: A Theory of Wages, Interest and Profits*. New York: Kelley & Millman Inc.

Coyle, Diane. 2007. *The Soulful Science: What Economists Really Do and Why It Matters*. Princeton, NJ: Princeton University Press

Drabenstott, Mark, Mark Henry, and Kristin Mitchell. 1999. "Where Have All the Packing Plants Gone? The New Meat Geography in Rural America." Kansas City, MO: Federal Reserve Bank of Kansas City.

Edwards, Richard. 1979. *Contested Terrain: The Transformation of the Workplace in the Twentieth Century*. USA: Basic Books.

Henry, John F. 1995. *John Bates Clark: The Making of a Neoclassical Economist*. New York, NY: St. Martin's Press, Inc.

Mankiw, N. Gregory. 2008. *Principles of Macroeconomics*, 5th ed. Mason, OH: Thomson South-Western

Phelps, Edmund. 1967. "Phillips Curves, Expectations of Inflation and Optimal Unemployment Over Time." *Economica*. August: 254-81.

Robinson, Joan. 1962, 1964. *Economic Philosophy*. Garden City, NY: Anchor Books, Doubleday & Company, Inc.

Salop, Steven. 1986. "A Model of the Natural Rate of Unemployment." In *Efficiency Wage Models of the Labor Market*, edited by George Akerlof and Janet Yellen. Cambridge, UK: Cambridge University Press, 93-101.

Shapiro, Carl, and Joseph Stiglitz. 1986. "Equilibrium Unemployment as a Worker Discipline Device." In *Efficiency Wage Models of the Labor Market*, edited by George Akerlof and Janet Yellen. Cambridge, UK: Cambridge University Press, 45-56.

Solow, Robert. 1986. "Another Possible Source of Wage Stickiness." In *Efficiency Wage Models of the Labor Market*, edited by George Akerlof and Janet Yellen. Cambridge, UK: Cambridge University Press, 41-44

Stiglitz, Joseph. 2013. *The Price of Inequality: How Today's Divided Society Endangers Our Future*. New York: W.W. Norton & Co.

Wolff, Edward. 2009. *Poverty and Income Distribution*, 2nd ed. Chichester, West Sussex, UK: Wiley Blackwell

❖ 11

The Banking System and Poverty

In a book on poverty, it may seem ~~key mech to~~ irrelevant to consider money, money creation, and the banking system. The poor generally can't qualify for bank loans, and many don't have bank accounts. However, orthodox economists have suggested government policies to reduce poverty that are critically dependent on their view of how the banking system functions.

Once again, the heterodox and orthodox models differ considerably, and once again, the orthodox model is built on a couple of highly unrealistic assumptions. As it is with the policies that come from the orthodox model of labor markets, the macroeconomic policies that come from the orthodox model of money creation help the rich rather than the poor and middle class. To evaluate these policies, however, we first need to know how the banking system operates and in particular, how banks create money in the process of making loans.

We'll start by looking at what money is. Then we will layout the two theories of money creation. Once we have this information on hand, we will then turn our attention to the orthodox solutions to poverty that depend on their idea of a "fixed pie of loanable funds."

What is Money?

Money is what we use to purchase goods and services and to pay off debts. Historically, societies have used three types of money—commodity money, representative commodity money, and credit money. Over time, as the confidence in money, banks, and the financial system grows, society tends to move from one form of money to the next.

Commodity money is a form in which the item used as money has the same value in use as it does in exchange. The first commodity monies appear to have been grains (Wray 1990). However, grains are unwieldy and rot over time. Eventually, metal coins were used. The fact that the first monies are commodity monies is not surprising. When the concept of money is new, whatever object we accept in exchange has to be worth at least as much in use as what we give up in case no one else is willing to accept that object as money.

With representative commodity money, the object itself has little or no value, but it can be exchanged for gold or silver that is equal to its face value. In the nineteenth century, banks in the US issued pieces of paper known as bank notes. People could take these notes to the bank that issued them and exchange them for gold or silver coins. Until 1933, currency issued by the US government could also be exchanged for gold.

Credit money—or debt money—refers to "any money, except representative full-bodied [commodity] money, that circulates at a value greater than the commodity value of the material from which it is made" (Goldfeld and Chandler 1986). Like representative commodity money, this money has little or no actual value, but unlike representative commodity money, it cannot be exchanged for gold or silver coins. All of the money currently used in the US—currency, checking accounts, and even our coins—is credit money. Approximately 95% of our money is now in the form of checking accounts.

Another definition of credit money, which is narrower and more technical but useful in thinking about how money is created in a modern capitalist society, is that credit money is "the liability of the issuing bank and is backed by borrowers' liabilities (IOUs) in the bank's possession. The supply of credit money varies with changes in the demand for bank credit" (Moore 2003). Expansions in the money supply come about through increases in the volume of checking accounts that are triggered by increases in the demand for loans by creditworthy customers.

If money is what is used to purchase goods and services, then how do debit cards and credit cards fit into this definition of money? When we pay with a debit card, money comes directly out of our checking accounts. It is like having a reusable plastic check. To understand how credit cards work, we will have to wait until the end of the next section to answer that question.

Two Theories of Money Creation

Among economists, there is no debate about where the creation of money takes place. All economists of every stripe believe that money is created—comes into existence—during the process of banks making loans to their customers, and that money is destroyed—disappears—when bank customers pay back their loans.

What economists disagree on is how much freedom banks have to make loans anytime they choose. To illustrate the difference between the two theories, it may be helpful to think about a metaphor of a dog on a leash. The dog represents the banks. The dog's master, the one holding the leash, is the Federal Reserve, which is often referred to as "the Fed."

In the vision painted by orthodox economists, the master has tight control of the dog who is on a very short leash. The banks can only make loans and create money when the Federal Reserve wishes them to do so. Even though the dog and the business community might be straining to take off and run by making more loans to more people, the master keeps a tight grip. In the orthodox vision, the Fed targets the amount of money they wish to have in the economy. The Fed thus takes great care to make sure that banks don't create more or less money than the targeted amount. While the Fed can change its target, most orthodox analysis assumes that the Federal Reserve keeps its money target constant.

In the heterodox vision, the dog has the ability through asset and liability management to slip out of its collar and run free. The master is not bothered by this. Dog and master are in a field, and as long as the dog is well behaved its running and playing is good for the economy. If the master believes the dog is getting too far afield by making too many loans, he can whistle by increasing interest rates or enforcing regulations to bring the dog back closer to the master. In the heterodox model, banks are free to make loans any time they believe it will be profitable.

To fully understand how money is created in the process of making loans and to fully understand the difference between the heterodox and orthodox theories of money creation we need to learn about a bank's balance sheet.[92]

In an introductory class, there is a strong tendency to simplify the balance sheet to contain only those items that are important for the lesson at hand. For example, the asset side of a real bank balance sheet contains the value of buildings owned by the bank. No introductory textbook includes this item in its balance sheet because it isn't important for explaining how money is created. Therefore, some items are on real bank balance sheets that aren't in the balance sheets used in introductory economics textbooks.

In the heterodox bank balance sheet, there are six items. In the orthodox bank balance sheet, there are only four items. Two items that heterodox economists believe are important for explaining how money is created are completely absent from the orthodox balance sheet. As we shall see, it is the lack of these two items from the orthodox balance sheet that transforms our metaphor from one where the dog runs free to one where the dog is on a short leash.

Balance Sheets

A balance sheet is a statement of the assets and liabilities for a business or household. The sum of assets and the sum of liabilities need to be equal — in balance. With a bank's balance sheet, an asset is what the bank owns, either a physical object like a building or a piece of paper saying someone owes the bank money. A liability is what the bank owes to someone else, such as funds in checking accounts that it owes to its depositors.

Below is the balance sheet of the fictitious Left Bank, where the units are millions of dollars. In order to be able to discuss each asset and liability on both the heterodox and orthodox balance sheets, our balance sheet contains all six items — three items on the asset side and three items on the liability side. The assets are reserves, loans, and T-bills. The liabilities are checking accounts, borrowed funds, and net worth.

Assets

Reserves: In order to have sufficient cash on hand to pay depositors, banks must keep a percentage of their deposits on reserve, either as cash in their vaults or in their accounts at the Federal Reserve. Because reserves don't earn interest, banks face a trade-off. The more reserves they hold, the less revenue they receive. However, the more reserves they hold, the smaller is the chance that the bank is unable to pay depositors if a large number ask for their money at once.

If we leave that decision solely in the hands of individual banks, the amount of reserves will differ considerably from bank to bank. Some place a higher value on profitability, and others value safety. Part of the Federal Reserve's job, however, is to ensure the safety of the banking system as a whole. As a result, the Fed requires all banks to hold a minimum of 10% of their checking account funds on reserve. Anything above that amount is referred to as excess reserves.

Given the low level of excess reserves that are normally held in the US banking system, it is assumed that most banks prefer to hold less than the Fed's minimum, and, therefore, these banks will not hold any excess reserves.

Left Bank just meets its reserve requirement—10% of its $200 million worth of checking accounts is $20 million. Because most banks do not like to hold excess reserves, they lend them out, often on the federal funds market, which is the market where banks borrow and lend to each other.

Loans: In essence, loans are IOUs signed by the bank's customers. They promise to repay the bank the borrowed amount plus interest. Many think of a loan as having two steps—the borrower promising to pay the bank back with interest and then the bank giving money to the borrower. On a balance sheet, however, the item "loans" is just the first step, the promise to repay. The second step, giving the customer money, appears elsewhere on the balance sheet.

T-bills: This is the asset that is not on the orthodox balance sheet. Banks hold a variety of securities, including state and local bonds, Treasury bonds (T-bonds), and Treasury bills (T-bills). A T-bill or a T-bond is a promise by the US Treasury to pay the holder the face value of a bill or bond at particular date. T-bills when sold have a maturity date of one year or less, and for T-bonds, the maturity date is more than one year. Banks can buy and sell securities like these at any time. For simplicity, we assume that in this example, Left Bank only holds T-bills.[93]

Liabilities

Checking accounts: Bank customers can deposit money into either a checking account, which is used primarily for making payments, or a savings account, which is used primarily for earning interest. In essence, checks are promises by the bank to pay the receiver of the check whatever amount is written on the check—as long as the bank customer has sufficient funds in their checking account. Savings accounts are also liabilities, but because they don't play a role in money creation, we will assume that Left Bank only has checking accounts.

Borrowed funds: This is the liability that is not on the orthodox balance sheet. Borrowed funds are funds that the banks borrow on the open market. Banks can borrow from a variety of sources—corporations, fund managers, other banks, the overseas Eurodollar market, and the Federal Reserve. The borrowing of these funds tends to be short-term, from overnight to two years. Bank can readily increase or decrease their level of borrowed funds at any time. For this simple example, Left Bank has only borrowed on the federal funds market — the market where banks borrow and lend to each other.

Net Worth: Net worth, which is also referred to as capital or bank capital, is the difference between a bank's assets and liabilities. It is placed in the liability column so that the balance sheet balances. This is the value of what a bank's stockholders own. A healthy bank generally has a net worth of between 4% and 8% of assets. With its $250 million worth of assets, Left Bank's net worth of $20 million is 8%.

In the next section we will show how money is created in the process of a bank making a loan. We will use the heterodox balance sheet, but we could just as easily use the orthodox balance sheet because T-bills and borrowed funds don't come into play at the moment that new money comes into existence. However, the making of the loan causes the bank—in this case, Left Bank—to have a problem. The difference between our two theories is how they hypothesize banks deal with this problem. The theory that correctly identifies what real banks actually do is the one that has the best chance of being correct.

The Creation of Money

One of the features of a balance sheet is that it always balances, so any time we work with a balance sheet, an excellent internal check of our work is to make sure it balances at every step. As we can see in figure 1 on the next page, the assets and liabilities columns add to $250 million.

We'll assume that Clair Voyant comes to Left Bank and asks for a $10 million loan. The bank asks Clair for a lot of information to determine if she is creditworthy. Her creditworthiness depends on the quality of her

Assets		Liabilities	
Reserves	20	Checking Accts	200
Loans	140	Borrowed Funds	30
T-bills	90	Net worth	20
Total	*250*	*Total*	*250*

Figure 1. Simple balance sheet for Left Bank, in millions of dollars.

business plan, her business experience, and whether the bank believes she will have sufficient demand for her product.

Using information about the business, Left Bank determines that Ms. Voyant is creditworthy, so it approves the loan. Clair then fills out a series of papers, essentially IOUs to the bank, which state when and how much she will repay the bank.

In exchange for these IOUs, Left Bank gives Clair money. It could give her cash out of its vaults, but the money given to borrowers almost always comes in the form of a checking account, and that's what happens here. If Ms. Voyant already has an account at Left Bank, as is normally the case, Left Bank makes the loan by adding $10 million to it. If she doesn't, Left Bank creates a new account and enters $10 million. For example, if Clair had $237,874 in her checking account before the loan, then the bank would type in a 1 and a 0 into the eighth and seventh columns, making the funds in her checking account $10,237,874.

This loan transforms the balance sheet, increasing both loans and checking accounts by $10 million.[94] Figure 2 illustrates these changes, which are shown in bold on the balance sheet. It is worth pointing out that although "loans" is an item on the asset side of the balance sheet, the actual process of making a loan involves both the asset and liability sides. To make a loan, the borrower first promises to repay the bank by signing an IOU. This IOU goes on the asset side. The bank then creates a checking account in the borrower's name, and this goes on the liability side. As we can see, this fits perfectly with Moore's definition of credit money.

Assets			Liabilities		
Reserves	20		**Checking Accts**	**210**	
Loans	**150**		Borrowed Funds	30	
T-bills	90		Net worth	20	
Total	*260*		*Total*	*260*	

Figure 2. Impact of Clair Voyant's loan on the balance sheet for Left Bank, in millions of dollars.

With a few critical keystrokes, checking accounts at Left Bank—and in the US economy—just increased by $10 million. Left Bank created this money out of thin air. Any of the nearly five thousand banks in the US can do the same at any time and for anyone they choose. There is no commodity, no gold, no *anything* to back up this new money. The only thing that holds the system together is the confidence that people have in accepting checks as payment for goods and services.

When you use your credit card to make a purchase, you are getting a loan from a bank. A credit card is a legally binding line of credit. Many businesses set up loan agreements with banks in the form of a line of credit. This allows the firm to borrow from the bank up to a specified amount any time it chooses. The reason for these lines of credit is that a firm's expenditures are often not well matched with its revenue flows. For example, a firm may need to pay workers before it receives the revenue from selling its product. A credit card works similarly except that it's for individuals. When one charges a purchase on a credit card, one is contracting a loan from a bank.[95]

The Heterodox Theory

Looking at figure 2, we notice the Left Bank now has a problem. The amount in checking accounts is $210 million. With a 10% reserve requirement, Left Bank should have $21 million in reserves, but it only has $20 million. That means that Left Bank must increase reserves by $1

Assets		Liabilities	
Reserves	**21**	Checking Accts	210
Loans	150	Borrowed Funds	30
T-bills	**89**	Net worth	20
Total	*260*	*Total*	*260*

Figure 3. Selling $1 million in T-bills and moving it into reserves means that Left Bank again holds 10% of checking accounts in reserve.

million.

In the heterodox theory, banks don't need excess reserves in order to make loans. They can accommodate the needs of their loan customers by adjusting their balance sheets through a process known as asset and liability management. Left bank can increase its reserves in one of two ways. One option is that the bank can sell $1 million in T-bills and put the proceeds into reserves. Figure 3 shows how these changes, in bold, solve the problem.

The other option for Left Bank is to borrow an additional $1 million on the federal funds market and put those proceeds into reserves, as we see in figure 4.

However, what happens to Left Bank's balance sheet when Clair Voyant spends her loan money by purchasing lumber from Uncle Buck to build her psychic supply store? If Uncle Buck also banks at Left Bank, then when he deposits Clair's check, Left Bank deducts $10 million from Ms. Voyant's account and adds it to Uncle Buck's. The total amount of checking deposits at Left Bank has not changed, so nothing extra needs to be done.

If Uncle Buck has a checking account with Right Bank, however, we have a different situation. In that case, Uncle Buck deposits Clair's check at his own bank. Right Bank adds $10 million into Uncle Buck's account, and then it sends the check to Left Bank and asks for the money. Left Bank deducts $10 million from Ms. Voyant's account and sends $10 million from reserves to Right Bank. In this case, instead needing to

Assets		**Liabilities**	
Reserves	21	Checking Accts	210
Loans	150	**Borrowed Funds**	**31**
T-bills	90	Net worth	20
Total	*261*	*Total*	*261*

Figure 4. Borrowing $1 million from the federal funds market and moving it into reserves means that Left Bank again holds 10% of checking accounts in reserve.

raise $1 million, Left Bank now needs to obtain $10 million. However, the process is the same. Left Bank uses asset and liability management to adjust its portfolio to meet whatever situation they face.[96]

As a result, in the heterodox model, banks can make loans and create money any time they believe that a project has a very good chance of being profitable. In this model, banks are free to make loans anytime they choose. Going back to our dog and leash metaphor, asset and liability management allows the dog to slip its collar and run free. Therefore, in the heterodox model, "investment is almost never constrained by a lack of loanable funds, but only by a lack of creditworthy investment projects."

Now let's look at the exact same problem that we started this section with. This time, however, we'll use the orthodox balance sheet. Let's see what effect eliminating T-bills and borrowed funds will have on the economic analysis.

The Orthodox Theory

Having dropped two items off the balance sheet, the first thing we need to do with the orthodox model is to change the numbers from figure 2 slightly to make our balance sheet balance. As is apparent in figure 5, we still have the same basic problem. Left Bank has $210 million in checking accounts and only $20 million in reserve. Under these conditions, what

Assets			Liabilities	
Reserves	20		**Checking Accts**	**210**
Loans	220			
			Net worth	30
Total	240		*Total*	240

Figure 5. The orthodox version of the balance sheet, adapted from figure 2.

can Left Bank do to solve its problem? Nothing! Left Bank will soon be in trouble with the Federal Reserve for being below its reserve requirement.[97] In the orthodox model, banks cannot make additional loans if they don't have the excess reserves to cover those loans.

Where could these excess reserves come from? One possibility is a customer of Left Bank could deposit a check written by a customer of Right Bank. However, this would increase the reserves at Left Bank by decreasing the reserves at Right Bank by the same amount. This would not increase the level of reserves for the banking system as a whole and would not increase the amount of loans in the nation.

Another possibility is that relatives of old Aunt May might find money stuffed into her mattress after she passes away. If the relatives deposit these funds into Left Bank, the reserves at Left Bank will go up without the reserves of any other bank going down. Left Bank can thus increase its loans without any other bank having to decrease their loans. As a nation, however, we can hardly depend on periodic discoveries of mattress money for the expansion of our economy.

The primary source of additional reserves for the banking system is the Federal Reserve. In the orthodox model, in order for the banking system to make additional loans, the Federal Reserve must first supply additional excess reserves. We can now see the metaphor of the dog on a short leash.[98]

The Federal Reserve could increase the level of reserves freely so that there is always large amounts of excess reserves. In such a case, we recreate the metaphor of the dog running freely, with banks making loans anytime they think it will be profitable. However, that is not what the orthodox theory assumes. In that model, the Federal Reserve targets the growth rate of money. By having a target for money growth, the master keeps a tight grip on the dollar amount of loans banks can make.

Unrealistic Assumptions

Two important assumptions are necessary to create the dog on the short leash metaphor, and both are false. The first assumption is actually a set of assumptions that work together. The orthodox theory assumes that banks don't own securities — T-bills — or borrowed funds and that they don't actively manage the assets and liabilities in their portfolios to meet their ever-changing required level of reserves. It's hard to imagine any economist asserting that banks in the real world don't own securities or borrow funds on the open market. No economist who is familiar with banking would ever assert that banks don't actively use asset and liability management to meet their reserve requirement. If banks do actively use asset and liability management — and they do — then they don't need excess reserves to make loans.

The second assumption is that the Federal Reserve targets the money supply. Unfortunately for orthodox economists, the Federal Reserve doesn't do that. The Federal Reserve targets a short-term interest rate — the Federal Funds rate. In the post-World War II period, there are only three years where the Federal Reserve attempted to target the money supply (1979–82).[99] In all the other years, they targeted an interest rate. In so doing, the Fed lets go of any ability that it might have to control the money supply and bank lending.[100] Banks in the real world will therefore make loans to any and all customers that they deem to be creditworthy.[101]

Predictions

If you have model that has an unrealistic assumption, the place to test that model is at a point where the economic analysis is heavily dependent on that assumption. These two unrealistic assumptions give us one of the basic features of the orthodox theory of money creation, that banks are unable to make new loans unless they have excess reserves. This is the feature that we will test.

Legally binding lines of credit[102] and credit cards are different from other types of loans because once negotiated, banks no longer have any control over when the loans occur or how large loans are for—as long as these loans are for less than the customers' credit limits. Because, in the orthodox model, banks can't make loans without excess reserves, the model predicts that either of the following results:

- The banking system will hold large levels of excess reserves in order to be able to meet any surge in loan demand from legally binding lines of credit or credit cards.

- There will be few or no legally binding lines of credit or credit cards in our society.

In the heterodox model, banks don't need excess reserves in order to make loans. Therefore, this model is consistent with an economy where the banking system has little or no excess reserves and has a large number of legally binding lines of credit and credit cards.

As it turns out, the number of lines of credit in our economy is large and so are the number of credit cards. Furthermore, during normal time periods, the level of excess reserves in the banking system has been small. Therefore, the orthodox model mispredicts what happens in our society, and it mispredicts badly. The orthodox theory of a dog on a short leash can never be true in a country with a large number of legally binding lines of credit and with a large number of credit cards. This isn't a small miss by the orthodox model. It goes to the very heart of how our economy works.

On the other hand, the heterodox theory of money creation is perfectly consistent with the existence of legally binding lines of credit and credit cards. If banks believe a customer is creditworthy they will give them a loan. In the heterodox theory, "investment is almost never constrained by a lack of loanable funds, but only by a lack of creditworthy investment projects."

Solutions for Poverty

Having these two theories of money creation in mind, it is now time to see how the orthodox theory is used to generate a series of macroeconomic policy suggestions to reduce poverty. Given that the orthodox theory of money creation is built upon two false assumptions, we shouldn't be surprised that these policy suggestions are highly questionable.

Orthodox economists have suggested the following macroeconomic policies as a way to reduce poverty:

1. Changing from an income tax to a sales tax

2. Reducing the capital gains tax

3. Reducing corporate taxes

4. Reducing the income tax, especially for the rich

5. Eliminating Social Security or Medicare

6. Reducing government spending, thus reducing budget deficits

The basic question that we need to ask is how are these policies are supposed to work. As we will see, the orthodox theory of money creation—the dog on a short leash—plays an important role.

When it comes to discussing economic policies with the general public, economists often use a metaphor rather than arguing with a complex set of graphs or equations. The metaphor orthodox economists often used in discussing banks and money can be labeled as the "fixed pie of loanable funds." This metaphor is a description of the loanable funds market. Businesses, consumers, and the government demand loanable funds. Household and business savings combined with money created by the banking system is the supply of loanable funds. However, as we have seen, orthodox economists assume that the Federal Reserve targets the money supply. Therefore, additional loanable funds created by the banking system will not be forthcoming. This leads to the metaphor of a fixed-pie where there is only so much pie to go around.

Given the size of the pie, banks and other financial firms then allocate these scarce funds to businesses, households, and government. The amount of business investment is thus constrained by the size of the pie. Policies to increase investment must either increase savings—the size of the pie—or reduce the demand for loanable funds by the other two actors. With the latter, what is normally suggested is a reduction in government spending.

The 2017 tax overhaul plan is an example of an actual government policy whose rationale was, at least in part, that it would reduce poverty through the reduction of corporate income taxes. Notice how the fixed-pie metaphor shows up and plays a pivotal role in the mechanism by which this policy is supposed to reduce poverty:

1. Because corporate taxes are lower, profits are higher, and these higher profits flow into the pockets of corporate shareholders.

2. Because shareholders tend to be wealthy and thus have a higher MPS than others in society, savings rise.

3. As savings rise, more money is available for loans as the supply of loanable funds goes up.

4. As the supply of loanable funds increases, interest rates fall.

5. As interest rates fall, investment increases.

6. As investment increases, workers have more and better capital equipment at their fingertips and become more productive.

7. As workers become more productive, wages increase.

8. As wages increase, the number of people who are poor or near poor decreases.

While some of steps in this mechanism are correct, steps three and four are not.[103] These steps depend on the orthodox theory of money creation to produce a theory where the quantity of loanable funds is scarce — the fixed-pie metaphor.

While some are skeptical about how giving more to the wealthy will reduce poverty, the above mechanism has garnered a certain level of support because the fixed-pie of loanable funds metaphor resonates with the general public. The reason it is effective is that for the average person, it describes their daily lives. For most people, expenditures are constrained by income. Unless they borrow money, which will be even more constraining in the future, average citizens face a fixed-pie income. The more they spend in one area, the less they have leftover to spend in other areas. The only way to spend more on housing is either to spend less on food or get a raise. According to orthodox economists, the supply of loanable funds is determined by the savings of households and businesses. If we want more funds for investment, we either need to increase the level of savings or spend less on government.

We know that statements like these are false because real banks have portfolios with securities and borrowed funds. Real banks can and do asset and liability manage their balance sheets. Real banks can and do make loans to any and all customers that they deem creditworthy. In the real world, the supply of loanable funds is not fixed. It expands to whatever size is necessary to support the economy.

The proper metaphor for envisioning the banking system is not a fixed pie but a bathtub.[104] The level of water in the bathtub is the amount of money in the economy — the money supply. Water flows into the bathtub whenever banks make new loans to creditworthy borrowers. Water flows down the drain and out of the bathtub whenever borrowers pay back their loans.[105]

Because banks continuously make loans and customers continuously pay them back, the inflow and outflow of money into and out of the bathtub is constantly occurring. The water level rises when banks make new loans faster than borrowers pay them back, which normally happens during expansions. The water level falls when borrowers pay back their loans faster than banks make new loans, which tends to happen during recessions.

The important point of the bathtub metaphor is that the money supply, the amount of loanable funds, is always at whatever level is required for the functioning of the economy. As the demand for loans by creditworthy businesses expands, the banking system expands the money supply to meet that demand. Investment by firms into new plant and equipment is almost never constrained by a lack of loanable funds.[106] It is only constrained by a lack of creditworthy investment projects.[107]

True Beneficiaries

Many economic policies to reduce poverty have been suggested and enacted based on the fixed-pie of loanable funds metaphor. However, as we have seen, in a modern capitalist banking system, business investment is almost never constrained by a lack of loanable funds. Therefore, policies aimed at increasing investment by increasing the amount of savings or by reducing government spending are ineffective and possibly harmful to society.

While we can understand why the fixed-pie of loanable funds metaphor resonates with the general public, we must ask why orthodox economists would invent a model that is so obviously false. Why would professional economists use the fixed-pie of loanable funds metaphor to advocate to the general public certain policies?

A reasonable first reaction to experts pushing ideas that are clearly false is to wonder if these ideas are serving some powerful constituent in society. A good first step to unravel this mystery, then, is to ask who benefits from these policies.

According to the fixed-pie metaphor, any policy that increases the size of the pie or reduces the demand for loanable funds by consumers or the government results in greater investment. The policies below and ones like them have been suggested to increase investment and lower poverty. Let's look at who benefits from each:

1. Changing from an income tax to a sales tax: If we assume the amount of taxes collected stays the same, the poor and middle class, who spend most of their income, will see their tax burden go up. The rich, who save a higher percentage of their income, will see their tax burden go down.

2. Reducing the capital gains tax and **3. Reducing corporate taxes**: These taxes fall heavily on the rich, so reducing these taxes heavily benefits the rich.

4. Reducing the income tax, especially for the rich: Everyone likes to see their taxes reduced, but if the major emphasis is reducing the taxes of the rich, they are obviously the ones who benefit the most.

5. Eliminating Social Security or Medicare: Eliminating Social Security or Medicare reduces the security of the general population and makes people far more dependent on their employers. The more conservative elements of the business community are in favor of that because it reduces their tax burden and promotes a more subservient workforce.

6. Reducing government spending and budget deficits: Discussion of reducing government spending tends to focus on cutting programs that help the general public. These government spending cuts tend to reduce the security of the poor and middle class.[108]

Looking at who benefits from these policies, we might reasonably conclude that the orthodox theory of money creation and the fixed-pie metaphor were constructed and continue to exist because they are so helpful to the interests of the rich.[109]

Further evidence that orthodox economists use the fixed-pie metaphor to defend the interests of the well-to-do comes from a potential policy that orthodox economists don't advocate. This policy flows naturally from the fixed-pie metaphor, but it works against the interest of the rich: Don't allow people to borrow money for the purchasing of stocks, bonds, or other financial instruments.

Using the fixed-pie metaphor, this policy works the same as a reduction in government spending — it increases investment by reducing the demand for loanable funds by non-business borrowers. However, this policy would hurt those who have the ability to borrow money for the purchasing of stocks and bonds by reducing the amount of stocks and bonds they can purchase. The group that is primarily hurt by this policy is the rich. Therefore, orthodox economists are willing to use the fixed-pie of loanable funds metaphor to advocate for the policies that benefit the rich, but they are unwilling to use the fixed-pie of loanable funds metaphor to advocate for policies that injure the rich.

Conclusion

Orthodox economists primarily use microeconomics to analyze the causes and solutions to poverty. However, there is a set of macroeconomic policies that have been suggested whose goals are, in part, to reduce poverty. These policies are supposed to work by increasing the level of investment. However, for these policies to actually be effective, the orthodox theory of money creation must be true. Unfortunately, this theory rests on two assumptions that are clearly false.

These false assumptions and the orthodox theory that is derived from them create an alternative universe where there is a fixed amount of loanable funds — the fixed-pie of loanable funds metaphor. The level of investment is, as a result, constrained by a lack of loanable funds. The only way to increase investment and reduce poverty in this theory is either to increase the amount of loanable funds by increasing amount of household and business savings or to reduce the demand for loanable funds by non-business entities.

In the heterodox model, these two false assumptions have been removed. In this theory, banks can create loanable funds for whomever they choose. The amount of loanable funds is therefore essentially unlimited as long as banks consider their loan customers to be creditworthy — the bathtub metaphor.[110] In the heterodox model, investment is almost never constrained by a lack of loanable funds, only by a lack of creditworthy business ventures. In the heterodox vision, the policies suggested by orthodox economists would be completely ineffective at increasing investment and completely ineffective at reducing poverty. Not surprisingly, when these two models are tested against reality, the orthodox model fail miserably, while the heterodox model appears accurate.

References

Furey, Kevin. 2013. "A Reading on Money and Money Creation." *Forum for Social Economics* 42, no. 1: 38–58.

Goldfeld, S., & Chandler L. 1986. *The Economics of Money and Banking*. New York: Harper & Row.

Greider, William. 1987. *Secrets of the Temple: How the Federal Reserve Runs the Country*. New York: Simon & Schuster Paperbacks.

Moore, Basil. 1988. Horizontalists and Verticalists: The Macroeconomics of Credit Money. Cambridge: Cambridge University Press.

Moore, Basil. 2003. "Endogenous Money." in *The Elgar Companion to Post Keynesian Economics*, edited by John E. King. Northampton MA: Edward Elgar Publishing, 117-21.

Ravn, Ib. 2015. *"Explaining money creation by commercial banks: Five analogies for public education." Real-world economics review*, Issue 71: 92-111.

Sinkey, Joseph. 1989. *Commercial Bank Financial Management: in the Financial Services Industry*. New York: MacMillan Publishing.

Wray, L. Randall. 1990. *Money and Credit in Capitalist Economies: The Endogenous Money Approach*. Northampton, MA: Edward Elgar.

Appendix – The Loanable Funds Market and Our Two Metaphors

We said that the fixed-pie of loanable funds metaphor, and the bathtub metaphor are simplified depiction of the loanable funds market. For some, the understanding of this chapter is enhanced if our metaphors can be transformed into supply and demand diagrams of the loanable funds market.

As figure 6 below shows, the x-axis in the loanable funds markets is the quantity of loanable funds. The y-axis is the interest rate. The demand for loanable funds, by creditworthy borrowers, is the sum of the demands by businesses, consumers and governments to borrow money. It is assumed that as interest rates go up these groups will reduce the amount they wish to borrow and if interest rates go down, they will increase the quantity they demand. Thus, the demand curve for loanable funds is downward sloping and this will be true for both metaphors.

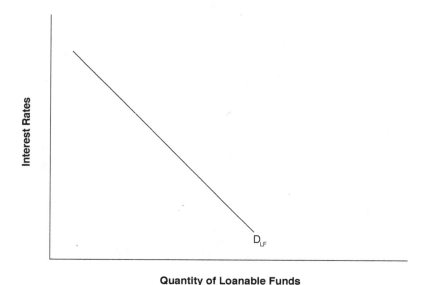

Quantity of Loanable Funds

Figure 6. The demand curve for loanable funds for both metaphors.

But what does the supply curve look like? That depends on which theory of money creation one uses. The supply of loanable funds is the combination of household and business savings plus the amount of loanable funds (money) created by the banking system.

In the orthodox model, the dog on a short leash, the banking system either doesn't add any loanable funds or they add some fixed amount determined by the Federal Reserve's money supply target. In orthodox introductory textbooks it is assumed that the banking system doesn't add any loanable funds. Thus, any changes in the supply of loanable funds will be as a result of changes in household or business savings. If interest rates rise it is assumed that households and businesses will increase their savings by some small amount, and if interest rates go down, they will decrease their saving by some small amount. As a result, the supply curve in the orthodox model is upward sloping and steep, as shown in figure 7.

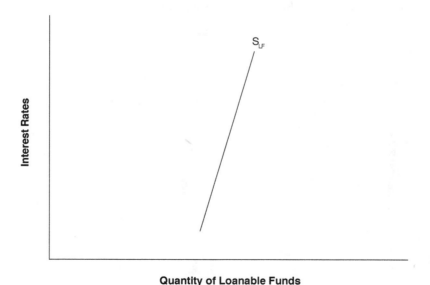

Quantity of Loanable Funds

Figure 7. The supply curve for loanable funds in the fixed-pie of loanable funds metaphor.

In Figures 8 and 9, we can see the standard orthodox results that we obtained with the fixed-pie of loanable funds metaphor. In figure 8, if we cut government spending, this results in less government borrowing, and the demand curve for loanable funds shifts down. At the original interest rate i_0 this results in a surplus of loanable funds. Market mechanisms then kick in and this causes a decline in interest rates and an increase in borrowing by households and businesses. The borrowing by business is assumed to be for investment--the purchasing of new plant and equipment. Thus, a decrease in government spending leads to an increase in investment. In the long-run, this is supposed to lead to an increase in the average standard of living and to a reduction in poverty, as the MP_L and VMP_L are supposed to increase with the increase in investment. An increase in government spending would have the opposite effect, increasing interest rates and "crowding out" investment.

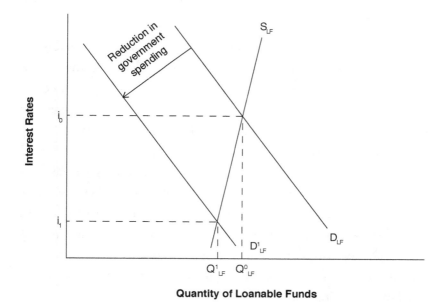

Quantity of Loanable Funds

Figure 8. The effect of a decrease in government spending in the fixed-pie of loanable funds metaphor.

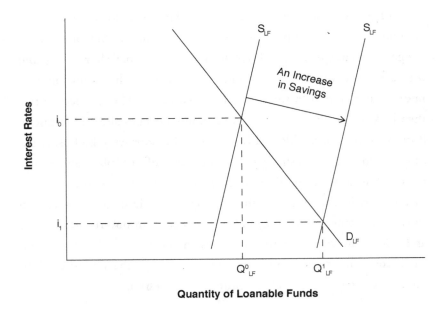

Figure 9. The effect of an increase in savings in the fixed-pie of loanable funds metaphor.

In figure 9, a decrease in corporate taxes leads to an increase in saving, and thus an increase in the supply of loanable funds. The result is a decrease in interest rates and an increase in borrowing by both households and businesses. Once again in the orthodox model, the suggested policy will increase investment, which will increase our standard of living and decrease poverty.

While we can see the fixed-pie of loanable funds results in these loanable funds market diagrams, it must be remembered that these results are dependent on the assumptions of the orthodox model: that banks can't and don't asset and liability manage their balance sheets, and that the Federal Reserve targets the money supply. Both assumptions are necessary to obtain the steep, positively sloping supply of loanable funds curve, and both assumptions are false.

In the heterodox model it is assumed that banks can and do asset and liability manage their balance sheets in order to meet their reserve

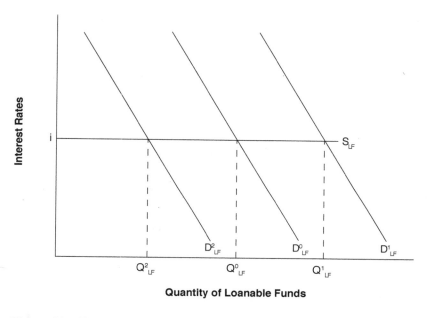

Figure 10. The effects of an increase (D^1_{LF}) and a decrease (D^2_{LF}) in government spending in the bathtub metaphor

requirement. Further, it's assumed that the Federal Reserve targets an interest rate. In that case, the supply curve of loanable funds is a horizontal line, as shown in figure 10. Here we can see the bathtub metaphor. The quantity of loanable funds is whatever creditworthy borrowers demand. If government borrowing increases or decreases in this model, the amount of loanable funds simply increases or decreases to meet that in the demand. It has no effect on the ability of households or businesses to borrow money. Investment is never constrained by a lack of loanable funds; investment is never crowded out by government spending.

Furthermore, cutting taxes to increase savings would have no effect on the availability of loanable funds. More saving would reduce the need for bank loans, but in figure 10 and bathtub metaphor, the level of loanable funds is always whatever level is demanded by creditworthy borrowers. Thus, policies to increase savings or to decrease government spending would be completely ineffective at increasing investment.

❖ 12

[handwritten: not to do this chapter. for exam]

The Consequences
of Being Wrong

When the purpose of economic analysis is to develop public policy, a primary question should always be how much damage would result from using solutions generated by an incorrect model. Economists rarely if ever answer this question, but that is what we will do in this chapter for all three of our perspectives — the heterodox model, the conservative orthodox model, and the liberal orthodox model.

We have no history of any of these programs ever being fully implemented.[111] As a result, there is a sense that we're engaged in an exercise of science fiction writing, especially when dealing with the liberal orthodox perspective. However, by thinking within models, we can at least get a sense of possible consequences for implementing policies that are based on the solutions of an incorrect model.

But what is more important here is that this chapter gives us another opportunity to practice thinking within models. Given the models they use and their starting assumptions about human nature, all three perspectives are logically consistent. We have used these models to generate solutions, and then we have observed how, with each perspective, these solutions have led to the elimination of poverty. It has been like reading fairy tales where the knight in shining armor (economic policy) always saves the damsel in distress (the poor).

In this chapter, we switch from fairy tales to horror stories, in which government policy goes badly wrong. This chapter provides us with another chance to use our models to determine the effects of government policy.

Heterodox Solutions

Suppose that we implement solutions from the heterodox model, and it then turns out that the orthodox model of labor markets is actually the correct model. If the orthodox model is correct, then resources are scarce. There is the full utilization of both labor and capital. Society is at full employment or the natural rate of unemployment. Heterodox economists, on the other hand, believe that unemployment can be lowered further. If the orthodox model is correct, what damage would the heterodox solutions cause?

One part of the heterodox solution is decreasing unemployment by increasing aggregate demand. To keep this simple, let's achieve that by increasing government spending. Once the policy is implemented, the demand for goods and services is greater than the nation's ability to produce them. The demand is now at a point that is outside the PPF. The nation thus faces shortages in both the goods and services markets and labor markets. The result is an increase in the inflation rate.

Inflation objectively makes borrowers such as mortgage owners better off, while making lenders such as banks and the wealthy worse off. Subjectively, however, the vast majority of the population dislikes inflation. Inflation injects a degree of anxiety and uncertainty into everyone's lives. While people may be objectively better off, for many of these people, the

benefits are more than offset by the psychological costs inflicted by inflation. Higher inflation rates are thus politically unpopular.

However, let's assume that the backers of this policy find an excuse to
not blame the increase in inflation on the increase in aggregate demand.
In the case of the heterodox solution to poverty, they do not have to look
far for a likely scapegoat. Another part of the heterodox solution is a
sizable increase in the minimum wage. Everyone predicts that an increase
in the minimum wage will increase in inflation at least for the first year.
The effect of a one-time increase in the minimum wage on inflation will
disappear quickly, but it still provides a plausible explanation for inflation. Policymakers will use that explanation to push aside arguments that
inflation is the result of the demand for goods and service being greater
than what society can supply (AD > AS). This allows the policy to continue.

However, according to orthodox theory, if aggregate demand continuously exceeds aggregate supply, then the rate of inflation continuously climbs (Friedman 1968). If the heterodox policy is implemented
in the current inflationary climate, with inflation averaging around 2%
per year, then based on the events of the late 1960s to the early 1980s,
we might assume that when the inflation rate climbs to between 5% and
10%, the political blowback will finally end the policy. Leaning on the
side of maximum damage caused by the heterodox policy, let's assume the
inflation rate climbs to 10%.

The two groups most hurt by inflation are those on fixed incomes
and lenders. The first group is made up of people who have partial or fully
fixed incomes. Those who are retired, for example, may receive pension
income that is a fixed dollar amount that doesn't adjust with inflation.
As prices go up, what they can buy with their fixed income goes down.

While this first group is not unimportant politically, they don't
have the same clout as the second group, the lenders—banks and the
wealthy. If the inflation rate becomes greater than the interest rate, then
the money lenders are repaid will purchase less in the way of goods and

service than the original money they lent out. Lenders are essentially losing money by lending it out. These are institutions and individuals of great political influence. We can assume that this group will react to the failed heterodox policies by mounting a major push to return inflation rates to their previous levels.

The Federal Reserve currently sees itself as the institution primarily responsible for fighting inflation. To restore the nation to the former low levels of inflation, the Federal Reserve will most likely need to throw the economy into recession by significantly increasing interest rates. The higher the inflation rate, the harder the Federal Reserve is going to have to squeeze the economy. In the worst-case scenario, where inflation rates end up near 10%, we are likely to see a recession like a double-dip recession of the early 1980s, which had a peak unemployment rate over 10%.

Overall, the damage from instituting the heterodox solutions when the orthodox theory of labor markets is correct can be broken down into four components.

1. Damage done by inflation: More people are better off monetarily because the mortgage payments of homeowners now constitute a smaller percentage of their budgets. However, the main costs of inflation are psychological. Almost everyone becomes anxious due to uncertainty caused by higher rates of inflation. The reason for the anxiety is real. Assuming zero growth in the economy, the average increase in people's income is equal to the increase in inflation. However, there is nothing to guarantee that your income will increase by this average. It could be more, or it could be less. Therefore, people worry that inflation will reduce their standard of living, that their wages won't keep up with the rising prices of goods and services. While psychological costs cannot be measured, they are nonetheless very real.

2. Damage done by the recession that follows: With recessions, we get an increase in unemployment, business failures, foreclosures, and poverty. That leads to increases in robberies, heart attacks, strokes, murders, child abuse, and spousal abuse. The deeper the recession, the worse these problems become. It is possible that the recession that following a failed heterodox policy could be deep. It depends on how high inflation went and on how high the Federal Reserve decides they need to raise interest rates to fight that inflation.

3. Increases in the federal budget deficit and national debt: Because labor markets are at full employment outside of the PSE in the inner cities, Appalachia, and Native American reservations, the increase in government spending does not increase employment. Therefore, government expenditures are a waste because the money spent doesn't accomplish the goal of lowering poverty. In addition, the federal government has higher expenditures after the failed anti-poverty programs end because the Federal Reserve's higher interest rates cause the government to pay out more in interest payments on the money it borrows to finance the national debt. Both the federal budget deficit and the national debt would rise.

4. Crowding out of the private sector: Because all resources are fully employed, the only way the federal government can add new programs is to bid resources away from the private sector. Thus, the public sector gets larger, and the private sector becomes smaller. For many, especially conservatives, this is considered an undesirable result.

Conservative Orthodox Solutions

The conservative orthodox solution to poverty is to eliminate all government aid programs to the poor and near poor. According to conservatives, government aid programs enable the poor to be lazy. If these programs are removed, the poor have no one but themselves to rely on. They are thus forced to get jobs and then work hard to keep them. For those who have jobs and are still poor, eliminating government aid programs like the Supplemental Nutritional Assistance Program forces these individuals to not be lazy. They work harder and become more productive in order to receive a livable wage.

For the conservative solution to work, there must be jobs for the poor to obtain, and higher productivity must lead to higher wages. However, if the heterodox theory of labor markets is correct, then even before the implementation of the conservative orthodox solution, there are more job seekers than there are jobs. The elimination of government assistance programs will result in a decrease in government spending that further exacerbates the situation by causing aggregate demand to decrease. This further reduces employment at the same time as the number of job seekers is rising. Therefore, in a world where the number of job seekers outnumbers the number of jobs, the implementation of the conservative solution increases the number of job seekers while decreasing the number of jobs. For those who don't have a job, what little income the state provided will now be stripped away. Poverty will increase and deepen.

The poor, however, will not allow themselves and their children to starve without a fight. They will attempt to obtain food and income any way they can. Because the legal way, getting a job, is not available, many will turn to their only other alternative—crime. A crime wave will thus ensue, and given the number of jobless adults on public assistance, it is likely to be a large crime wave. If we add to this group those who are involuntarily working part-time at low wages and receiving some form of public assistance, the crime wave grows even larger.

We assume that with the first appearance of a crime wave, the policymakers who implemented this policy will not change course. They will find some rationale for continuing the policy. We can easily envision Senator Soulless giving a speech that goes something like this: "Some of the poor are so lazy that they won't or can't get a job. So rather than doing the hard work required, they have taken the easy way out by pursuing a life of crime. But we shouldn't be bullied into giving these criminals public assistance. We should simply build more prisons. In the beginning, the elimination of welfare will be hard, but for the benefit of all, we need to soldier on."

The crowd may cheer its approval of the senator's passion, but as the new anti-poverty program continues, crime will also continue to increase. It won't just affect poor neighborhoods, either. Increasing fear will seep into every corner of the country. Everyone will feel it.

While the increased crime will become an electoral topic, it is unclear when the conservative solutions can be reversed. Almost everyone is against higher inflation. Once heterodox anti-poverty programs are seen as the cause of the higher inflation, building a political movement to end those programs is relatively easy. With crime, however, it will take longer to understand that the cause of the crime is a lack of jobs rather than lazy or corrupt people. Reversing the anti-poverty policies of conservative economists will most likely take a long time.

The damage from instituting the conservative orthodox solution when the heterodox theory of labor markets is true can be broken down into five parts.

1. Increases in unemployment and poverty: Remembering the simple Keynesian model, a decrease in government spending causes aggregate demand to go down, real GDP to go down, and unemployment to go up. As a result, poverty will increase. If the money saved by cutting social safety net programs is spent on other government programs, there will be no fall in aggregate demand or increase in poverty. However, this is unlikely to happen as it goes against the conservative ethos of small government.

2. Increases in crime: Beyond the damage done to those who are assaulted and robbed, whole neighborhoods will be plagued with drugs, prostitution, and violence. There are also psychological costs from the increased fear and mistrust of strangers. The entire nation will become a less trusting and less pleasant place to live.

3. Social division: The conservative solution will increase the social divisions that already exists. The elimination of these programs will make the poor feel as if the rich have abandoned them. With the increase in crime, the rich will become ever more fearful of the poor. Moreover, because the poverty rates are higher in black and Latinx neighborhoods, minorities will feel like white America no longer cares what happens to them. As crime rates in those neighborhoods increase, the distrust of minorities by white middle-class America will also increase.

4. Increase in the proportion of the population that is incarcerated: New prisons will have to be built. If this is financed by cutting other government programs, then this is another loss of useful government services. What may be of even more significance is a greater proportion of the population will turn their inventiveness and mental energies to criminal pursuits.

5. Loss of social services: Not only will there a loss of income from public assistance, but medical care provided by state Medicaid programs will be gone. A guaranteed level of food provided by the Supplemental Nutritional Assistance Program will vanish. If households cannot fully replace these services and income through criminal activity, then the provision of these critical goods will now compete with other household needs. With the meager budgets of the poor and near-poor, life will become harder, meaner, and more anxiety-ridden for these adults and their children. For young children, high levels of stress and a poor diet also impairs their neural development and can affect the architecture of their brains and central nervous systems in a variety of ways that affect memory, language development, cognition, and socio-emotional skills (U of M 2016, CEA 2016). We will thus have an even larger than normal subgroup of less capable citizens, and the reduction in quality food and medical care, on average, will take years off their life spans.

Over the past forty-five years, there have been a couple of time periods — 2001-07 and 2017-19 — when conservatives controlled both houses of Congress and the presidency. However, conservatives have never made a serious attempt to pass a bill containing the conservative orthodox economists' solution to poverty. We should suspect that one reason for this inaction is that many conservative politicians fear that the above effects would be the actual outcome.

Liberal Orthodox Solutions

The liberal orthodox solution is essentially a sizable expansion of existing government programs. The cost will vary depending on the exact programs in their solution. However, liberal economists have rarely, if ever, expensed out the full cost of eliminating poverty.

In this section, we make some assumptions about the expense and damage of implementing the liberal orthodox solutions when the heterodox model of labor markets is correct. What follows does not include Medicaid expenditures or any estimates as to what would happen to Medicaid expenditures if poverty is eliminated.[112]

In 2016, approximately twenty-three million working-age adults lived below the poverty line. In the liberal solution, all would receive substantial levels of government expenditures either directly or indirectly.[113] Estimating the per-person cost of eliminating poverty is largely a guess. At $5,000 per person per year, these programs would cost $115 billion per year, or 3.7% of total federal government expenditures for the 2016 fiscal year. At $10,000 per person per year, the costs would be $230 billion, or 7.4% of total federal government expenditures.

If these programs really eliminate poverty, then some might think that they are a bargain. According to liberals, the cost of some of these programs will fall over time because the initial successes of the education and training programs result in fewer individuals who need education and job training.

Evaluating the damage caused by implementing the liberal orthodox solutions when the heterodox model is correct depends on how these programs are financed. One option is for the federal government to reduce other government programs so that total change in government spending and aggregate demand is zero. At the other extreme, the federal government could borrow the money to pay for these programs, greatly increasing the federal budget deficit and the national debt. This method of financing leads to a significant increase in aggregate demand. The government can also choose some in-between position, but for our purposes, we'll focus just on these two extreme options.

No Increases in Government Spending

There are numerous elements to the liberal orthodox solution. Some of these elements are consistent with the solutions suggested by heterodox economists. Giving sufficient support for those who can't work is part of the heterodox solution. Raising the after-tax wages of those who are working at low-wage jobs is also part of the heterodox solution to reduce poverty from low wages.[114] However, the main weapon for combating long-term poverty in the liberal orthodox theory is to increase the VMP_L of the poor through formal education and job training programs. If the heterodox model is correct, these programs will be completely ineffective at reducing poverty.

Formal education and job training programs will fail for two reasons. First, improved education and job training do not increase the number of jobs. Second, they do not change the wages paid to workers because these programs will not change the percent of jobs in the primary and secondary markets. In the heterodox model, workers' wages depend on the jobs they hold. It is not equal to their productivity ($VMP_L \neq W$). These programs have no effect on either the shape or height of Hotel America, our strangely shaped income hotel. As a result, efforts to improve education may change the characteristics of those who occupy each room, but they do not change the number of rooms on each floor. These programs are completely ineffective at increasing employment and completely ineffective at increasing wages and thus are completely ineffective at reducing poverty.

In the zero-change funding option, aggregate demand and employment stay the same. The funding comes from cutting or eliminating government programs that provide positive benefits to society, such as programs that provide loans to college students or funding to repair roads and bridges, and replacing them with questionable anti-poverty programs. Given the size of the liberal orthodox solution, that means cutting or eliminating a large number of programs that provide benefits to U.S. citizens. It may take quite a long time, however, before people see that these new programs are ineffective. There are three reasons for this.

First, because there are parts of the liberal solution that are the same as the heterodox solution, these parts of the liberal solution are effective and poverty rates will fall. While improvements beyond that point will not be forthcoming, this initial victory propels the general program forward for a time.

Second, business cycles make it difficult to separate out changes in the level of poverty that are caused by the implementation of a new anti-poverty program and the changes that naturally occur because of the business cycle. In the business cycle, expansions are longer than recessions, so it's more likely that a new anti-poverty program is initiated during an expansion. Just as we saw after the implementation of a new, conservative-leaning program in 1996, there is a natural tendency for proponents of the program to credit the program for all of the reduction in poverty rather than to credit the expansion in the economy and the resulting increase in the number of jobs. This may delay for years the recognition of the ineffectiveness of new educational and training programs.

Third, while educational and training programs have no effect on poverty, they do shuffle who gets which rooms in our income distribution hotel. Those who operate training programs can justify their existence by tracking what happens to those who go through their programs. If the training is at all helpful, those who go through it have an increased chance of getting a job that pays enough to get them out of poverty. Those running the training programs can then proclaim that each of their graduates who has gotten a job has reduced poverty by one.

However, because the training programs don't create any jobs, for each individual pulled out of poverty, there is another individual who is bumped *into* poverty.[115] Because these programs can point to individuals who have been pulled out of poverty, it may take a long, long time for people to recognize that educational and training programs just rearrange who is in poverty without affecting the level of poverty. Therefore, these programs may damage the US economy for years and years.

Increases in Government Borrowing

If we finance the programs of the liberal orthodox economists by borrowing, then those programs will be more successful—but not for the reasons expounded by liberal orthodox economists. The successful parts of the liberal program discussed in the prior section still hold true. In addition, poverty rates will fall because the increase in aggregate demand causes unemployment to fall.

The liberal program thus looks like a poorly executed version of the heterodox solution:

- Help for the disabled and for young mothers
- Added after tax income for low wage workers
- A large decrease in unemployment due to a large increase in government spending

What is missing from most liberal orthodox solutions is the employer of last resort function played by PSE programs. Their solutions also make no attempt at producing a full employment society with the excess capacity necessary to allow the economy to grow during expansions. Because increasing the after-tax income of low-wage workers is paid for by the taxpayer, their programs are also more expensive. Perhaps most importantly, while the heterodox solution uses government spending for things that improve society beyond just increasing employment, a large portion of the government spending in liberal solutions is for relatively worthless job training.

Consequences

The successes and damages from instituting the liberal orthodox solution when the heterodox theory of labor markets is true can be broken down into four consequences:

1. Reduction in poverty for those who can't or shouldn't work: Supporting those who can't work or shouldn't work is successful at reducing poverty. This provision is essentially the same in both the liberal orthodox and heterodox solutions, and it is aimed at supporting those who are disabled and single parents with children below the age of X.

2. Reduction in poverty due to low wages: Efforts to increase after-tax wages for the poor are successful at reducing poverty from low wages. However, there is a difference between liberal orthodox and heterodox solutions. Most liberals suggest either employer subsidies or Earned Income Tax Credits. The cost of both programs falls on the government. Heterodox economists suggest increasing the minimum wage, whose cost falls directly on businesses — and to the extent that business can pass along these costs, it falls indirectly on consumers. [116] For liberal orthodox economists, the question again becomes how these government expenditures are financed. The options and the consequences are the same as we discussed earlier.

3. Ineffective training programs: Educational and training programs are ineffective at reducing national poverty rates. If educational and training programs are financed by cutting other government programs, the cost is the loss of a massive amount of government services in exchange for programs that have no effect in lowering the national poverty rate. That is a large loss to society.

If educational and training programs are financed by borrowing, the cost is a significant increase in the size of the national debt and in the interest payments made to the holders of that debt. As these expenditures increase, the federal government must either cut into other government programs or increase taxes. A benefit of this method of finance is that the poverty rate falls because aggregate demand rises. Unemployment rates fall because these programs employ people to give education and job training to the poor.

It may take the public a long time to understand the damaging effect of training programs. As a result, these ineffective programs may continue for many years. Regardless of how they are financed, they damage the US economy and that damage could continue for a long time.

4. More educated population: While formal education programs do not reduce poverty, there are a number of social benefits from a more educated population. Businesses benefit when they have more educated workers to choose from. Society benefits from the greater inventiveness that a better educated population provides. In theory, a more educated population will also produce more informed voters, although given the corporate news media that feed us information that's not likely to happen.

Over the past seventy years, the US has instituted many, if not all, of the anti-poverty programs suggested by liberal orthodox economists but at levels far short of what is necessary to end poverty if the liberal orthodox economists are correct. The size of these programs changes with the political winds. They tend to be cut but not eliminated during conservative time periods and expanded but not fully funded during liberal time periods.[117]

Over the past forty-five years, there have been several time periods — 1977-81, 1993-95 and 2009-11 — when liberals have controlled both houses of Congress and the presidency, but liberals have never made a serious attempt to pass a bill containing a sufficient level of funding to produce the liberal orthodox economists' solution to poverty. We should suspect that liberal politicians fear that suggesting an expensive anti-poverty program is a sure path to electoral defeat.

It is important to recognize that there is no economic theory that says that the approach of the last seventy years has any hope of solving the problem of poverty. Those who have instituted these programs are not attempting to eradicate poverty. They are only trying to manage the level of poverty. It is a cynical balancing act, providing enough support so that the poor don't riot but not so much that the taxpayers revolt at the voting booth.

References

Council of Economic Advisors. 2016. *Economic Report of the President, 2016*. Washington D.C.: Council of Economic Advisors.

Domhoff, G. William. 1983. "The New Class War," *Social Policy*, Winter.

Friedman, Milton. 1968. "The Role of Monetary Policy." *American Economics Review*, 72: 1–24.

Jenkins, J. Craig, and Barbara Brents. 1989. "Social Protest, Hegemonic Competition, and Social Reform: A Political Struggle Interpretation of the Origins of the American Welfare State." *American Sociological Review*, 54. 6.

Piven, Frances Fox, and Richard A. Cloward. 1971, 1993. *Regulating the Poor: The Functions of Public Welfare*. New York, NY: Vintage Books.

University of Minnesota Libraries. 2016. *Social Problems: Continuity and Change*. http://open.lib.umn.edu/socialproblems/.

❖ 13

Testing the Models

For a model to be effective at discovering the causes and developing solutions to social problems, it must be able to mimic the actions of the real world. If it can't, then the solutions that the model generates have little or no chance of being successful.

We should not assume that "experts" always choose the right model or that their solutions always make the situation better. In the 1980s and 1990s, the International Monetary Fund (IMF) had a long and awful record of suggesting or requiring debtor nations to pursue economic policies that turned out to be disastrous. The reason those policies turned out so badly is because of the unrealistic economic models used by the IMF.

Our focus has been to determine, from the point of view of an economist, the causes of and the solutions to poverty. We have used two very different economic models to analyze poverty, and those models produce very different solutions. Which path should we follow? The model that stands the best chance of eliminating poverty is the model that best mimics the actions of the real world. Our goal in this chapter is to determine which model does a better job of predicting economic outcomes and explaining how the real world works.

What to Test

The predictions of heterodox and orthodox economists are based on their respective models of labor markets. The heterodox business cycle model says that rising costs and the amplifying effects normally bring expansions to an end before reaching full employment. There are thus always or almost always more people looking for work than there are jobs. The segmentation theory also predicts that wages tend not to fall during recessions.

In the orthodox model, two market mechanisms force nominal wages down when unemployment occurs. These market forces act to reestablish either full employment or the natural rate of unemployment. They also drive the economy back a point of scarcity on the PPF. As we discovered earlier, these mechanisms for market clearing are strongly dependent on unrealistic assumptions.

In economics, the gold standard for testing models is to determine how well the model *predicts* real world events. For example, the orthodox model predicts that when unemployment is high—as occurs during a recession—that nominal wages will fall. However, for the majority of the scientific world, the gold standard for testing models is to determine how well the model *explains* how the real world works. A model should be able to explain, for example, why employers form internal labor markets or why firms give yearly performance evaluations.

The distinction between predictions and explanations is not as clear-cut as it may seem. What makes something a prediction and something else an explanation is hard to separate. Models do both. They explain how the real world works, and they make predictions about outcomes of certain events. In the orthodox model, there is the feature that employees and not employers determine the number of hours that employees work. Do we consider this a prediction of the model or do we consider it an explanation of how the real world works? It isn't clear which category it belongs to. However, keeping this difficulty in mind, we will first look at two predictions of our models:

Two predictions:

1. What happens to nominal wages during recessions?
2. In the long-run, do labor markets converge to full employment
   or the natural rate?

There are two tests for this second prediction:

1. A comparison of vacancy rates and unemployment rates

2. An analysis of the pattern of unemployment rates over the business cycle

We will then look at three explanations of our models:

1. Why do firms form internal labor markets, and why do internal labor markets have certain features?

2. Who determines how many hours an employee works?

3. Observing the use of capital, does the US economy face scarcity or is it an excess capacity society?

Testing the Wages Prediction

The first prediction we will test is the prediction of what happens to nominal wages during recessions.

The orthodox model predicts that nominal wages fall when labor supply exceeds labor demand — when there is a surplus of labor.[118] It is difficult to find a method for determining when there is a surplus of labor that all economists agree upon. However, most agree that in the depths of a recession, there is a substantial surplus of labor. If the orthodox model is correct, we should observe a decrease in wages during the high unemployment periods that occur with recessions. This prediction holds true for both full employment and natural rate orthodox economists. Furthermore, the deeper the recession, the greater the surplus, so the more wages should fall.

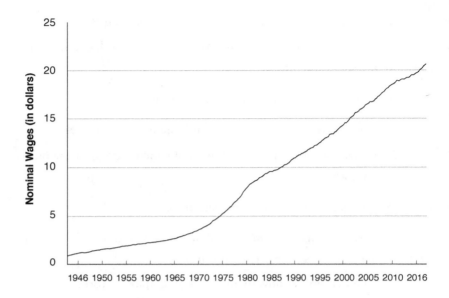

Figure 1. Nominal wages, 1946–2016.

While it is not as clear-cut, the heterodox model predicts that the likelihood of wages falling during a recession in the post-World War II period is small. This is because a large percentage of jobs have wage-setting mechanisms that don't allow for a decline in wages. These wage-setting mechanisms covered few jobs before the late 1930s, but they cover a large percentage of jobs after World War II.

The first wage-setting mechanism is internal labor markets, which contain the majority of jobs in America. As Wolf (2009) points out, the internal consistency of their wage structure is more important than external consistency. Wages in an internal labor market thus tend not to fall with high levels of unemployment. Employers may feel no urgency to raise wages under those conditions, but they steer clear of demoralizing their workers by lowering their wages. For efficiency reasons, these firms don't wish to risk an increase in turnover or damage to worker moral, which would result if nominal wages were decreased.

The second wage-setting mechanism is the minimum wage. In secondary labor markets, a large portion of jobs have wages that are influ-

Start	End	Fall
1949 Quarter I ($1.26)	1949 Quarter IV ($1.243)	1.30%
1954 Quarter I ($1.667)	1954 Quarter II ($1.653)	0.80%
1962 Quarter II ($2.27)	1962 Quarter III ($2.263)	0.30%
2011 Quarter I ($18.933)	2011 Quarter III ($18.883)	0.30%
2012Quarter II ($19.063)	2012 Quarter III ($19.05)	0.08%

Figure 2. During most recessions nominal wages increased, but in a few recessions (shown above) nominal wages fell modestly

enced or solely determined by the minimum wage, and the minimum wage has never gone down. The real minimum wage may go down but not the nominal minimum wage.

These two groups of jobs, those in internal labor markets and those affected by the minimum wage, make up a large percentage of the US workforce. Therefore, the chance that the overall wage rate for the nation will fall during a recession is small. If it does, we would expect the decline to be minor.

Our two models thus have very different predictions as to what happens to wages during recessions. The orthodox model predicts that wages will fall during and immediately after recessions when unemployment is high. The heterodox model predicts that wages will tend not to fall, and that if they do, they will not fall by very much.

We can test these predictions by looking at nominal wages, as shown in figure 1. Figure 1 presents the average hourly earnings of production and nonsupervisory employees, not seasonally adjusted, from the Bureau of Labor Statistics for the years 1946 to 2017. The original data is monthly, from which quarterly data was calculated.

This time period contains eleven recessions, three of which were very deep. As we can see, there are no significant declines in wages. While it may appear that wages continuously rose, they did fall during four recessions. However, as figure 2 shows, wages didn't fall for very long, and they didn't fall by very much.[119] The data on nominal wages solidly rejects the predictions of the orthodox model and is consistent with the predictions of the heterodox model.

Testing the Employment Prediction

The second prediction is whether, in the long run, labor markets converge to full employment or the natural rate of unemployment. We will test the orthodox and heterodox predictions with two sets of data—a comparison of vacancy rates and unemployment rates, and then an analysis of the pattern of unemployment rates over the business cycle.

Vacancy Rate Data

By the standard definition, equilibrium in a labor market occurs when the market achieves a wage where there is neither excess supply nor excess demand for labor. At that wage, everyone who wants a job has a job, and every firm that wishes to hire an employee has an employee to hire. This definition works well for static societies, but modern capitalist societies are dynamic. People are always in the process of leaving or entering the labor market, and firms are always in the process of expanding or shrinking. Even at full employment, there will be people who want work but do not have jobs, and there will be firms with unfilled job openings.

How should full employment be defined for a dynamic society? The definition that best fits an economy with a supply-and-demand labor market is one attributed to William Beveridge (1945): full employment occurs when the number of job vacancies equals the number of unemployed.[120] One method for determining whether labor markets clear is thus to compare vacancy and unemployment rates.[121] The unemployment rate where the number of unemployed equals the number of job vacancies is sometimes referred to as the full-employment unemployment rate (FEUR). US vacancy rates data can be broken into two time periods, before and after December 2000.

Prior to December 2000

In a 1983 *American Economic Review* article, Katharine Abraham analyzes the results of six studies between 1964 and 1980, that collected data on vacancies. Some of the studies were national, some covered particular states, and one was Canadian. Abraham discusses seven reasons why results from vacancy rate surveys tend to underestimate the number of vacancies, and she corrects for each. In her opinion, these adjustments are "very generous." In five of the studies, the results suggest the FEUR occurs at or below 3%. In the sixth study, the FEUR is between 3.6% and 4.0%.

While we can't extrapolate these results to other times or places with complete confidence, they do raise a warning flag for those who assume that labor markets operate like supply-and-demand markets. Over the past 60 years, the unemployment rate has never been below 3% and has only been below 4% during three periods, 1966–70, 2000, and 2018–19. As a check, Abraham uses an indirect method of estimating the unemployment to vacancy ratio. The results of this estimate are consistent with the direct measures of vacancies. She concludes her article by saying:

> Taken as a whole, the information compiled suggests that both the number of unemployed persons and the number of job seekers have consistently been much larger than the number of vacant jobs. If it could be assumed that the vacancy rate/unemployment rate relationships observed in the available survey data mirrored the vacancy rate/unemployment rate relationship prevailing in the United States over the same time period, reasonable estimates would be that there were roughly 2.5 unemployed persons for every vacant job during the middle 1960s, and an average of close to 4.0 unemployed persons per vacant job during the early 1970s and an average 5.0 or more unemployed persons

for every vacant job during the latter part of the 1970's. . . . In most situations, large reduction in the aggregate unemployment rate will only be achieved if more jobs can be create. . . . The most standard approach to new job creation is obviously aggregate demand stimulation. (p. 722)

The implication of Abraham's conclusion is that labor markets either don't operate as supply-and-demand markets, or, if they do, they adjust so slowly to equilibrium that it would be best not to use a supply-and-demand labor market in an economic model. Her study casts doubt on most of the macroeconomic and microeconomic models that have dominated orthodox economics for years.

To defend the use of supply-and-demand labor market models, there are two avenues for legitimately questioning the implications of Abraham's study. First, her study is dependent on the accuracy of her estimates of the vacancy rate. As mentioned before, vacancy rate data is normally biased low, and Abraham makes adjustments to overcome this bias. According to Abraham, if anything her adjustments overcompensate for this downward bias. However, if one can find a legitimate reason for believing her adjustments are too small, then one can cast doubt on her conclusions. Second, we can argue that the FEUR is much higher in periods not covered by Abraham's study.

What was the reaction of economists to Abraham's article? Did they produce a reason for believing her estimates of vacancies were low or that the FEUR was higher in other time periods? No. Abraham was an assistant professor at MIT who received her Ph.D. from Harvard. Her article was published in the world's most prestigious economic journal. Even so, economists largely ignored her. It was as if her study had never been published.

The only study critical of Abraham's analysis was done by Schwartz, Cohen, and Grimes (1986), who believe that Abraham's proxy estimate, and not the adjusted vacancy rate data, is biased low. They construct an alternative measure using Social Security data from 1973–81. Abraham

(1986), in a reply, offers two solid reasons why their results overestimate vacancies. However, even if their results are not overestimates, they confirm Abraham's conclusion that there are more unemployed workers than job vacancies. In 1973, the year with the lowest unemployment rate in their study, 4.9%, Schwartz et al estimate there are 2.1 unemployed for every job vacancy.

Zagorsky (1998) and Blanchard and Diamond (1989) have also developed proxy measures of vacancies by correcting for the downward bias in help-wanted advertising. Using ten years of data from Minnesota, Abraham (1987) shows that a corrected help-wanted index can successfully track vacancy rate date. Zogorsky's measure spans the years 1923 to 1994, and according to his estimates, the unemployment rate during the post-World War II period always exceeded the vacancy rate. Blanchard and Diamond have two estimates, one using downward-adjusted unemployment data and one with unadjusted data. The measure using an adjusted unemployment rate spans the years 1968 to 1981. According to their estimate, the economy was at full employment in the late 1960s but not after that. The estimate using an unadjusted unemployment rate, which runs from 1952 to 1988, always has the unemployment rate exceeding the vacancy rate, just as the heterodox model predicts.

December 2000 to Present

Since December 2000, the US Department of Labor has collected monthly data on vacancies as part of the Job Opening and Labor Turnover Survey (JOLTS). Figure 3 shows both vacancy and unemployment rates from December 2000 to December 2018.

The JOLTS data gives us important information about three expansions. The first few months of the survey, December 2000 to March 2001, were the last few months of a ten-year expansion. While unemployment drew close to the vacancy rate, it was always greater. Next is the 2001–07 expansion. Even though the recession of 2001 was relatively mild and the expansion lasted six years, the unemployment rate was still

Figure 3. Vacancy and unemployment rates, 2001–18.

considerably higher than the vacancy rate—1.1%. The third expansion is the current one.

As the book goes to press, this third expansion is in its tenth year. During 2018, for the only time in more than eighteen years of JOLTS data, the vacancy rate has become greater than the unemployment rate. Based on this data, we might conclude that during the current expansion the economy made it to full employment. However even if that is true, it isn't much of a victory for orthodox economists because it took nine years to get to full employment. The data suggests that either labor markets don't clear or they clear very slowly.

In conclusion, both the data from before December 2000 and the JOLTS data is consistent with the predictions of the heterodox model that there are always or almost always more people looking for work than there are jobs. This data suggests that either labor markets do not clear in the long run, or they clear very slowly. Therefore, it would be best not to assume a supply-and-demand labor market when preforming economic

Expansions	Unemployment, Vacancy Rate Gap
1949–53	0.2%
1954–57	2.0%
1958–60	3.1%
1961–69	0.6%
1970–73	2.0%
1975–80	2.8%
1983–90	2.8%
1991–2001	0.3%
2001–07	1.1%
2009–18	− 0.9%

Figure 4. The minimum difference between the unemployment rate and the vacancy rate.

analysis. Instead, we should use the heterodox models.

Unfortunately, this data can't be used as a definitive test of the natural rate hypothesis because in that view, the unemployment rate always exceeds the vacancy rate. However, it can be used to point to a strong inconsistency, one that should make us doubt the idea that the economy gravitates to some natural rate of unemployment.

If the natural rate hypothesis is correct, then at the point where the economy achieves the natural rate, the gap between the vacancy rate and the unemployment rate should be as close as it ever gets. That gap should also be reasonably consistent across different time periods. However, as figure 4 shows, that doesn't appear to be the case. During some periods, the gap is large. In other periods, it is near or less than zero.

Figure 4 shows the smallest gap between the unemployment rate and the vacancy rate for each expansion. For consistency, we use Zagorsky's estimates of vacancies for all the expansion before 1991 and the JOLTS data for the end of the 1991 to 2001 expansion and thereafter.

Because the vacancy estimates are made using different techniques, we need to be cautious about comparing the gap across these two time periods. However, within each time period, the size of the gap has been inconsistent.

In this next section, we will look at the pattern of unemployment rates over the business cycle. This data can be used to test whether the actual unemployment rate tends to gravitate towards some natural rate.

Patterns of Unemployment Rates

One way to differentiate between the orthodox and heterodox theory of labor markets is to look at the pattern of unemployment rates over the business cycle. Labor markets that clear or gravitate towards the natural rate exhibit a very different pattern than those that don't.

Hypothesized Patterns

For both models, unemployment increases when a recession strikes. In the orthodox model, excess labor supply causes wages to fall, which then causes the quantity of labor demanded to increase and the quantity of labor supplied to decrease. Both of these effects cause unemployment to fall. This process continues until we reach equilibrium—full employment or the natural rate of unemployment. After that, the unemployment rate varies around the FEUR until the next recession. Figure 5 illustrates this pattern.

Within orthodoxy, there is some controversy as to the length of time it takes the economy to return to full employment. Conservative economists believe the economy returns rapidly to full employment, but liberals believe this occurs more slowly. Analyzing the pattern of unemployment rates is the perfect test to resolve this controversy. If unemployment rates return quickly to FEUR, then conservatives are correct. If it takes several years, then liberals are correct. The fact that neither side has proposed using this test suggests that the results hurt both sides.

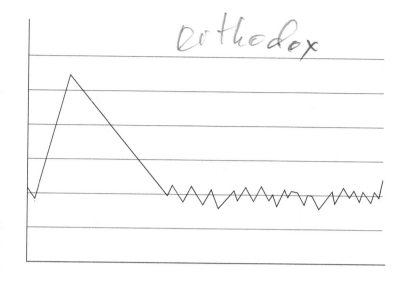

Figure 5. The predicted unemployment rate pattern of the orthodox model.

The heterodox theory of labor markets says that employment is determined by aggregate demand. In the US, under normal conditions, more people enter the labor market than leave, so the labor force is continuously growing. During an expansion, aggregate demand normally grows fast enough to employ all the additional individuals and then some. As a result, the unemployment rate tends to fall during the expansion. Heterodox economists believe that most expansions end before full employment is reached. Therefore, as figure 6 on the next page illustrates, the pattern of unemployment rates should take on a sawtooth shape, continuously falling over the expansion and then rising during the recession. Near the end of the expansion, the economy slows before turning negative, so the unemployment rate may stop falling just prior to the end of the expansion.

One of the problems with this method of testing is the possibility of a false positive—data that indicates full employment has been achieved

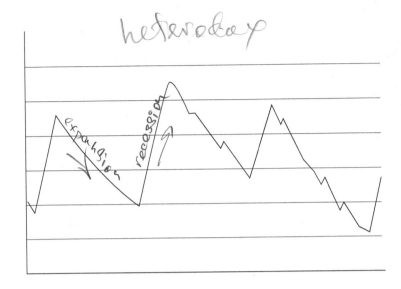

Time Measured in Years

Figure 6. The predicted unemployment rate pattern of the heterodox model.

when in fact it hasn't. This can occur if the economy is growing just fast enough to absorb the growing labor force and offset growths in productivity. The result is the economy continues to expand, but the unemployment rate stops falling. We know this occurred from February 1962 to March 1964 and from June 1984 to June 1986 because the two expansions later picked up speed, and the unemployment rate resumed falling.[122] We will look at other time periods where a false positive may have occurred just prior to a recession.

Actual Patterns

Figure 7 shows the actual unemployment rates from 1948 to 2018. During most cycles, unemployment continues to drop until near or at the end of the expansion. If we look at individual cycles, there are three that show a resemblance to what the orthodox model would predict. However, other information leads us to believe that at least two of these are false positives.

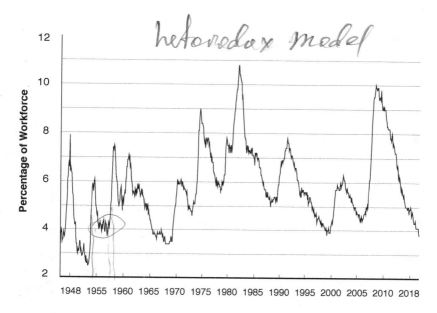

heterodox model

Figure 7. Unemployment rates, 1948–2018.

Taken as a whole, the pattern seems to fit the predictions of the heterodox model and not the predictions of the orthodox model.

Figure 8 illustrates the expansion of 1954–57. A year after the trough of the recession, the unemployment rate fell to 4.3% and varied between 3.7% and 4.4% for the next twenty-seven months until the next recession.

While this data fits the pattern predicted by the orthodox model, it is unlikely that this is the natural rate. We do not expect for the natural rate to stay constant over the years, but we do not expect it to change dramatically, either. This is especially true if the periods being compared are close to one another. Only a few years earlier, in 1951–53, the economy achieved unemployment rates below anything seen in the 1954–57 expansion for thirty straight months, culminating with an unemployment rate of 2.5%.[123]

Figure 9 shows the expansion of 1961–69. This one may not be a false positive. Five years after the trough, the unemployment rate stabilized,

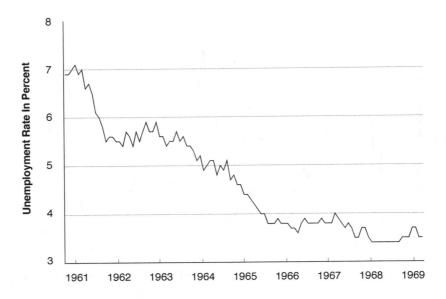

Figure 8. Unemployment rates during the expansion of 1961–69.

varying between 4.0% and 3.4% for nearly four years. Unemployment hovered in the upper part of that range at first and then in the lower part at the end. However, even if the economy did reach full employment/ natural rate, it took at least five years after a relatively mild recession to accomplish it. This certainly doesn't fit the conservative scenario, and it may be uncomfortably long for many liberals.

Figure 10 presents the expansion of 1983 to 1990. Five and one-third years after the trough of the recession, the economy settled into an unemployment rate that varied between 5.0% and 5.6% for twenty-eight months until the next recession, primarily varying between 5.2% and 5.4%.

This appears to be a false positive. In the next expansion, 1991–2001, the unemployment rate fell below 5% for forty-four consecutive months before the start of the next recession, reaching a low of 3.8%.

Of the eleven expansions, only one may have achieved what is predicted by the orthodox model. This means that at best there was one

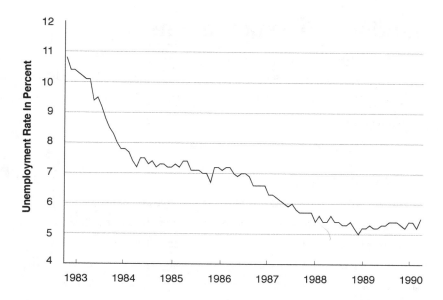

Figure 9. Unemployment rates during the expansion of 1983–90.

four-year stretch out of seventy years where the economy was at long-run equilibrium. We could also argue that the economy may have also achieved long-run equilibrium for a brief period during the last months of the 1949–53 expansion when unemployment declined to 2.5%, the end of the 1991—2001 expansion when the unemployment rate fell to 3.8%, and in 2018–19 of the current expansion.

Overall, however, the data on the pattern of unemployment rates over the business cycle is consistent with the heterodox model. For the most part, it is inconsistent with the orthodox predictions that in the long run, labor markets gravitate to either full employment or the natural rate of unemployment. Both the vacancy rate data and the pattern of unemployment rate data cast serious doubt on the idea that the supply-and-demand labor market model can accurately predict the most important outcomes of the modern labor markets, especially for issues revolving around poverty.

Testing the Explanations

For most of the scientific community, explanation is more important than prediction. How well do the orthodox and heterodox models explain the basic functioning of actual labor markets? That is what we will consider in this section.

Labor Markets can't explain it

The orthodox supply-and-demand labor market is set up like the orthodox supply-and-demand product market. In the market for corn, for example, when a household buys an ear of corn, there is not an on-going relationship between the household and the ear of corn. They eat the corn, and it's gone. If they paid fifty cents for the ear of corn today, and it is still sitting in the refrigerator tomorrow, they don't pay the shop owner another fifty cents. Once they pay for a product, it's theirs. They can do with it as they like—within reason.

Supply-and-demand labor markets are set up in the same way, as if the employer is purchasing day-laborers.[124] However, that isn't how real-world employment relationships work. Once workers are hired, relationship is established between the employer and the employees. In most cases, it is assumed that this relationship continues indefinitely until one party decides to break off the relationship. The orthodox supply-and-demand model can't explain this ongoing relationship unless the parties renegotiate the wage rate every day or the employee is to be paid the same wage forever. Furthermore, the employer doesn't own the workers. The employer is simply purchasing labor power—the workers' ability to do work. In most cases, the employer is not purchasing an amount of work. The amount of work received depends on how the employer organizes work and motivates the employees.

In addition, if the price for corn falls, the ears of corn don't become insulted and secrete a substance to make themselves taste worse. However, workers *can* be insulted by the wage paid or by some perceived violation of custom, and they can then decide to not work as hard. Furthermore, owners can institute workplace rules and employment structures to give workers an incentive to work harder. In a real-world labor market, employers have incentives to behave in ways that corn producers never contemplate.

This brings us to one of the major problems with the explanatory power of the supply-and-demand labor market model. This model is unable to explain the major feature of most employment relationships—that most employment is organized into internal labor markets. Therefore, supply-and-demand models can't explain many features of real-world labor markets, such as:

- Why firms have job openings where the only people competing for the jobs already work for the firm
- Why firms have yearly performance reviews
- Why the same job has multiple pay steps, which result in people doing the same job but being paid substantially different wages
- Why firms would have management by rules
- Why firms would give a preference in promotion to senior workers rather than basing promotions purely on merit

The orthodox supply-and-demand models are thus incapable of explaining the most important feature of the modern labor markets—the internal labor market and its standard features.

It is hard to overstate the importance of that fact. Using the standards set by the greater scientific community, this fact alone is sufficient to pronounce the orthodox supply-and-demand labor market model as unscientific. The evidence of its mispredictions is telling but also unnecessary. This inability to explain the existence and features of the internal labor markets is enough.[125] However, there is more that this model is incapable of explaining.

On the other hand, the heterodox segmented market model is built specifically to explain why certain employers have formed internal labor markets and pay high wages and why other firms don't form internal labor markets and generally pay low wages. The ability to explain what occurs in real world labor markets is the strength of the heterodox model.

Hours Worked

When comparing the differences between the orthodox and the heterodox models, one of the keys is that the orthodox model produces a world of scarcity. It produces full employment, and as a result, employers and employees meet in the marketplace as equals.

The heterodox model produces an excess capacity society. When there is excess capacity, more people are looking for work than there are jobs available. In that situation, the employer has the upper hand because a worker needs the job more than the employer needs a particular worker. In the heterodox model, the employer is thus able to dictate how many hours an employee works.

In the orthodox labor market model, workers choose how many hours to work. In his book, *Capitalism and Freedom*, the US economist Milton Friedman (1962) emphasizes that those who participate in a market exchange do so on a purely voluntary basis. What makes it voluntary is no one is forcing them to trade. They can choose to participate in market exchanges or not, as they see fit. In addition, there are many individuals with whom to trade. If one doesn't like the deal Vendor A is offering, there are Vendors B, C, D, and many others to trade with. It is the fact that one does not need to trade at all and the fact that there are many parties with which to trade that makes it so that each party meets as an equal.

One party in a transaction can't force the other party to sell more product than they wish. If Driller Dave, the local dentist, wishes to buy eight oranges and Rosy the Kindergarten Teacher only wishes to sell five oranges from her garden, then Dave can only buy five oranges from Rosy. He has to find another individual from whom he can buy the other three oranges. Rosy can't be coerced into selling eight oranges. This is how it is with the orthodox supply-and-demand labor market model. All parties meet voluntarily in the market place as equals, so the sellers of labor are the ones who determine how many hours they work—unless the seller wishes to work more hours than the buyer wishes to hire them for.

The only thing wrong with this idyllic picture is that it has nothing to do with the real world. Workers and employers don't meet as equals. For most people, the only way to earn a living is to sell their labor power for a wage or a salary. Very few own enough land to feed, house, and clothe themselves. Most workers sell their labor power because they have no other way to earn a living. It is not really voluntary because most workers don't have the option of not participating.

Furthermore, as the data from the testing section indicates, employers normally have more potential workers to choose from than workers have employers to choose from. In most situations, when an employer offers a worker a job, the worker has no additional job offers to choose from. The worker must either accept the offer or take their chances that there will be better offers—soon. In this highly unequal situation, the employer quite naturally dictates the terms of employment. In all but the rarest of cases, the number of hours a laborer works is either set by the employer or by a collective bargaining agreement. Once again, the heterodox model does a far better job of explaining what actually occurs in the real world.

Excess Capacity

In the orthodox supply-and-demand labor market model, firms use all their capital, and they use it all the time. There is never any excess capacity. In the orthodox model, this is the result of the magical transformation of capital that happens every time the amount of capital or the number of laborers changes. This is the result of the assumption of Play-Doh capital built into their model. By contrast, the heterodox theory characterizes capitalism as an excess-capacity society. In that society, there must be excess capacity in capital, labor, and loanable funds in order for business-people to be able to increase output during expansions.

As we saw earlier, the Federal Reserve has been collecting data on capacity utilization since 1967. During those more than fifty years, there has always been a substantial amount of excess capacity. In the lowest quarter on record, the fourth quarter of 1973, 11.5% of the capital stock was idle. The orthodox model says excess capacity never exist, but the data shows that substantial excess capacity always exists. Again, the orthodox theory is unable to explain reality, but heterodox theory is able to so effortlessly.

Test Results

These tests show us that time and time again, the orthodox supply-and-demand model is unable to explain the working of real-world labor markets. Its errors are not small, nor are its problems focused on insignificant features. The question is why it does so poorly. The answer is that the basic orientation of the orthodox model is flawed.

In this model, the major problem facing society is scarcity. The labor and capital markets work automatically to propel society into a position of scarcity—to a point on the PPF. At that point, society can only produce more of one good by taking productive resources out of the production of some other good. The operation of the capitalist system naturally results in all of society's resources being used efficiently.

The problem with this vision is that it is at odds with how an actual capitalist economy operates. It is also at odds with the data. Capitalist societies are excess-capacity societies, just as you would expect. In a capitalist society, the economy is never at equilibrium but is always either expanding or contracting. Most of the time, it's expanding. To grow, firms must have access to additional capital, labor, and loanable funds. And in all but the rarest of situations, society possesses excess quantities of all three.

In contrast, the heterodox model is an excess-capacity model. The business cycle model is a profit squeeze model. It assumes that expansions will always or almost always end before full employment is reached because as unemployment declines and raw material inventories fall, costs will rise to the point where profits fall and the expansion ends. Because it is an excess capacity model, its predictions and explanations line up with what occurs in the real world.

The labor segmentation model also plays a role in the correct predictions of the heterodox model. This model focuses on how issues of control and skill learning affect how firms structure their work places, and the wages and benefits firms pay their workers. This focus on how firms structure their work places allows the model to accurately explain features we observe in real-world labor markets. In addition, its focus on wage setting mechanisms allows the heterodox model to correctly predict that in the post-World War II era that nominal wages would either not fall during recession or would fall by only small amount.

References

Abraham, Katharine. 1983. "Structural/Frictional vs. Deficient Demand Unemployment: Some New Evidence." *American Economic Review* 73: 708–24.

Abraham, Katharine. 1986. "Structural/Frictional vs. Deficient Demand Unemployment: Reply." *American Economic Review* 76: 273–6.

Abraham, Katharine. 1987. "Help-Wanted Advertising, Job Vacancies, and Unemployment." *Brookings Papers on Economic Activity* 1: 207–43.

Beveridge, William. 1945. *Full Employment in a Free Society.* New York: W. W. Norton.

Blanchard, Olivier and Peter Diamond. 1989. "The Beveridge Curve." *Brookings Papers on Economic Activity* 1: 1–76.

Clark, John Bates. 1899, 1956. *The Distribution of Wealth: A Theory of Wages, Interest and Profits.* New York: Kelley & Millman Inc.

Clark, Kelly, and Rosemary Hyson. 2001. "New Tools for Labor Market Analysis: JOLTS." *Monthly Labor Review* 124, December: 32–37.

Clark, Kelly. 2004. "The Job Openings and Labor Turnover Survey: What Initial Data Show." *Monthly Labor Review* 127, November: 14–23.

Economic Policy Institute. 2002. "Unemployment and the US Jobs Deficit." *Economic Snapshot,* October 2: 1–3.

Friedman, Milton. 1953. "The Methodology of Positive Economics." In *Essays in Positive Economics.* Chicago: University of Chicago Press: 3–43.

Friedman, Milton. 1962. *Capitalism and Freedom.* Chicago: University of Chicago Press.

Mankiw, N. Gregory. 2009. *Principles of Macroeconomics,* 5th ed. Mason, OH: South-Western Cengage Learning.

Marx, Karl. 1867. *Capital.* New York: L.W. Schmidt.

Schwartz, Arthur, Malcolm Cohen, and Donald Grimes. 1986. "Structural/Frictional vs. Deficient Demand Unemployment: Comment." *American Economic Review* 76: 268–72.

Summers, Lawrence. 1986. "Why Is the Unemployment Rate So Very High Near Full Employment?" *Brookings Papers on Economic Activity* 2: 339–96.

Zagorsky, Jay. 1998. "Job Vacancies in the United States: 1923 to 1994." *The Review of Economics and Statistics* 80: 338–45.

❖ 14

Conclusion

"The purpose of studying economics is not to acquire a set of ready-made answers to economic questions, but to learn how to avoid being deceived by economists."
— Joan Robinson

As we've seen, while the heterodox models of business cycles and segmented labor markets may need more work and testing, they do a reasonably good job of modeling the operations of the real world. On the other hand, the orthodox model cannot mimic the operations of the real world and thus should not be used for determining the causes or solutions to poverty—or other social problems. This is no surprise, either, because we've seen that the orthodox model is built on a set of highly unrealistic assumptions.

Instead of being rejected as a guide for the solution of social problems,[126] the orthodox model has a virtual monopoly on giving economic advice.[127] How is this possible? The world is filled with smart people.

How is it that the orthodox model continues to be used when its predictions are continuously wrong, when it is unable to explain important features of the real world, and when it produces solutions that always fail? How is it that the heterodox model, which at least shows promise, is never even part of the discussion?

The answer isn't as difficult as one might suppose, and we will now conclude this book by looking at what stands in the way of implementing the solutions to poverty that we have identified in the heterodox model.

The Wealthy Favor Orthodox Models

Capitalist societies are societies of excess capacity. The downside of such societies is they are highly unfair. A segment of the population must be marginalized, set aside just in case their labor power is needed as the economy expands. This segment isn't always made up of the same people, but it is always present. In the absence of government policy to correct the problem, this segment is left in a state poverty or near-poverty.

Moreover, these underutilized workers put other workers in an unequal position in the market place for labor. These reserve armies of the unemployed and over-educated give employers the ability to dictate the terms of employment and exploit their employees. They pay employees less than the value of what they produce, and they take the remainder for themselves. The charge of exploitation may have been more explosive in the time of J.B. Clark when living standards were lower, but it is still fundamentally unfair.

It is not our intention to bash capitalism. Living standards have increased dramatically over the past 250 years, as have life expectancies. It isn't a historical accident that this rapid growth has coincided with the development of capitalism. It is the result of the basic structure of capitalism. How and why the structure of capitalism results in rapid change has not been covered in this book, but it is within the grasp of an introductory student. Our point is instead that while capitalism has produced tremendous increases in our standard of living, these advances come at a price. There is a dark side to capitalism. One of its problems is that, without concerted government action, it produces substantial poverty in the midst of plenty.

For those who most benefit from society, the idea of capitalism as an excess capacity society presents a problem. If it were general knowledge that what allows some to grow rich is that many others must remain poor, there would be general outcry that this is unfair and that something needs to be done about it. There would be a call for some remedy to the situation, for a change in the system that would allow everyone to work while still maintaining excess capacity.

The problem with any such plan is that it will transfer large amounts of income away from the wealthy. Most wealthy people are not particularly fond of plans that reduce their income by massive amounts. From their perspective, it is best if people don't know that the wealth they have obtained is the result of a system that naturally results in a large segment of the population being poor. It is better for them if they can blame the poor for their own poverty. It is best if they have an economic theory that does that for them.

Orthodox economic models that assume scarcity give results that are more amenable to the interests of the rich than models of excess capacity. At a minimum, the employers derive an advantage from unemployment and the subservient position it gives to workers. Models that assume scarcity never suggest that we need to solve the problem of unemployment because it doesn't exist in these models.[128] Even though the data from the real world shows otherwise, orthodox economists have steadfastly maintained that capitalism is not an excess capacity society but one in which all resources are naturally, through the magic of the market, used and used efficiently.[129]

How can a model that preforms so poorly, that appears to have been built to defend the interest of the rich, have come to dominate the study of economics?

The Dissemination of Ideas

The first step towards understanding how this could happen is to ask how ideas are transmitted within society. Henry (1990) writes:

> For ideas to be viable, to have significance, they obviously must be transmitted as well as developed. And it is the social process of dissemination that creates the greatest force in the power of ideas.... In sum, then, it is argued that ideas are themselves social products; that if ideas are to be popularly disseminated, they must have some appeal to those bodies controlling the mechanisms of transmission. Since the means of communication are economics units and are controlled by those who have economic interests in mind, then the ideas they advance must be favorably disposed toward those economic interests. And subversive ideas—those not favorably disposed toward prevailing authority—must seek other than the dominant channels of communication for their dissemination; so they will be in the minority. (p. 8)

Who controls the major avenues for the transmission of ideas and information in an advanced capitalist economy? Who owns the newspapers, television networks, publishing houses, magazines, and radio stations? The answer is large corporations, and these media corporations, like all corporations, have only one goal—to maximize their profits. The main source of revenue for most corporate media is advertising. The primary source of advertising dollars is other corporations. To defend their profits, those who control the major avenues for the transmission of ideas must defend the income and power of the business-owning class (Chomsky and Herman 1988).

Policies born from economic analysis using the heterodox model would greatly reduce the income and power of the business class. Businesspeople prefer a strong economy, but the heterodox solution of promoting full employment takes a good thing too far. When an economy approaches full employment, the power of workers to raise wages increases significantly, so the income of business owners declines. Significant increases in the minimum wage also reduce profits. The general public strongly favors the higher wages, lower unemployment, greater job security, and lower poverty rates.

However, these outcomes run counter to the interests of the business-owning class, so the theories and policies of heterodox economics are suppressed. Other theories that don't threaten the profits of owners are disseminated to the public instead. It doesn't matter whether or not these theories are scientifically accurate. What matters is that they don't threaten the interests of the business class. If a scientific theory cannot be found, then a fraudulent theory must be developed and disseminated, and orthodox economics is the fraud that has been developed.[130]

Orthodox Economists

If orthodox economics is a fraud, it raises the question of whether the thousands of professional orthodox economists, especially those teaching in colleges, are willing and active participates in the fraud.[131] Can we assume that underneath their demure exterior, these academics are consciously misleading students and the public into accepting policies that favor the rich at the expense of the majority?

Unfortunately, we have no data to draw upon, and we can't ask this question of orthodox economists and expect a truthful answer. We are thus left to speculate based on the observation of a small subset of orthodox economists.[132] Those who developed the far-fetched models of orthodox economics are clearly conscious class warriors. Other economists, born into upper-class families, who defend their own class interests, are probably conscious of their role, too. However, the majority of orthodox economists don't come from the upper-class, and they are not the primary developers of the orthodox models. So why do they participate in the fraud?

In his book on the euro, Joseph Stiglitz (2016) asks a similar question about why the officials of the European Union continued to insist on austerity programs in the face of mounting evidence of their failures:

> One possibility—a real one—is that the architects of austerity truly believed in the economic doctrines that they espoused, in spite of the overwhelming evidence against them accumulated over more than three-quarters of a century.
>
> Advances in behavioral economics and psychology provide some explanation for the persistence of such beliefs—the theory of *confirmation bias* holds that individuals discount information that is not consistent with prior beliefs. And in our complex world, it is easy to do so. It is hard, of course, to deny the decrease in Greece's GDP. But it is possible to find alternative explanations—Greece didn't do everything that it should have done. (p. 308-09)

We also find support for this idea that people are blinded by ideology from the field of cognitive science and linguistics. George Lakoff emphasizes that people do not think logically. They think within frames and metaphors. If orthodox theory is good at anything, it is good at supplying easily digested frameworks such as supply-and-demand analysis, the production possibilities frontier, the money multiplier story, and so on. According to Lakoff, "Facts can be assimilated into the brain only if there is a frame to make sense out of them" (2006a). Therefore, if "a fact is inconsistent with the frames and metaphors in your brain that define common sense. Then the frames or metaphors will stay, and the fact will be ignored" (2006b).

Can we really blame the behavior of orthodox economists on the fact that they learned a series of models when they were young, that they are now so ideologically crippled that they are incapable of discerning the failures of their own models? I think not. The prediction errors are too large. The inability to explain how the real-world works is too great.

The assumptions in their models are too absurd and unrealistic. No one can be professor of economics and *not* serious question the validity of orthodox economics. Stiglitz himself appears to question the validity of being blinded by ideology:

> I had seen such rationalizing on the part of the IMF in the multiple failed programs in developing countries and emerging markets. The programs were well designed, it was argued; the failure was one of implementation on the part of the country. Such arguments, I believe, are disingenuous — an attempt to shift the blame for the failure of the program to the victim of the program. (p. 309)

Why then do orthodox economists participate in the fraud? Are they conscious of their role? Do they see themselves as class warriors? Our suspicion is that they are taking the path of least resistance, that for so very little, orthodox economists have simply sold out.

For a smart individual who is good at math, a career as an economics professor is an excellent option. Once tenured, the work environment is pleasant. There is great latitude to use your creative abilities in teaching your classes and developing your research agenda. The salary is mediocre, but there is a special respect accorded to college professors. For the most part, it is a busy but pleasant life.

However, with a few exceptions, PhD-granting institutions are purely orthodox. Most new PhDs are thus orthodox economists. For those who become college professors, the next six years are dedicated to getting tenure. That requires a mixture of teaching economics courses and producing peer-reviewed journal articles. The articles provide the greatest barrier to receiving tenure. Each article requires a high degree of specific knowledge and a large amount of effort. For most economists, this is not the time for dabbling with new theories. They have to stick to what they know and make sure they get tenure.

Once tenured, college professors finally have the ability to pause and take an objective look at orthodox economics and its alternatives. An orthodox economist with any curiosity should have at least questioned the reason for scarcity being the starting point for this approach. There are also many unrealistic assumptions within the models. It should have at least crossed the mind of every orthodox economist that there are problems, and potentially major problems, with orthodox theory. On the surface, at least, we might expect that all tenured orthodox economists would have investigated heterodox economics and the problems associated with orthodox economics.

However, what are the costs and benefits of converting to heterodox economics? For the newly tenured professor, they are almost all costs. Most or all of the other members of the department are orthodox economists. Abandoning orthodox economics strains working relationships with others in their department. They tend to become isolated. Everyday life becomes little less pleasant, and for some, a lot less pleasant. Receiving a promotion from an associate professor to full professor requires the recommendations of colleagues. By switching sides to heterodox theory, the newly-tenured professor is now in jeopardy of not getting good recommendations from orthodox colleagues.

Converting to a new approach is also a lot of work. In their fields of orthodox economics, the newly tenured professors are experts. As heterodox economists, they're novices. It takes years to become an expert in an area of heterodox economics. There is likely to be a long gap with no publications, which hurts their chances of promotion.

Moreover, depending on their area of specialization, it's difficult to convert to being a heterodox economist gradually, at least in the classroom or in making public statements. There are some areas of economics where one can dabble in heterodox economics without abandoning orthodox economics everywhere else. But in other areas, especial those that are associated with the core micro and macroeconomic theories, it is difficult, if not impossible, to gradually make the change. For example, you can't be a heterodox economist when comes to money creation and use an orthodox model for the rest of macroeconomics. The two simply don't fix together. If one is faced with making the jump all at once, it may seem overwhelming and therefore not worth attempting it at all.

For first-tier economists, certain prestigious jobs, such as being a member of the Federal Reserve's Board of Governors, are reserved for those who believe in the orthodox theory. As a heterodox economist, the probability of landing one of these plum jobs is reduced to zero. Moreover, the ability to influence economic policy, to take part in serious policy discussions, is generally limited to orthodox economists.

These costs add up. As for the benefits, outside of soothing one's conscience, there are none. For those trained as orthodox economists, life is more comfortable, with higher income and greater recognition, if they continue to be orthodox economists. This, we suspect, is how they sell out for so very little. However, they aren't just selling out themselves. They are also selling out other people—lots of other people—millions and millions, if not billions, of other people.

While there is no oath, nor any courses in ethics for social scientists, professional academics have an implicit obligation to pursue truth, to use their position, as best as they are able, for the betterment of society. When performing their cost/benefit analysis, they must consider the benefits of all the other people who are affected by their calculations. Society depends on academics to stand up for what is best for society as a whole. If that requires personal sacrifice, then that is the price they must pay for the privilege of being academics. It is their moral obligation.

The Solutions to Poverty

Is poverty the worst problem facing America? If it isn't, then it is close. A host of social problems are linked to and made worse by poverty. Poverty is associated with a greater risk of divorce, domestic violence, child abuse, and child neglect. Children of the poor have lower levels of educational attainment. Young children who live in poverty have a greater chance of neural development that will negatively impact their cognition, memory, behavioral skills, and mental health. The poor have more health problems, and poverty is also associated with higher crime rates.

Anything that significantly reduces poverty, then, improves the lives of most, if not all, US citizens. What then should we do to reduce poverty? The heterodox model offers these basic solutions:

1. Maintain the economy at or near full employment by using government policy to increase aggregate demand.

2. Provide public service employment for any citizen who wants a job at the minimum wage.

3. Significantly increase the minimum wage and then tie further increases to inflation and changes in productivity.

4. Establish special public service employment programs for geographically isolated areas such as the inner city, certain Appalachian regions, and Native American reservations.

5. Provide support for those who can't or shouldn't work.

6. Make changes to the legal definition of what constitutes an employee to make it more difficulty to have employees be independent contractors and so that corporations are more responsible for the workforce employed by subcontractors.

7. Substantially increase funding for the enforcement of labor laws.

However, capitalist economies are excess-capacity societies. To grow and thrive, there must be individuals who are available for businesses to hire as the economy expands. In a full-employment economy, excess capacity is provided by people working at jobs that don't fully use their skills and education, the reserve army of the over-educated, and by those who can be pulled from the public service employment. In this book, we have outlined two plans can be used separately or together to provide excess capacity in a full employment economy:

1. Construct a two-tiered minimum wage, one for the private sector and one for PSE jobs.

2. Once private sector employment has reached a particular threshold, reduce the size of government spending as the private sector expands further.

While this is necessary in the physical sense, however, it is not sufficient in the political or ideological sense. The reason poverty hasn't been reduced significantly over the past forty years is that policies to end poverty have been based on ideas generated by the orthodox model. According to Keynes (1936), the ideas of academics exert a more powerful influence than is generally recognized:

> But apart from this contemporary mood, the ideas of economists and political philosophers, both when they are right and when they are wrong, are more powerful than is commonly understood. Indeed, the world is ruled by little else. Practical men, who believe themselves to be quite exempt from any intellectual influences, are usually the slaves of some defunct economist. Madmen in authority, who hear voices in the air, are distilling their frenzy from some academic scribbler of a few years back. (p. 383)

Henry would most likely modify Keynes's quote by injecting the words, "those who can get their ideas disseminated."

However, to successfully rid ourselves of poverty, it isn't sufficient to merely push for the heterodox solutions. We also need to rid ourselves of the economic theory that underlies conventional wisdom. We will need to rid ourselves of the theory that has produced a succession of failed policies. We need to rid ourselves of the theory that is blocking the path to progress. We need to rid ourselves of orthodox economics.[133]

References

Chomsky, Noam, and Edward Herman. 1988. *Manufacturing Consent: The Political Economy of the Mass Media*. New York: Pantheon Books.

Henry, John F. 1990. *The Making of Neoclassical Economics*. Winchester MA: Unwin Hyman Inc.

Keynes, John M. 1936. *The General Theory of Employment, Interest and Money*. New York: Harcourt, Brace and Company.

Lakoff, George. 2006a. *Thinking Points: Communicating Our American Values and Vision*. New York: Farrar, Straus and Giroux.

Lakoff, George. 2006b. *Whose Freedom? The Battle Over American's Most Important Idea*. New York: Farrar, Straus and Giroux.

Lekachman, Robert. 1966, 1975. *The Age of Keynes*. New York, NY: McGraw-Hill.

Robinson, Joan. 1962. *Economic Philosophy*. London: C. A. Watts & Co. Ltd.

Routh, Guy. 1989. *The Origin of Economic Ideas,* 2nd ed. Dobbs Ferry, NY: Sheridan House.

Stiglitz, Joseph. 2016. *The Euro: How a Common Currency Threatens the Future of Europe*. New York: W.W. Norton & Company.

Endnotes

Chapter 1: Finding Solutions to Poverty

1. The goal of Social Security is to reduce the number of impoverished elderly, and it has been highly successful. However, the focus of this book is on the working-age poor and their children. As a result, discussions of the elderly poor and the successes, failures, and future of Social Security are completely absent from these pages.

2. The data comes from the U.S. Census Bureau Current Poplulation Survey, Annual Social and Economica Supplements, Tables P-1 and H-3.

3. In recent years much has been written about the growing income inequality in the US. There have been many books and they present a lot of statistics. But perhaps just a couple of statistics can give the reader a sense of what has happened. For households in the bottom 20% of the income distribution their share of the nation's income fell from 4.1% in 1970 to 3.1% in 2016. For those in the next 20% their share fell from 10.8% to 8.3%, and for households in the middle 20% their share fell from 17.4% to 14.2%. The share going to those in the top 20% went from 43.3% to 51.5%.

   But what does this mean in dollar terms? In 2016, the average income for households in the bottom 20% was $12, 943. Had their share been the same as it was in 1970, their average income would have been $17,062. For those in the next 20%, their average income was $34,504. If their share had remained the same, their income would have been $44,945. For the middle 20%, their average income in 2016 was $59,139, but had their share remained the same, it would have been $72,412. For those in the bottom 60% of the income distribution, their lives would have been much better off had the distribution of income stayed the same as it was in 1970.

4. This, in and of itself, is both odd and telling.

5. e.g. Danziger and Gottschalk (1995), Phelps (1997), Mangum, Mangum and Sum (2003), Lang (2007), Schiller (2008), Wolff (2009), Rycroft (2013), Ravallion (2016), Murray (1984). Murray is not an economist but is often cited as if he is one for his numerical analysis.

6. The former group is sometimes referred to as non-orthodox economists, but due to efforts of Frederic Lee (2009) and others, the name heterodox economics now appears to be the preferred term.

7. An example of a skill mismatch is when the job openings require a college degree and the unemployed have only high school diplomas. In that situation, the jobs remain unfilled, and the jobless remain unemployed. An example of a geographic mismatch is when the job openings are in South Carolina and the unemployed are in Nevada. That's a tough commute.

8. There is no consensus among conservatives as to whether the government should provide short-term unemployment insurance or not.

9. It is worth mentioning the extreme myopia necessary for someone to make this argument. People today wouldn't even be able to produce 1% of what they produce without the thousands upon thousands of inventions, improvements, and discoveries made by others over the past fifteen thousand years. Most of what we can produce is the result of the efforts of others, but we give only a small fraction of our income to these individuals and their descendants. Their knowledge and ingenuity is what society has bequeathed to us free of charge. Any income that we might earn above what our ancestor earned fifteen thousand years ago we owe to society as a whole. Therefore, any tax rate of less than 99% is a gift. We are being left with more income than we could have earned without the help of others. We're not arguing that we should have tax rate of 99%, only that those who view taxes as some sort of immoral government theft haven't thought very deeply about the issue.

10. America is a freedom-loving country. We talk about it all the time. However, what exactly does the word "freedom" means? That is not so simple because the word has been used in many different ways to support many different causes. For the sake of simplicity, we can divide

definitions of this word into two camps, the negative and the positive definitions of freedom.

The negative definition of freedom tends to run along the lines of freedom being a lack of constraints. Those who use this definition tend to focus on the government, with its laws and regulations, as the greatest barrier to freedom. Quite naturally, this definition is favored by large corporations. The only countervailing force that is large enough and powerful enough to prevent large corporations from doing whatever they want is the government. Most government regulations are the result of some abuse of power by businesses.

The positive definition of freedom tends to run along the lines of freedom being the ability to do things. In the US, where few goods and services are provided by the government, the ability to do things is dependent on one's income. Activities normally require the purchasing of goods and services necessary to do that activity. The positive definition tends to focus on income and the distribution of income. One of the problems with mass poverty is that large portions of the population lack some of the basic freedoms enjoyed by the rest of society. Especially for children, who can in no way be blamed for their poverty, this seems highly unfair. To the extent that we talk about freedom in this book, we use the positive definition of freedom.

11. The actual poverty line varies slightly based on the family make up. For example, a family of three with two adults and one child has a poverty line of $19,318 while a family of three with one adult and two child has a poverty line of $19,337. Notice you can also have a family of three with three adults, which has a poverty line of $18,774. The poverty lines reported in figure 2 are the weighted averages of the all different poverty lines for that size of family as calculated by the US Census Bureau.

12. The lowest poverty line was encountered in a working paper by Haveman and Mullikin (1999), who were surveying alternative poverty measures. The poverty line using this measure was 55.5% of the official poverty line. Using this measure there were still approximately 22 and a half million people below the poverty line in 2016.

Chapter 2: Economic Models

13. The terms "simplifying" and "conditional assumptions" (Henry 1983) sometimes bring to mind a clearer image of what these assumptions are trying to accomplish. However, Musgrave's designations "negligibility" and "domain assumptions" are more universally used.

14. There are times when a negligibility assumption is found not to be negligible and is converted into a domain assumption. This can have

interesting ramifications as explained by well-known philosopher of science Alan Musgrave (1981):

> Suppose a scientist makes a negligibility assumption, embeds it in a theory, tests that theory, and finds that its predictions are false. He may pin the blame on his negligibility assumption, and decide that the factor F whose effects he had assumed to be negligible does have significant effects after all. And he may conclude that his theory will only work where factor F is absent, and restrict its applicability to cases of this kind. He may retain the 'assumption' that F is absent, but now use it to specify the domain of applicability of his theory. Let us call assumptions of this second kind, domain assumptions.

> What begins as a negligibility assumption may, when it gets refuted, turn into a domain assumption. And the interesting thing is that this quite radical change in the theory may go unnoticed because the same form of words is used to express both assumptions. An economist who says 'assume the government has a balanced budget' may mean that any actual budget imbalance can be ignored because its effects on the phenomena he is investigating are negligible. But he may also mean precisely the opposite: that budget imbalance would have significant effects, so that his theory will only apply where such an imbalance does not exist.

15. Depending on which model we wish to examine, the bicycle example may be too simplistic. The assumption about the chain is like a light switch. Either the chain is on, and the rear wheel spins when the pedals move, or the chain is off, and the rear wheel does not spin when the pedals moves. There is no in-between. However, with many domain assumptions, there is an in-between. We could, for example, make the domain assumption that a market is made up of many small powerless firms (perfect competition). However, let's say that the market we wish to study is made up of several large firms. Clearly, the domain assumption is incorrect, and the model will mispredict—but how badly will it do so? While the market is not a free-for-all between a large number of powerless firms, it is also not a monopoly. The question becomes how closely a model with the assumption of perfect competition approximates the real world. There are many situations like the above where there is a continuum of possible states and the question is how closely does the domain assumption match reality.

16. Some orthodox economists believe that there are obstructions that prevent market forces from driving the economy to a market-clearing position. They believe that market forces will drive unemployment down to the "natural rate of unemployment" but no further. We will meet these economists later in the book.

17. John Bates Clark, who infused into the orthodox model of labor markets his assumption of Play-Doh capital, come close to admitting publicly that his model was developed for ideological reasons. Writing in 1899, Clark was aware of the potentially destabilizing effects that could occur if the general populace thought the distribution of income was unfair. He noted:

The right of society to exist in its present form, and the probability that it will continue so to exist, are at stake. These facts lend to this problem of distribution its measureless importance. The welfare of the laboring classes depends on whether they get much or little; but their attitude toward other classes — and, therefore, the stability of the social state — depends chiefly on the question, whether the amount they get, be it large or small, is what they produce. If they create a small amount of wealth and get the whole of it, they may not seek to revolutionize society; but if it were to appear that they produce an ample amount and get only a part of it, many of them would become revolutionists, and all would have the right to do so. The indictment that hangs over society is that of "exploiting labor." "Workmen," it is said, "are regularly robbed of what they produce. This is done within the forms of law, and by the natural working of competition." If this charge were proved, every right-minded man should become a socialist; and his zeal in transforming the industrial system would then measure and express his sense of justice. If we are to test the charge, however, we must enter the realm of production. We must resolve the product of social industry into its component elements, in order to see whether the natural effect of competition is or is not to give to each producer to amount of wealth that he specifically brings into existence. (p. 3-4)

Clark recognizes the importance for the stability of society of having a model that "shows" that laborers are not exploited. He then goes on to produce such a model whose main result — laborers are not exploited — is critically dependent on one of the weirdest assumptions in all of economics, Play-Doh capital, which is discussed in Chapter 10. It is one of the clearest examples of a model being produced for purely ideological reasons.

18. Friedman uses a bifurcated set-up to make this argument. It is an argumentation style that we see elsewhere in economics, and therefore, it is worthwhile for students to be able to recognize this type of argumentation when they see it. It starts by setting up the opposing position in a way that is easy to defeat. Friedman states:

The difficulty in the social sciences of getting new evidence for this class of phenomena and of judging its conformity with the implications of the hypothesis makes it tempting to suppose that other, more readily available, evidence is equally relevant to the validity of the hypothesis — to suppose that hypotheses have not only "implications" but also "assumptions" and that the conformity of these "assumptions" to "reality" is a test of the validity of the hypothesis different from or additional to the test by implications. This widely held view is fundamentally wrong and productive of much mischief. (p. 14)

A clear weakness in the position "a hypothesis can be judged solely by the reality of their assumption" is that it's unclear who gets to judge when an assumption or set of assumptions is too unrealistic to be part of a scientific model, and how unrealistic these assumptions need to be to disqualify the model. Friedman then sets up his position as the only alternative, with no middle ground. Once the straw position is destroyed, the only thing left is Friedman's position — the sole test of a hypothesis is whether it predicts accurately.

However, there is clear middle ground, and had Friedman delineated the difference between negligibility and domain assumptions, the existence of this middle ground would have been obvious. Unrealistic assumptions cannot be used as the sole bases for disqualifying a hypothesis. They do, however, give us strong reasons for doubting a hypothesis and can point towards those areas that deserve the most scrutiny and testing.

19. Many economists appear disingenuous by stating that prediction is what determines the worthiness of a theory or model while at the same time ignoring the data that shows that their theory or model mispredicts. However, this is not the point we are attempting to make here. The point is that while economists have enthroned prediction as king, for much of the scientific world, explanation is king.

20. Hesse (1967), Webb (1987), Haack (2003).

Chapter 3: The Simple Keynesian Model

21. We will see these differences in the chapter on money creation.

22. Businesses also purchase intermediate goods used in the production of goods and services. However, to avoid double-counting aggregate demand, we only track the purchases of final goods and services by each actor. Plant and equipment are the only final goods and services brought by businesses.

23. This can take place in one of two ways. First, the government can purchase goods and services directly from private firms, such as tanks from General Motors or fighter jets from Boeing. Second, they can hire workers and purchase supplies to produce goods and services themselves, as with public education.

24. For orthodox economists, the most important factor affecting investment is the interest rate.

25. Even when investment is financed by an internal flow of funds, interest rates have an effect. The alternative use for those funds is to purchase some financial instrument, such as a bond, that pays the firm interest. When interest rates are high, the firm may forgo using its internal funds to purchase plant and equipment and instead purchase bonds with that money.

26. Unfortunately, those who collect data on investment add building residential housing to the purchasing of plant and equipment. The purchasing of houses is very responsive to changes in interest rates.

27. Because the flow of revenue coming from the sale of goods and services doesn't always occur at the same time as the firm's expenditures for labor and supplies, businesses take out what are known as working capital loans in order to cover their expenditures until their revenues come in.

28. The prime rate is currently 3% higher than Federal Reserve's target for the Federal Funds rate. When the Federal Reserve changes its target for the Federal Funds rate, banks tend to change their prime rate by the same amount.

29. The Federal Reserve also reports this data monthly. The highest monthly capacity utilization rate was in January of 1967 at 89.4% (10.6%). The highest quarterly capacity utilization rate is 88.5% from the fourth quarter of 1973. The average excess capacity rate is the average of the June capacity utilization rates from 1967 to 2016 subtracted from one. The Federal Reverse has also collected capacity utilization data for manufacturing back to 1948.

30. An increase in taxes causes disposable income and consumption to fall but not by as much as government spending increases. That's because the MPC is less than one. For example, if government spending and taxes both increase by $100, then government spending increases by $100, and disposable income decreases by $100. The decrease in consumption equals the decrease in disposable income times the MPC. If MPC is 0.95, consumption falls by $95. If government spending increases by $100 and consumption falls by $95, then aggregate demand increases by $5, and as a result employment increases. Therefore, the lawn signs that say "increases in state taxes will kill jobs" are incorrect.

31. On May 31, 2019, the actual exchange rate was $1=108.92¥.

Chapter 4: Business Cycles

32. The term "business cycle" is a bit misleading. It brings to mind the regular, symmetric cycles on an oscilloscope. However, the length and strength of expansions vary considerably, as do the length and depth of recessions.

Combined with the fact that expansions tend to be considerably longer than recessions, a pattern to US business cycles emerges which looks far different than cycles on an oscilloscope.

33. In looking at individual firm data, Fazarri (1993) found that investment increases with increases in profits and increases in the internal flow of funds. He found little or no support for the idea that investment increases as a result of decreases in business taxes.

34. Others explain this effect differently. During an expansion, the share of income going to workers falls and the share going to owners increases. Because owners have a lower MPC, total consumption falls short of the total production of consumption goods (Sherman et al 2008). Because the data doesn't currently support the idea of underconsumptionism, it doesn't seem important to determine the most accurate form of the argument.

35. With technological improvements, economies become more productive over time. The same number of workers can produce more goods and services. Furthermore, the number of people in the labor force grows over time. Thus, for the unemployment rate to decline during an expansion the economy must grow faster than some rate X that varies somewhat depending on the time period. During an expansion, RGDP normally grows faster than rate X. However, there have been time periods when RGDP has not grown that fast. The result is an expanding economy where unemployment is either constant or rising. The beginnings of the last three expansions and a two-year period in the mid-1980s are examples of such periods.

36. Normally, the unemployment rate peaks at the end of the recession. However, with our last three recessions (1990–91, 2001–02 and 2007–09), the peak unemployment rate did not occur until as much as a year after the end of the recession.

37. For evidence of profits declining just before the end of the expansion, see Boddy and Crotty (1975) and Tapia Granados (2012).

38. Minsky's description of this process is more complex than what is presented here.

39. There are other economists who believe the Federal Reserve, acting as an agent for the business class, deliberately brings the expansion to an end. This position is attributed to the famous Polish economist Michael Kalecki (Wilber and Jameson 1983). In this view, as the expansion continues, workers worry less and less about day-to-day job security and become progressively more militant and assertive. Feeling threatened, the business class, through the apparatus of the state—in this case,

the Federal Reserve—engineers a recession to restore the proper labor discipline through higher rates of unemployment and job insecurity. Without being a mind-reader, it is impossible to determine whether the Federal Reserve's true reason for raising interest rates at the end of an expansion is to head off inflation or if it is to re-establish the profitability of the business class by reducing workers' bargaining and political power.

40. According to Wolfson (1986), while small firms and firms with short credit histories have their access to credit reduced or eliminated, "big banks try to meet the needs of their established customers."

41. Wolfson (2003) presents a clear and straightforward model of credit rationing that is consistent with the views expressed in this chapter and the chapter on money creation, Chapter 11.

42. With the Great Recession, the size of the US national debt increased rapidly from $8.68 trillion at the beginning of 2007 to $22.03 trillion on May 30, 2019. As we discussed, we never have to pay off the national debt. However, we do have to pay interest on the national debt. In 2017, the US government paid $459 billion in interest payment on debt. That constitutes more than 14.4% of total federal expenditures. While that's a large number, it could be a lot larger and no doubt will be in future. Current interest rates are low. In 2017, the federal government paid an interest rate of approximately 2.3% on the national debt. If in preparation for the next recession, the Federal Reserve were to increase interest rates as they have during past expansions, then that number would increase considerably. In 2006, the federal government paid $451 billion in interest payments on a much smaller debt. The interest rate paid in 2006 was approximately 4.8%. If the Federal Reserve increases interest rates so that we were paying the same interest rate on the national debt now, the US government's expenditures on interest payments for the debt will be a little over one trillion dollars. Almost 32% of federal expenditures would go to pay interest on the debt.

The Fed has been slow to raise interest rates during the current expansion. Their claim has been that they want to see a stronger labor market before raising interest rates. However, one wonders if the Fed's inaction maybe an attempt to keep the cost of financing the national debt low by keeping interest rates low. If this is the new unstated policy of the Federal Reserve, then they will have little ability to fight recessions in the future.

By the way, when reporting government revenues and expenditures, in order to make the federal debt situation look better than it is, some people add Social Security into the government's budget. This is illegitimate. Social Security is a separate entity. By doing so, these people can make the above calculations look much smaller for two reasons. First, total government expenditures will be greater if you count retirement benefits paid out by Social Security. As total expenditures rise, the percent paid on the debt falls. Second, a sizable portion of those interest payments are made to Social Security, thus net interest payments — total interest payments minus interest payments to Social Security and other government entities — look much smaller than total interest payments.

43. The "T" in "T-bill" stands for the US Treasury. "Bills" have maturity of one year or less, while "bonds" have a maturity of more than one year. The US Treasury sells bills and bonds to the public with maturities ranging from thirty days to thirty years. This is the main way the US borrows to finance the national debt.

44. Why is this happening? The purveyors of austerity claim that these programs will jump-start growth, but there is good reason to believe that they are being disingenuous. First, the theoretical case for austerity producing sizeable increases in consumption and investment is shaky at best. Second, there is no historical evidence that austerity programs have ever worked, and they are not working now in any of the European countries that have enacted them. However, the purveyors of austerity continued to call for ever more austerity even as their economies fell into recession. In the face of all the evidence to the contrary, one might ask why they insist on more austerity. The real reason appears to be that a certain affluent segment of society is taking advantage of high budget deficits — caused primarily by the financial crisis of 2007–09 — to call for dismantling social safety net programs. While these programs are beneficial to most members of society, they cost the rich money in higher taxes and lower profits. The tendency of certain groups to take advantage of economic or natural disasters to make policy changes that would be impossible under normal conditions is outlined in great detail with numerous historical examples in Naomi Klein's book, *The Stock Doctrine: The Rise of Disaster Capitalism* (2007).

45. By contrast, in recent recessions that appear to have followed the basic mechanism (1991 and 2000–01), the Federal Reserve has raised interest rates by an average of only two percentage points.

46. Defining when recessions start and end can be difficult. Instead of defining the entire period from 1980 to 1982 as one long recession, the National Bureau of Economic Research, which is the group charged with defining the start and end of recessions, decided that there was a six-month recession in 1980, followed by a one-year expansion, follow by an 18-month recession. Many have referred to this period as a double-dip recession.

47. Economists often talk as if an additional unit of capital is like an additional unit of a consumer good — something you can just buy off the shelf, like a can of Spam. This gives the impression that units of

capital are homogenous like cans of Spam. This is sometimes true, such as when a firm wishes to expand and what the firm needs to expand are more personal computers. However, most of the time, an additional unit of capital is a one of a kind item, made to fit the unique needs of that firm. For example, if the They Oughta to Name a Drink After You Saloon wants to purchase new capital by expanding their establishment to add the Kick Up Your Heels Dance Hall, they can't just buy that off the shelf. It has to be specifically made for the firm. Therefore, while economist tend to talk about firms buying an additional unit of capital in the same manor that they discuss consumers buying an additional shirt, you should understand that in most cases, they are discussing firms purchasing non-homogenous, firm-specific additions to plant and equipment.

48. In the Harvey/Davidson model, there are more than two variables that affect the demand for new capital. In order to keep this model simple, we only discuss two variables. These two variables were chosen because they are the ones that drive the business cycle in the Harvey/Davidson model.

49. The growth rate in RGDP has been especially slow since 2000. Capacity utilization rates have also been unusually low for expansions during this time period.

50. A number of studies have shown that there is a strong spillover effect between wages paid by union firms and the wages paid by non-union firms (Wachtel 1988). As union wages go up, they pull non-union wages up with them.

51. Brown (2008) also emphasizes how increasing inequality of income leads to a less stable economy. He cites different channels than those cited by Stiglitz. In particular, Brown emphasizes how increasing inequality leads to increasing debt loads across the income spectrum. With increased debt loads comes an increased possibility of default.

52. One negative effect of greater income inequality is that life expectancies fall (Montague 1998).

53. This major result contains the qualifying words "almost always." However, the prior discussion should give you an idea why we can't say simply "always." If there is a strong countervailing push on aggregate demand from the government, as occurred during World War II and the Vietnam War, then the economy can reach full employment. While there is debate as to whether we reached full employment during the Vietnam war, there is no debate about the World War II. If the government pushes aggregate demand up hard enough, then this might overcome the tendency for investment to decline and for the nation to fall into recession before full employment is reached.

54. Among industrialized countries, the US pays the lowest unemployment benefits and pays them for the shortest amount of time.

Chapter 5: Wage Determination

55. There are some primarily sector jobs where part of one's pay is based on productivity. Those are jobs that pay bonuses. Most of these jobs have a base pay, which normally constitutes a major of one's compensation. If their performance exceeds some measure of productivity, then the individuals receives some additional pay — a bonus. Sometimes it's a company-wide bonus: if the company makes a profit greater than X, everyone gets a bonus. The more that profits exceed X, the greater the bonus. Other times it's an individual bonus. In the case of salespeople, if their sales are more than Y, they get a bonus. The more sales exceed Y, the greater the bonus.

56. As Weil (2014) notes, this system is actually more profitable for the large corporations if the small subcontractors are financially unstable:

> Although the lead company is not liable in such an instance, contractors will end up forcing it to bear some of these potential costs in the form of higher prices up front. However, if the contractors are financially unstable, they become "judgment-proof" — that is, they will not face the costs of tort actions brought against them, because they will have few or no assets to claim. Such insolvent subcontractors will therefore price their services at a lower level. Hence, lead companies have incentives not only to shift their risk through contracting but also to select agents who are more likely to behave poorly because of their judgment-proof status. (p. 189)

57. Premier Warehousing Ventures claimed that after the California Labor Department forced them to obey the law, they could no longer operate profitable and asked Schneider to renegotiate its contract. Schneider refused, and Premier Warehousing Ventures laid off its workers.

58. The figures on real wages and net total output per hour come from David Cooper (2015).

59. Based on the estimates of Neumark and Wascher (1992), a 10% increase in the minimum wage caused young-adult employment to fall by 1.5% to 2.0%. Therefore, even though their estimates show employment falling, minimum wage workers as a whole receive a significant increase in income. For example, if the minimum wage is $10.00 per hour and workers work 100 hours per month, their income is $1,000 per month. If the minimum wage increases by 10% to $11.00 per hour, and if employment falls by 2%, the workers work ninety-eight hours per month. Therefore, their monthly income increases to $1,078 per

month, a 7.8% increase. Of course, if the firm instead lays off two of its one hundred workers, then for ninety-eight workers, their incomes are $1,100 per month, and for two workers, their incomes are $0.

60. These studies rarely, if ever, show no effect on employment. They either show a small increase or a small decrease. However, the changes are so small that they are not statistically significant. Therefore, based on the rules and customs of scientific research, when the effect of the minimum wage on employment is not statistically significant, then the study reports that there is no effect on employment.

61. There can also be other avenues by which an increase in the minimum wage effects employment.

Chapter 6 Heterodox Solutions

62. The simple Keynesian model is also built into more complex orthodox macroeconomic models.

63. Not surprisingly, the number of people who are involuntarily working part-time because they can't find full-time work goes down during expansions and up during recessions. For example, during the peak of the last recession in 2009, approximately 8.9 million laborers were involuntarily part-time, which was 5.8 percent of the labor force. By 2018, that number had fallen to approximately 4.8 million or 2.9 percent of the labor force.

64. It seems reasonable say that those who end up in the lower end of the secondary market, or who are continuously unemployed, are those who rank at the bottom of the list of secondary market employers — the bottom of the bottom. However, that's not the case. According to Doeringer and Piore (1971), secondary market employers don't spend much time or effort ranking potential employees:

> Entry into secondary employment is less characterized by a queueing process than it is in primary employment. Many employers do not appear to draw distinctions between one secondary worker and another except on the basis of sex or physical strength. Employers almost seem to be hiring from an undifferentiated labor pool. Because turnover is high and the right to discharge is relatively unrestricted, more careful pre-employment screening is not generally warranted. (p. 168)

65. Current and past discrimination also affects other variables such as the quality of education, the amount of education, and the number of connections.

66. There are laws against employment discrimination. However, proving discrimination can be difficult, especially against small firms. The proof

of discrimination often comes from statistical patterns of employment. For this type of evidence to pass muster in court of law, there must be a large sample size to show a discriminatory pattern. Most small firms don't hire a sufficient enough number of people to create a large enough sample size to prove discrimination. Large firms, however, which hire thousands and thousands of workers a year, must take the anti-discrimination laws seriously.

67. There is a thorny debate about how old children should be when parents are required to return to work. This clearly needs to be solved along with how to best provide affordable child care before this provision can be instituted.

68. The author spent a good part of his childhood in one of those cities, Greenbelt, Maryland.

69. Higher education in many states is currently focused on a "completion agenda." Among state officials, there is a sense that higher education is failing students and that it must make institutional changes that will increase the percent of students who go to college and the percent who graduate. Unfortunately, the strategies that have been suggested, such as performance-based funding and programs to increase the number of college credits awarded in high school, threaten to undercut the quality of a college education. In the future, we may have many more college graduates, but the quality of their education and the skills that they possess may be much lower.

70. It is actually somewhat greater because there are those working part-time but wishing to work full time. For 2018, this was 2.9% of the labor force. These individuals could supplement their part-time private sector employment with part-time public-sector employment.

71. Nixon proposed a negative income tax in 1969. The idea was voted down by Congress.

Chapter 7: Scarcity and Choice

72. We might think that the gap will become smaller over time as technological improvements increase our ability to produce goods and services. However, as Veblen (1899) explains, the forces of pecuniary emulation and conspicuous consumption will keep expanding that list of goods and services people wish to have.

73. Agricultural goods have the problem that we can't change the rate of production very rapidly. In most cases, farmers need to wait an entire year. Furthermore, while most agricultural products fit the domain assumptions for supply, they don't always fit the domain assumptions for demand. For some crops, there are only a few large corporate buyers.

As a result of these problems, some economic textbooks use "widgets" to illustrate supply-and-demand markets, just as we do. Because there is no such good as a widget, students can't raise the objection that classroom discussions don't fit with reality.

74. Heterodox economists also use marginal analysis, but because orthodox economists assume that households and firms have perfect knowledge, there are many more opportunities in orthodox theory to use it.

Chapter 8: The Orthodox Model of Labor Markets

75. In economics, exploitation is often defined as a situation in which laborers are paid wages below their VMP_L ($VMP_L > W$). In such a situation, workers don't receive the full value of what they creates. The owner, having underpaid the workers, has in essence stolen part of what the worker produced.

76. Again, for simplicity, we assume that the only payment made to labor is a wage.

77. In addition, as the wage goes up, the number of workers who do the training necessary to participate in this market goes up.

78. How long it takes to return to the equilibrium is a point of contention between liberal and conservative orthodox economists. Conservatives believe the process happens rapidly, but liberals believe that it occurs more slowly.

79. Remember, because people are always entering and leaving the labor market and because it takes time to find a job even if jobs are plentiful, the unemployment rate will never be zero.

Chapter 9: Orthodox Solutions to Poverty

80. Here the term "racist" takes on a very specific definition: "One who believes that one race is biologically inferior to another." Unlike social inferiority, the use of biological inferiority means that no change in the social situation can ever bring the one group on par with the other. Therefore, there is no reason to devise programs to assist the "inferior" group in catching up.

81. Phelps (1997) actually falls into a gray area between conservatives and liberal orthodox economists. Phelps is generally viewed as a conservative, but in his book, he states that

Eliminating the welfare system would carry a large risk. We cannot have any reliable idea of how society would fare without food stamps, Medicaid and the rest.... We must assume at least a minimal welfare system, despite its side effects on unemployment, wages, self-reliance, and self-respect. (p. 105)

Phelps's solution to poverty is a sizable government subsidy to employers of low-wage workers. Beyond this, however, there is little in Phelps' arguments that lines up with liberal orthodox economists.

82. For the purpose of this book, we will assume that liberal orthodox economists are attempting to devise an anti-poverty program whose goal is to eliminate or nearly eliminate poverty. In reading liberal economists, however, it is sometimes unclear whether their goal is to eliminate poverty or simply to reduce poverty by some incremental amount.

83. There are some liberal orthodox economists who in theory believe in the value of job-training programs as a part of a program to greatly reduce poverty. However, according to these individuals, the government hasn't or can't effectively provide these programs. Therefore, training programs are not a part of their solution.

Chapter 10: Questionable Assumptions

84. For employees in internal labor markets, it is unclear whether work effort rises or falls as the economy approaches the peak of the boom. There are three effects, but there is a strong reason to believe that the one leading to increased work effort will dominate.

1. The chances of being fired are less, so work effort falls.

2. For employees who have gotten promotions, there is still a cost of being fired because they are unlikely to find a job that pays as much as their current job. Thus, their work effort tends not to change.

3. Employees in an ILM see these positions as careers. Promotions are dependent on work evaluations over a number of years. Slacking off because the probability of being fired falls may jeopardize future promotions. Boom periods probably do not result in a decrease in work effort. In fact, the peak of the boom requires the firm to produce more output. Those in an ILM are probably under pressure to increase work effort during these periods.

This third effect may be the most important, and it is likely to be one of the reasons why US productivity is procyclical over the business cycle — that is, output per worker increases during expansions and decreases during recession.

85. Even at full employment, it takes time to find a new job. From the moment when workers are unemployed until they are hired, they are considered unemployed.

86. In the introduction to their book, Akerlof and Yellen's state, "Without equivocation or qualification, we view efficiency wage models as providing the framework for a sensible macroeconomic model, capable of explaining the stylized facts characterizing business cycles. Such a

macroeconomic model must have at least five features: It must have involuntary unemployment; shifts in aggregate demand must change equilibrium output and employment, at least in the short run; over the course of the business cycle, productivity must behave procyclically; more skilled workers must have lower unemployment rates; and the quit rates should decrease with higher unemployment.... although as yet no model has been constructed with all of these features simultaneously." They should have added no orthodox economic model has been constructed with all the features. All these features are part of the heterodox business cycle/segmented market theory.

87. Orthodox economists like to describe themselves as dispassionate observers of the world. Their analysis is given purely to help society as whole operate better. However, their models, and in this case their choice of words, is a giveaway as to whose side they are actually on. The word "shirking" means "to neglect or evade a duty." According to these economists, workers have a duty to work as hard as possible. To do less is to evade their duty to their employer. Those who don't bring that level of work effort to the job are thus labeled by the derogatory term "shirker." Employers evidently don't have same duty to society. Employers who steal wages from their employees, pollute the environment, or evade paying taxes by shifting their tax burden to a Caribbean island, are not referred to by a derogatory name. They are simply maximizing profits given the constraints. However, when workers maximize their well-being given the constraints, they are given the name "shirkers."

88. As illustrated by Gregory Mankiw's (2008) introductory textbook, the natural rate of unemployment has become a rather slippery concept over the years. On page 313, Mankiw defines the natural rate of unemployment as the "normal rate of unemployment around which the unemployment rate fluctuates." On the next page, he provides data on CBO's calculation of the natural rate and the actual rate of unemployment. The natural rate appears to be approximately the average unemployment rate "around which the unemployment rate fluctuates." Krugman and Wells also use a similar definition.

On page 503, Mankiw changes his definition: "What is so 'natural' about the natural rate of unemployment? Friedman and Phelps used this adjective to describe the unemployment rate toward which the economy gravitates in the long run." This second definition is akin to how we have been using the term. Market forces drive the economy towards a particular "natural" rate of unemployment. It is based on the economic theory we have been discussing. The first definition is not. There is nothing "natural" about the average unemployment rate, except that any group of numbers naturally has an average. An increase in government spending could reduce unemployment in the long run without causing inflation. No policy can be built from this definition. In other words, it is meaningless. The only advantage to using the first definition over the second, as we will see later, is the actual unemployment rate doesn't gravitate towards any unemployment rate. You can't use the second definition if we are going to display any actual data.

89. It is worth remembering the famous British economist Joan Robinson's (1962) observation about exploitation: "The misery of being exploited by capitalists is nothing compared to the misery of not being exploited at all."

90. For more detail on Clark's assumption and how he developed it over a series of papers, see John Henry's (1995) *John Bates Clark: The Making of a Neoclassical Economist*.

91. There are other places in orthodox economics — isocost-isoquant analysis — where the substitution of capital for labor and vice versa are a part of the predictions of the model. These two parts of orthodox theory are clearly in contradiction with one another.

Chapter 11: The Banking System and Poverty

92. As with any business, a bank's goal is to maximize profits. This requires keeping total revenues as high as possible above total costs. A bank's sources of revenue are the interest paid on loans and securities and the payment of fees by customers. The bank's costs include the interest paid on deposits and borrowed funds, wages and salaries paid to employees, and the cost of purchasing buildings and equipment. Loans that are repaid are a bank's biggest source of profits. However, it isn't just the favorable interest-rate spread that makes business loans so valuable to banks. Establishing a customer relationship with borrowers, especially corporate borrowers, can enhance bank profits because such borrowers "are associated with valuable deposit balances and the use of ancillary services that generate fee income. Banks' attempt to get existing customers to use more bank services is referred to as cross-selling" (Sinkey 1989).

93. Banks hold securities because securities provide both returns and liquidity. T-bills are held primarily for liquidity because they can be easily converted to reserves with little price risk, but they have a low return. State and local bonds and long-term T-bonds are held primarily for their returns. Medium length T-bonds play an in-between role (Sinkey 1989).

94. For simplicity, interest payments are left out of the examples. In reality, loans increase by $10 million plus interest to be paid on the loan, checking accounts increase by $10 million, and net worth increases by the interest to be paid.

95. Some cards are not directly issued by banks, but the issuers have agreements with banks to make the payments.

96. Approximately 75% of this money initially flows to other banks (Moore 1988).

97. There are penalties for falling below the required level of reserves. However, to fall below means to average below the bank's reserve requirement over a fourteen-day period. Being momentarily below the reserve requirement is not a problem.

98. The money creation process in orthodox textbook is wrapped around what is called the money multiplier. In the heterodox theory there is no money multiplier. Therefore, if the heterodox theory is correct, then there is no such thing as a money multiplier.

99. While the goal in 1979 to 1982 was to hold the growth rate of the money supply constant, it vacillated wildly during this period (Appendix of Greider 1987), calling into question whether it is even possible for the Federal Reserve to be able to maintain a constant money growth target.

100. The Fed does have some indirect control over the money supply via moving their interest rate targets. If they think the money supply is growing too fast, they can raise interest rates hoping to slow the demand for loans, and if they think the money supply is growing too slowly, they can lower interest rates. However, it appears that it is the fear of inflation that spurs the Fed to raise rates and the fear of rising unemployment and recession that prompts them to lower rates.

101. For an introductory-level explanation of how the Federal Reserves' policy of interest-rate targeting automatically leads to the Federal Reserve supplying whatever level of reserves that the banking system requires, see Furey (2013).

102. A large volume of industrial bank loans is made through legally binding lines of credit. On average, roughly half of these lines of credit are unused (Moore 1988). Businesses thus have at their discretion the ability to greatly increase their borrowing, and banks are obligated to supply that credit in the blink of an eye.

103. As we saw in Chapter 10, the connection between an increase in productivity and an increase in wages appears at best to be very weak. Therefore, the seventh and eighth steps of this mechanism are also highly questionable.

104. Using simple metaphors to help describe how the banking system works is an idea that was inspired by an article written by Ravn (2015). The bathtub metaphor is taken directly from Ravn's article.

105. Some struggle with the idea that paying back a loan destroys money, so let's consider a simple numerical example. Motorcycle Mark takes out a

one-year loan from the Bank of Big Joe Williams for $100,000. Mark agrees to pay 5% interest on the loan. Mark signs the IOUs, and Big Joe types $100,000 into Mark's checking account. Mark then spends the money to start his Raiders memorabilia business, and his checking account goes to zero. Slowly but surely, Mark adds money back into his checking account from the profits from his business until after one year, it reaches $105,000. He then writes a check to the Bank of Big Joe Williams for $105,000. Big Joe cancels Mark's IOUs and reduces Mark's checking account by $105,000. Motorcycle's account went from $105,000 to zero, and no one else's account went up. Therefore, when Motorcycle Mark paid back his loan, that money vanished from the economy. Notice that at the time the loan was made, Mark promised to pay Big Joe $105,000, and Big Joe gave Mark $100,000. The difference, $5,000, was logged into Mr. William's balance sheet as net worth.

106. The freezing of financial markets is one reason why creditworthy businesses might not receive loans. Other reasons revolve around either the decisions of regulators or the need to meet certain regulations. In these cases, the bank wishes to give certain businesses loans but is prevented from expanding its loan portfolio. These events, like the freezing of financial markets, are infrequent.

107. By no means does this system work perfectly. There have been periods when banks made systematic mistakes about borrower creditworthiness, and the Federal Reserve and other regulatory agencies have made mistakes by allowing financial institutions to take on too much risk. The results can be catastrophic, as we witnessed in the financial crisis of 2007–09. However, the fact that banks are unable to judge creditworthiness perfectly doesn't invalidate the basic conclusion of this chapter that investment is almost never constrained by a lack of loanable fund but only by a lack of creditworthy investment projects

108. In addition, the fixed-pie metaphor is used to increase paranoia of foreigners when its adherents trumpet fears that the US is beholden to and at the mercy of China or some other country because they have essentially lent the US large sums of money by purchasing our T-bills and T-bonds.

109. In addition, besides the redistribution of income from the poor and middle class to the rich, these policies are likely to have other effects on the economy. To the extent that these policies reduce aggregate demand—and options 1, 5, and 6 clearly would—then they would decrease output, increase unemployment and increase poverty. As a result, these policies would also run the risk of depressing the animal spirits and reducing investment.

110. This statement gives the impression that the level of loanable funds could grow indefinitely. During most time periods, we never encounter any limits to the nationwide expansion of loanable funds. However, certain banks do encounter limits, and thus it is theoretically possible that the system as a whole could encounter a limit to the expansion of loanable funds if all the banks were in a position where they had to restrict borrowing. The way this happens to an individual bank is when a bank grants a loan, it tends to become more "illiquid," and if it becomes sufficiently illiquid, it must restrict further increases in loans. What does it mean for a bank to become illiquid? Keeping it simple, we can discuss how this would happen to a bank that is an asset manager and how it would happen to a bank that is a liability manager.

For a bank that is primarily an asset manager, it sells T-bills and other securities to meet its reserve requirement. As the bank makes more loans, which tends to happen during an expansion, it normally has to sell securities to cover those loans. We say "normally" because it depends on the amount of funds that flow into the bank from other banks compared to the amount of funds that flow out. However, if the expansion goes on for long enough, it is possible that the bank could run out of securities. At that point, they have to stop making loans because if they go below their reserve requirement, there is nothing they can do to meet it. Having securities to sell provides liquidity to the bank, and as the number of securities becomes low, the bank is said to have become illiquid. In actuality, though, the bank will start restricting loans well before their securities reached zero.

For a bank that is primarily a liability manager, it borrows money on the open market to meet their reserve requirements. However, to borrow money, you need people who are willing to lend money, which means the lender is taking the risk that the bank will pay them back. If an expansion goes long enough, a bank may end up with a large amount of borrowed funds. If others start to worry that the amount that this bank has borrowed is too large, they may become unwilling to lend to the bank because they worry that the bank might not be able to pay them back. If this becomes widespread, then our liability manager bank will face a crisis that might cause the bank to go out business. Banks who are primarily liability managers will limit or stop lending before they to reach the point where they believe their level of borrowing will cause those who lend to them concerns. For banks who are primarily liability managers, the ability to borrow funds is what provides them with liquidity. Having too much borrowing on their balance sheets make these banks illiquid.

Chapter 12: The Consequences of Being Wrong

111. There was a time, many years ago, when there were no government anti-poverty programs. However, looking at that time period doesn't seem like a good model of what will happen now if we eliminate all government anti-poverty programs. We are now a much more urban society, so there is no retreating to the family farm if times get tough. We also have millions of people receiving income or services from anti-poverty programs. To compare a world where all these people are cut off from assistance programs to a world in which they have never had them doesn't seem very useful.

112. For the 2016, the federal government's expenditures for Medicaid were approximately $344 billion.

113. A number of the near poor also receive benefits from attempts to increase after tax wages.

114. While they are a minority, some liberal economists suggest using PSE programs. This is also part of the heterodox solution. However, liberal economists don't appear to wish to use these programs as the employer of last resort.

115. That particular family may not end up in poverty. They may get a lower-level job, bumping someone else into an even lower job, and so on, until we get to the one who is bumped into no job.

116. We know that businesses can't perfectly pass on these costs because of the fierce opposition of the business community to increases in the minimum wage. If businesses could pass all those costs along to the consumer, then there would be no reason to oppose increases in the minimum wage.

117. Piven and Cloward (1971, 1993) have argued that the process is more complicated, that expansions in these programs have occurred in response to protests and rising civil disorder. Domhoff (1983), and Jenkins and Brents (1989) agree with Piven and Cloward's basic contention, but they argue that protests have been more effective when there is a greater division between business conservatives and business liberals.

Chapter 13: Testing the Models

118. An orthodox economist might object that we have depicted the orthodox theory of labor markets inaccurately, and to a certain extent we have. However, this inaccuracy does not change the basic conclusions of this section.

In introductory orthodox textbooks, the orthodox labor market theory is often depicted as a nominal wage theory in order to keep the arguments simple. However, the actual orthodox theory of labor markets is in terms of real wages. That is, it hypothesizes that what is on the y-axis—what firms and workers actually react to—are changes in real wages and not nominal wages. Real wages are nominal wages divided by the price level. The price level is some measure of all the prices for goods and services purchased by consumers.

The reason for having real wages on the y-axis is that orthodox economists hypothesize that workers do not increase or decrease the number of hours that they supply to the market because the nominal wage goes up or down, but they do so only if that increase in nominal wage can buy more goods and services. Therefore, a 2% increase in nominal wages only results in an increase in the quantity supplied of labor if the price level goes up by less than 2%, thereby increasing real wages. If the price level goes up by more than 2%, then real wages fall and workers offer to work fewer hours. The same is true of the firm's demand of labor. It is not how much they have to pay to workers in nominal terms that matters but what firms can buy in terms of goods and services with those nominal wages. The greater the firm's sacrifice is in terms and goods and service, the less willing it is to hire workers and vice versa.

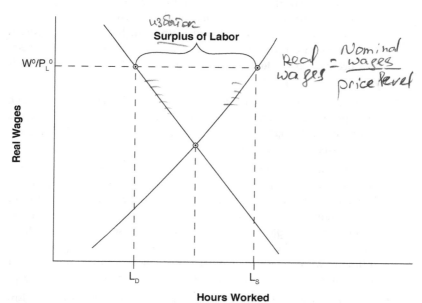

Figure 1. A surplus of labor in a real wage model.

However, reforming the orthodox supply and demand labor market model into a real wage model doesn't change how firms are supposed to react when the economy falls into recession. What happens in this model when a surplus of labor exists? As figure 1 shows, real wages must fall to clear the market. Either nominal wages must fall or the price level must rise. However, only one of the two is a market mechanism, and the other is not. Orthodox theory is based on individual maximization. The consumers or workers maximize their satisfaction or utility based on the prices they face, the wages they receive, and the income they may obtain from other sources. Firms maximize their profits based on the demand for their product, the price or prices they can charge for their products, and the cost of labor, capital and so on.

As events unfold, changes occur in the economy. As firms and households learn of these changes, they adjust their behavior to maximize their profit and satisfaction under the new reality. If a recession occurs, a surplus of labor appears, and in the orthodox model, firms react by lowering the nominal wage they pay their workers. Additionally, unemployed workers, desperate for work, offer their services for a lower nominal wage. However, neither of these groups can control the real wage because neither group controls the overall price level. The price level is the result of the pricing decisions of all firms within the economy. No market mechanism controls it. Nominal wages are the only variable in real wages that workers and firms can directly control.

The conclusion is that it doesn't matter whether orthodox theory is framed in terms of nominal wage or real wages. The market mechanism that occurs in orthodox theory when an excess supply of labor exists is that nominal wages fall.

119. Wages also fell during two periods that are not associated with the high unemployment of recessions. In 1959, they fell between the second and third quarters by 0.8% and between the fourth quarter of 2005 and the first quarter of 2006 by 0.07%.

120. Actually, according to Beveridge, "The full employment that is the aim of this Report means more vacant jobs than unemployed men.... It is not enough to say that there must be more vacant jobs than idle men—more or about as many.... Full employment, in any real sense, means that unemployment in the individual case need not last for a length of time exceeding that which can be covered by unemployment insurance without risk of demoralization. Those who lose jobs must be able to find new jobs at fair wages within their capacity, without delay."

121. The point where the vacancy rate equals the unemployment rate isn't actually where the market clears. That is because there are always a substantial number of individuals who are employed part-time but who want to work full-time. In May of 2018, this described nearly 3% of the workforce. However, factoring this information into the calculation of the unemployment rate is unnecessarily cumbersome. Even without making this adjustment to the unemployment rate, the data on the

vacancy and unemployment rates show that at best, labor markets rarely clear.

122. The well-known orthodox economist Lawrence Summers, who served in a number of important positions, including chief economist of the World Bank, President Clinton's Treasury Secretary and President Obama's Director of the National Economic Council stated in 1986, "Today, four years into an economic recovery, the unemployment rate hovers around seven percent.... Even most forecasts that call for steady growth over the next five years do not foresee unemployment rates dipping back below six percent.... Where Kennedy-Johnson economists set four percent as an interim full-employment target, contemporary policymakers would regard even the temporary achievement of six percent unemployment as a great success." Two years later, the unemployment rate was hovering just above 5%.

123. Furthermore, vacancy rate estimates by Zagorsky, and Blanchard and Diamond during the 1954-57 expansion are all below 2.5%. Thus, there is a considerable gap between the vacancy rate and the unemployment rate.

124. It is actually set up as if they were purchasing slaves.

125. As we saw earlier, orthodox economists have attempted to modify their models to take account of some of the realities of the modern workplace. However, the perceived need to produce equilibrium models in which the optimal wage achieves equilibrium has prevented orthodox economist from creating models that address the complexities of the real world. Their models are constructed in a way that firms can solve problems of control and skill-learning without forming internal labor markets. Therefore, they are unable to explain the actions of most firms in the real world.

Chapter 14: Conclusion

126. Neither the liberal nor the conservative solution has been fully implemented, but time and time again, the legislative solutions to poverty are derived from either liberal or conservative variants of the orthodox model. Time and time again, these solutions fail to make any serious improvements.

127. The orthodox monopoly on giving economic advice isn't restricted to the area of poverty. It is everywhere, from the membership to the Federal Reserve, to President's Council of Economic Advisors, to the World Bank, and to the IMF. Many have argued that this advice has led to or aided in many of the problems that we see currently: stagnating wages, slow growth, continuous and high trade deficits, and rising inequality.

Sometimes orthodox advice and actions have had devastating effects, as in the 2007–09 recession. A large share of the blame for that recession has been laid at the feet of the Federal Reserve for its efforts to deregulate financial markets and its inaction in curbing risky activity in financial markets. After the financial house of cards collapsed, the longtime Federal Reserve Chairman Alan Greenspan mused that perhaps he had used the wrong model.

128. The orthodox model produces a world of scarcity and full employment. The primary problem in this model is not unemployment but inflation. For the rich, inflation is a far greater evil than unemployment. The rich by definition have lots of money. Inflation reduces the purchasing power of money, so inflation reduces the wealth of the rich. In the heterodox model, whose operation produces a world of excess capacity, the primary problem that public policy needs to solve is unemployment. For workers, unemployment is a far greater evil than inflation.

129. How do orthodox economists defend themselves against those who point out the obvious—that our society is not one of scarcity? What do they say to those who call for an end to unemployment and poverty? From the view point of orthodox economists, these people need to be marginalized. For non-economists, orthodox economists simply state these people just don't understand the deep complexities of economics, so they can be ignored. But what about heterodox economists? What is to be done with them? This is why orthodox economists like Diana Coyle state that only those who have models with "the combination of rational maximizers and the equilibrium concept" are economists. Heterodox economists, who insist that capitalism is an excess capacity society with no equilibrium, are simply not economists. Heterodox economists, and their ideas and data can thus be ignored as well. Models of scarcity can then reign supreme without interruption.

130. Orthodox theory is not a science because its main tenets cannot be refuted by evidence. In other words, it does not matter how many times the model is shown to falsely predict. The main core of the theory can never change, and its disciples can never admit to the possibility of its failure. Evidence that refutes the model is simply ignored. However, the ideas, notions, and theories that are not part of the central core of the theory can be and are refuted by evidence. In some arenas, therefore, orthodox economics does appear to be scientific, and most orthodox economists believe, at least outwardly, that they are scientists.

131. How do we know that each and every orthodox economist is aware that their theory is fraudulent? One method of demonstrating this would be if we could find evidence that every economist knows, and if that evidence

proves that the orthodox theory is false, then this would indicate that each and every orthodox economist knows that his or her theory is fraudulent. We have two of these pieces of evidence in this book.

First, orthodox theory is based on scarcity. However, labor markets don't gravitate towards any natural rate of unemployment, or if they do, this occurs very slowly. As a result, there is almost always substantial amounts of unused labor. Furthermore, data gathered by the Federal Reserve shows that there is always a substantial amount of unused capital. This information is known to all economists. Therefore, every orthodox economist knows that the economy is never at a point of scarcity.

The second piece comes from the chapter on money creation. Most orthodox macroeconomic theories assume that the Federal Reserve targets the level of the money supply. It doesn't! It is as simple as that. The Federal Reserve targets a short-term interest rate and has done so for seventy of the past seventy-three years. Further, The Fed can't target both the money supply and interest rates simultaneously. The financial pages discuss the Fed's interest rate target all the time. No economist is ignorant of this piece of information. The assumption of money targeting is important in generating results favored by the well-to-do. Orthodox economists can't change these models even though having this assumption in their model makes them look foolish.

There is a third example that is not in the book, but it routinely shows up in introductory macroeconomics classes. While not as critical to orthodox theory as the preceding two examples, the Fisher equation is standard fare. According to the economic theory built into the Fisher equation, the interest rates that we observe in the market are the addition of the real rate of interest and the expected inflation rate, neither of which we can observe. While we cannot observe it, according to orthodox theory, real interest rates must always be positive because no one would lend money if they did not expect the money they received back to buy more goods and services than the money they lent. Measuring whether long-term real interest rates are always positive as the Fisher equation predicts, is difficult because it is hard to know what the populations' long-term expectations are for inflation. However, we can make very close estimates of the short-term real interest rates. Orthodox theory says that real interest rates can never be negative, but for many years in the 1970s and 2010s, the short-term real interest rates were negative. Therefore, the Fisher equation must be false, and every economist knows that short-term real interest rates were negative during those time periods. Even so, orthodox economists continue to teach the Fisher equation to their students.

We don't need to have the results of a survey or to be mind-readers. Simple pieces of evidence can tell us that all orthodox economists know that their theory is a fraud.

132. These conclusions are not based solely on the observation of a small subset of orthodox economists but are also drawn from observing a group that shares several attributes with orthodox economists. This group is known as the "puppet lords." A puppet lord is one who is in charge of a fiefdom and is in a position to make independent or nearly independent decisions over their fiefdom. For example, a college president or a director of a state agency. By the nature of their position, this person is charged with protecting the interests of the public and those in their fiefdom. However, instead of making decisions based what would be good for the public, puppet lords sometimes make decisions based on what they perceive will most benefit their careers in the long-run. Thus, instead of being the true lords of the manor, they dance like puppets on a string to whomever or whatever they believe will best further their careers.

Orthodox economists and puppet lords are both smart. Both profess to only to be operating in the public's interest. The puppet lords claim to be focused on the goal of student success. The orthodox economists profess to be only interested in a dispassionate, unbiased analysis of the economy, focusing on "what is" and not on what they personally think "should be." However, when critics of orthodox economics bring up the fact that models used by orthodox economists are unrealistic and are rigged to defend the interest of the rich, orthodox economists, being in a position of power, simply ignore their critics. The critics have no mechanism for forcing orthodox economists to debate with them.

Unions and other public groups can, on certain occasions, force puppets lords to interact by showing that Policy X is best for the public. The puppet lords, knowing this information, then use all manners of deceit and underhanded tricks in an attempt to implement Policy Y. Thus, the puppet lords — proclaiming to serve the goal of student success — actively work to implement policies that they know are damaging to students, normally by undermining the quality of education. Both puppet lords and the orthodox economists claim to be operating in the interest of the public. However, both appear to be acting based on a cost/benefit analysis that doesn't take the public interest into consideration. Only their own interests seem to matter.

133. Throughout the book we have used the labels heterodox models/ economics and orthodox models/economics. This is largely because these are the names that are traditionally used to describe these models. But the names by themselves don't impart much information. I would suggest changing these names so that the general public could instantly understand whose interest these models serve. For instance, I would change the name heterodox economics to "the people's economics." Not

because these models were devised specifically to help the average person. They were invented to try explain how real capitalist systems operate. However, in so doing they generally suggest economic policies that help the general public. I would also change the name of orthodox economics to "the rich people's economics." These models were developed and promoted because they produce economic policies that generally favor large corporations and the rich.

CPSIA information can be obtained
at www.ICGtesting.com
Printed in the USA
FSHW010749110919
61912FS